Joel Westerdale
Nietzsche's Aphoristic Challenge

Monographien und Texte zur Nietzsche-Forschung

Begründet von
Mazzino Montinari, Wolfgang Müller-Lauter
und Heinz Wenzel

Herausgegeben von
Günter Abel (Berlin) und
Werner Stegmaier (Greifswald)

Band 64

Joel Westerdale

Nietzsche's Aphoristic Challenge

—

DE GRUYTER

Contents

List of Abbreviations and Sources

Abbreviations of Nietzsche's Works

References to the *Kritische Studienausgabe* of Nietzsche's works (KSA) will be made according to volume and page (for example, KSA 6:365 means page 365 of volume 6), except in the case of those books composed of texts numbered according to a single continuous sequence (*The Birth of Tragedy; Human, All Too Human; Assorted Opinions and Maxims; The Wanderer and his Shadow; Daybreak; The Gay Science; Beyond Good and Evil; The Antichrist*), which are referred to according to section number preceded by an abbreviated title of the work in which they appear. References to the preface and three treatises of *On the Genealogy of Morals* consist of "Preface" or the Roman numeral I, II or III, followed by the section number.

Where no reference to a published English translation is provided, the translation is my own.

A	*The Antichrist*, PN 565–656.
AC	*Der Antichrist* (The Antichrist), KSA 6:165–254.
AOM	*Assorted Opinions and Maxims*. In: *Human, All Too Human*. Translated by R. J. Hollingdale. Cambridge: Cambridge University Press, 1996, 215–299.
BAW	*Historisch-kritische Gesamtausgabe. Werke*. 5 vols. Edited by Hans Joachim Mette and Karl Schlechta. Munich: Beck, 1933–44.
BGE	*Beyond Good and Evil*, BWN 179–435.
BT	*The Birth of Tragedy*, BWN 1–144.
BT Self-Criticism	Attempt at a Self-Criticism
BWN	*Basic Writings of Nietzsche*. Edited and translated by Walter Kaufmann. New York: The Modern Library, 1992.
CV 1	"Ueber das Pathos der Wahrheit" (On the Pathos of Truth), KSA 1:755–760.
CW	*The Case of Wagner*, BWN 601–645.
D	*Daybreak*. Translated by R.J. Hollingdale. Edited by Maudemarie Clark and Brian Leiter. Cambridge Texts in the History of Philosophy. Cambridge: Cambridge University Press, 1997.
D Preface	Daybreak, Preface
DS	David Strauss (= *Unfashionable Observations*, First Piece).
EH	*Ecce homo: How One Becomes What One Is*, BWN 671–791.
EH Clever	Why I Am So Clever
EH HH	Human, All Too Human
EH Destiny	Why I Am a Destiny
EH Wise	Why I am So Wise

EH Zarathustra	Thus Spoke Zarathustra
EH	*Ecce homo. Wie man wird, was man ist*, KSA 6:255–374.
EH klug	Warum ich so klug bin
EH MAM	Menschliches, Allzumenschliches
EH Schicksal	Warum ich ein Schicksal bin
EH weise	Warum ich so weise bin
EH Zarathustra	Also sprach Zarathustra
FW	*Die fröhliche Wissenschaft* (The Gay Science), KSA 3:343–651.
GD	*Götzen-Dämmerung* (Twilight of the Idols), KSA 6:55–161.
GD Alten	Was ich den Alten verdanke
GD Sokrates	Das Problem des Sokrates
GD Sprüche	Sprüche und Pfeile
GD Streifzüge	Streifzüge eines Unzeitgemässen
GM	*On the Genealogy of Morals*, BWN 437–599.
GM Preface	On the Genealogy of Morals, Preface
GM	*Zur Genealogie der Moral*, KSA 5:245–412.
GM Vorrede	Zur Genealogie der Moral. Vorrede
GS	*The Gay Science*. Translated by Walter Kaufmann. New York: Vintage, 1974.
GT	*Die Geburt der Tragödie* (The Birth of Tragedy), KSA 1:9–156.
GT Versuch	Versuch einer Selbstkritik
HH I	*Human, All Too Human (I)*. Translated by Gary Handwerk. In: *The Complete Works of Friedrich Nietzsche*, vol. 3. Stanford: Stanford University Press, 1995.
JGB	*Jenseits von Gut und Böse* (Beyond Good and Evil), KSA 5:9–243.
KGB	*Briefwechsel. Kritische Gesamtausgabe*. Edited by Giorgio Colli and Mazzino Montinari. Berlin/New York: De Gruyter, 1975–.
KGW	*Werke. Kritische Gesamtausgabe*. Edited by Giorgio Colli and Mazzino Montinari. Berlin/New York: De Gruyter, 1967–.
KSA	*Sämtliche Werke. Kritische Studienausgabe*. Edited by Giorgio Colli and Mazzino Montinari. 15 vols. Munich/Berlin/New York: DTV/De Gruyter, 1999.
KSB	*Sämtliche Briefe. Kritische Studienausgabe in 8 Bänden*. Edited by Giorgio Colli and Mazzino Montinari. 8 vols. Munich/Berlin/New York: DTV/De Gruyter, 1986.
M	*Morgenröte* (Daybreak), KSA 3:9–331.
M Vorrede	Morgenröte, Vorrede von 1886
MA I	*Menschliches, Allzumenschliches I* (Human, All Too Human I), KSA 2:9–366.
NL	Nachlass (writings from Nietzsche's literary estate), KSA vols. 7–14.

PN	*The Portable Nietzsche*. Edited and translated by Walter Kaufmann. New York: Penguin, 1982.
PT	"On the Pathos of Truth (1872)," in: *Philosophical Writings*. Edited by Reinhold Grimm and Caroline Molina y Vedia. New York: Continuum, 1995, 83–87.
RWB	Richard Wagner in Bayreuth (= *Unfashionable Observations*, Fourth Piece).
SE	Schopenhauer as Educator (= *Unfashionable Observations*, Third Piece).
TI	*Twilight of the Idols*, PN 463–563.
TI Maxims	Maxims and Arrows
TI Ancients	What I Owe to the Ancients
TI Socrates	The Problem of Socrates
TI Skirmishes	Skirmishes of an Untimely Man
TL	"On Truth and Lying in an Extra-Moral Sense (1873)," in: *Friedrich Nietzsche on Rhetoric and Language*. Edited and translated by Sander L. Gilman, Carole Blair and David J. Parent. Oxford/New York: Oxford University Press, 1989, 246–257.
UB	*Unzeitgemäße Betrachtungen I–IV* (Unfashionable Observations I–IV), KSA 1:157–510.
UO	*Unfashionable Observations*. Translated by Richard T. Gray. In: *The Complete Works of Friedrich Nietzsche*, vol. 2. Stanford: Stanford University Press, 1995.
VM	*Vermischte Meinungen und Sprüche* (Assorted Opinions and Maxims), KSA 2:367–534.
WA	*Der Fall Wagner* (The Case of Wagner), KSA 6:9–53.
WL	"Ueber Wahrheit und Lüge im aussermoralischen Sinne" (On Truth and Lying in an Extra-Moral Sense), KSA 1:873–890.
WP	*The Will to Power*. Edited by Walter Kaufmann. Translated by Walter Kaufmann and R. J. Hollingdale. New York: Vintage, 1968.
WS	*The Wanderer and His Shadow*, In: *Human, All Too Human*. Translated by R. J. Hollingdale. Cambridge: Cambridge University Press, 1996, 301–395.
WS	*Der Wanderer und sein Schatten* (The Wanderer and His Shadow), KSA 2:534–704.
Z	*Thus Spoke Zarathustra*, PN 103–439.
Z I Despisers	On the Despisers of the Body
Z I Reading	On Reading and Writing
Z I Prologue	Zarathustra's Prologue
Z I Women	On Little Old and Young Women
Z II Self-Overcoming	On Self-Overcoming
Z III Gravity	On the Spirit of Gravity

Z III Return	The Return Home
Z III Tablets	On Old and New Tablets
Z	*Also sprach Zarathustra* (Thus Spoke Zarathustra), KSA 4.
Z I Lesen	Vom Lesen und Schreiben
Z I Vorrede	Zarathustra's Vorrede
Z I Verächtern	Von den Verächtern des Leibes
Z I Weiblein	Von alten und jungen Weiblein
Z II Selbst-Ueber- windung	Von der Selbst-Ueberwindung
Z III Heimkehr	Die Heimkehr
Z III Schwere	Vom Geist der Schwere
Z III Tafeln	Von alten und neuen Tafeln

Abbreviations of Works by Georg Christoph Lichtenberg

All quotations from Lichtenberg's *Waste Books* (Sudelbücher) are from Georg Christoph Lichtenberg, *Schriften und Briefe*. Edited by Wolfgang Promies. 3 vols. Munich: Carl Hanser, 1980. Passages are identified by the abbreviation "Sudel-", followed by a letter and a number indicating notebook and passage respectively, e. g., Sudel-F 1219. Notebooks A through L (except G) appear in Volume I. Passages from Sudel-G and those marked with the subscript $_{II}$ appear in volume II. All English translations are my own.

Timeline of Key Publications Discussed and their Publishers

7 May 1878   *Menschliches, Allzumenschliches. Ein Buch für freie Geister* (Human, All Too Human. A Book for Free Spirits); published by Ernst Schmeitzner, Chemnitz.

20 March 1879   *Menschliches, Allzumenschliches. Ein Buch für freie Geister. Anhang: Vermischte Meinungen und Sprüche* (Human All Too Human. A Book for Free Spirits. Supplement: Assorted Opinions and Maxims); Schmeitzner, Chemnitz.

18 December 1879   *Der Wanderer und sein Schatten* (The Wanderer and his Shadow); Schmeitzner, Chemnitz.

Late July 1881   *Morgenröte. Gedanken über die moralischen Vorurtheile* (Daybreak. Thoughts on Moral Prejudices); Schmeitzner, Chemnitz.

10 September 1882   *Die fröhliche Wissenschaft* (The Gay Science, Books I–IV); Schmeitzner, Chemnitz.

End of August 1883   *Also sprach Zarathustra. Ein Buch für Alle und Keinen* (Thus Spoke Zarathustra. A Book for All and None); Schmeitzner, Chemnitz.

Late 1883/early 1884 *Also sprach Zarathustra. Ein Buch für Alle und Keinen, 2*; Schmeitzner, Chemnitz.

10 April 1884   *Also sprach Zarathustra. Ein Buch für Alle und Keinen, 3*; Schmeitzner, Chemnitz.

Early May 1885   *Also sprach Zarathustra. Ein Buch für Alle und Keinen. Vierter und letzter Theil* (Fourth and Final Part); printed by C. G. Naumann, Leipzig.

4 August 1886   *Jenseits von Gut und Böse. Vorspiel einer Philosophie der Zukunft* (Beyond Good and Evil. Prelude to a Philosophy of the Future); C. G. Naumann, Leipzig.

31 October 1886   *Die Geburt der Tragödie. Oder: Griechenthum und Pessimismus. Neue Ausgabe mit dem Versuch einer Selbstkritik* (The Birth of Tragedy. New Edition with the Attempt at a Self-Criticism); printed by E. W. Fritzsch, Leipzig.

31 October 1886   *Menschliches, Allzumenschliches. Ein Buch für freie Geister. Erster Band. Neue Ausgabe mit einer einführenden Vorrede* (Human, All Too Human. A Book for Free Spirits. First Volume. New Edition with an Introductory Preface); Fritzsch, Leipzig.

31 October 1886   *Menschliches, Allzumenschliches. Ein Buch für freie Geister. Zweiter Band. Neue Ausgabe mit einer einführenden Vorrede* (Human, All Too Human. A Book for Free Spirits. Second Volume. New Edition with an Introductory Preface); Fritzsch, Leipzig. NB: volume comprised of VM and WS.

Late 1886   *Also sprach Zarathustra. Ein Buch für Alle und Keinen. In drei Theilen* (Thus Spoke Zarathustra. A Book for All and None. In Three Parts); Fritzsch, Leipzig.

24 June 1887   *Morgenröte. Gedanken über die moralischen Vorurtheile. Neue Ausgabe mit einer einführenden Vorrede* (Daybreak. Thoughts on Moral Prejudices. New Edition with an Introductory Preface); Fritzsch, Leipzig.

24 June 1887   *Die fröhliche Wissenschaft. Neue Ausgabe mit einem Anhange: Lieder des Prinzen Vogelfrei* (The Gay Science. New Edition with a Supplement: The Songs of Prince Vogelfrei); Fritzsch, Leipzig. NB: this edition includes Books I–V.

16 November 1887   *Zur Genealogie der Moral. Eine Streitschrift* (On the Genealogy of Morality. A Polemic); C. G. Naumann, Leipzig.[1]

---

1 For a more comprehensive account of Nietzsche's publication history, see Schaberg, The Nietzsche Canon, which serves as the immediate source for this timeline.

Introduction. The Challenge

In 1878 Nietzsche published his first collection of aphorisms, *Menschliches, Allzumensch-liches* (Human, All Too Human). Years later he would portray this event as a challenge, claiming that he sent two copies to Richard Wagner at the same moment that Wagner was sending him the libretto for his own most recent project, *Parsifal*. According to Nietzsche's account, when the two texts crossed in the mail he heard an ominous sound: "Did it not sound as if two swords had crossed?" (EH HH 2; BWN 744).[1] Though this event may not have unfolded exactly as Nietzsche so dramatically depicts it in *Ecce homo* (he actually received his copy of *Parsifal* several months before *Menschliches, Allzumenschliches* appeared[2]), nevertheless conceptual swords did cross, and once they had, there would be no reconciliation between the philosopher and his former idol. A new phase of Nietzsche's career had begun. A cold scientific tone replaced the heated rhetoric of his earlier writings, a tone matched with a new scientific approach that contrasted the Wagnerian romanticism of those earlier works.

But *Menschliches, Allzumenschliches* presents a challenge to more than Wagner. Its aphoristic structure can be seen as a formal challenge to the dominant mode of *Systemphilosophie*. In presenting his philosophy in aphorisms, Nietzsche refused to subject his own views to the formal constraints imposed by systematic discourse. The aphorism collection, one might say, is a formal manifestation of Nietzsche's later vow in *Götzen-Dämmerung* (Twilight of the Idols, 1888) to "mistrust all system-atizers and [...] avoid them" on the grounds that the "will to a system is a lack of in-tegrity" (TI Maxims 26; PN 470).[3] The aphoristic volumes deliberately shun the formal conventions of academic writing, forgoing sustained argumentation in favor of an array of isolated texts ranging in length from a single sentence to several pages. Though numbered consecutively and at times loosely organized into thematic sec-tions, the aphorism books of Nietzsche's so-called Middle Period, which include not only *Menschliches, Allzumenschliches*, but also *Vermischte Meinungen und Sprüche* (Assorted Opinions and Maxims, 1879), *Der Wanderer und sein Schatten* (The Wanderer and His Shadow, 1879), *Morgenröte* (Daybreak, 1881), and *Die fröh-liche Wissenschaft* (The Gay Science, 1882), often come across as *disjecta membra* col-lected together without any necessary order. Erecting no edifice of sober argumenta-tion leading to a unified conclusion, but instead providing a compilation of discrete statements that the reader must interpret and assemble without any assurance of eventual resolution, Nietzsche's aphorism collections openly challenged the formal conventions of the systematic philosophical treatise. "I don't write treatises," he

---

1 "Diese Kreuzung der zwei Bücher – mir war's, als ob ich einen ominösen Ton dabei hörte. Klang es nicht, als ob sich Degen kreuzten?" (EH MAM 2; KSA 6:327)
2 Nietzsche received Wagner's libretto to *Parsifal* in January; *Menschliches, Allzumenschliches* did not appear until May of 1878; see Schaberg, The Nietzsche Canon, 58.
3 "Ich misstraue allen Systematikern und gehe ihnen aus dem Weg. Der Wille zum System ist ein Mangel an Rechtschaffenheit" (GD Sprüche 26; KSA 6:63).

would write in a note from 1885: "they're for jack-asses and magazine-readers."[4] Instead, he offered *Aphorismenbücher* – books of aphorisms.

Yet even as *Menschliches, Allzumenschliches* presented a challenge to Wagner and to the conventions of philosophical method, its aphoristic form also poses a significant challenge for Nietzsche's reader. The author later conceded in the preface to *Zur Genealogie der Moral* (On the Genealogy of Morals, 1887) that "the aphoristic form causes difficulty" (die aphoristische Form [macht] Schwierigkeit; GM Preface 8; GM Vorrede 8). With interconnections by and large withheld, contextual orientation is suspended, denying the reader even the pretense of the argumentative coherence and demonstrated development that characterizes more conventional academic and philosophical writing. Such a structure thwarts hermeneutic habit, unleashing a cascade of questions: What kind of text is this? What leads Nietzsche to write this way? How do these discrete statements fit together? How are they to be navigated? Does it matter where we start? What exactly are we supposed to do with such texts? The more one reflects on the form, the more the questions proliferate. Without recourse to the standards and expectations of academic convention, the reader must develop new rules of engagement to approach these works. Nietzsche acknowledged that the aphoristic form causes difficulty, but the difficulty, he contended, derives from the fact "that this form is *not* taken *seriously enough*" (dass man diese Form n i c h t s c h w e r g e n u g nimmt; GM Preface 8; GM Vorrede 8). The current study aims to remedy this situation, not only by itself taking the form seriously, but by investigating exactly why Nietzsche did, and what it means to do so.

 Note 7

The years since Nietzsche decried this neglect have done little to improve the treatment of the aphorism in Nietzsche scholarship. There are remarkably few book-length studies dedicated primarily to the works of Nietzsche's Middle Period at all, for scholars tend to read these works in isolated excerpts or simply as forerunners of Nietzsche's more mature philosophy.[5] Though there are notable exceptions,[6] these too invariably manage to circumscribe the issue of the aphoristic form rather than address it directly. There are those who openly disregard the aphorism, seeing it as a notion applicable only to a very narrow selection of Nietzsche's writings, despite the emphasis he

---

4 "Abhandlungen schreibe ich nicht: die sind für Esel und Zeitschriften-Leser" (NL 37[5], 1885; KSA 11:579).

5 Though the subtitle of Strobel, Das Pathos der Distanz (namely "Nietzsche's Decision in Favor of the Aphoristic Style") suggests that the study would address Nietzsche's initial turn to the aphorism, it focuses primarily on those works produced after *Also sprach Zarathustra*, particularly *Jenseits von Gut und Böse*, devoting only eight pages to a work associated with the Middle Period (and that is the fourth book of *Die fröhliche Wissenschaft*, i.e., a book on the cusp of Nietzsche's mature philosophy).

6 Most recently Franco, Nietzsche's Enlightenment; also Abbey, Nietzsche's Middle Period. A few studies focus on a single work from the period, for example Cohen, Science, Culture, and Free Spirits; Higgins, Comic Relief. Others have an even narrower focus, for instance Heller, Von den ersten und letzten Dingen; and the philosophical complement to Heller's study, Claesges, Der maskierte Gedanke.

placed on the form.[7] They contend that the term *Aphorismus* applies only to a very restricted subset of Nietzsche's works, and thus the generic designation is proportionally restricted. Such an understanding is inconsistent both with Nietzsche's use of the term and with the tradition of aphoristic writing in which he participates. In order to clear up this common misunderstanding, the current study begins with an examination of the genre of the aphorism itself. Part One, "Nietzsche and the German Aphoristic Tradition," argues for a broader understanding of the genre *Aphorismus*. The genre encompasses a variety of forms, and this formal diversity itself constitutes an integral part of the German aphoristic tradition's critical stance vis-à-vis systematic discourse. Not all of Nietzsche's aphorisms enjoy the pithy concision of the well-turned *Sentenz* (maxim), but their formal multifariousness and their excess of forms constitute a crucial moment of critique that aligns his aphorism collections felicitously with the larger tradition of aphoristic writing in German letters.

Part Two, "The Turn to the Aphorism," illuminates Nietzsche's initial conversion to aphoristic writing in *Menschliches, Allzumenschliches*. As a form often situated at the crossroads of literature and philosophy, the aphorism seems particularly suitable for a writer whose works straddle these two disciplines. But Nietzsche's turn to the form coincides with his burgeoning interest in the methods of the natural sciences. This too is in keeping with the German aphoristic tradition, though the form's more prominent association with literature and philosophy has long overshadowed this aspect. The German aphorism's origin in the natural sciences, I argue, is crucial for Nietzsche's turn to aphoristic writing in *Menschliches, Allzumenschliches*. Yet Nietzsche bends the form to suit his own purposes, and as his philosophy develops, the aphorism collection becomes a formal correlate to the Death of God, confronting his reader not only with the freedoms enabled by his developing philosophy, but also with the danger of chaos and nihilism that is its potential legacy.

Augmenting both the freedom and the danger of the aphorism collection is the fact that the author himself is not univocal in his account of the form or in the approaches he prescribes. Some readers gloss over the formal challenge by simply assuming there to be a coherence behind the aphoristic works, regardless of how the structure of the works may resist such a reading.[8] Even Franco's exemplary study devotes very little space to justifying such a methodology, citing Nietzsche's appeal in the preface to *Morgenröte* that one read him slowly and deliberately, "looking fore and aft" (rück- und vorsichtig)[9]; Franco reads this as an invitation to seek out a coherent philosophy from behind the disjointed texts of the *Freigeist*-trilogy.[10] Franco is

---

7 This position also emerges in one of the more recent studies dedicated specifically to the aphorism in Nietzsche's writing: Marsden, Nietzsche and the Art of the Aphorism.

8 Kaufmann promoted such an approach; Franco is its most recent and perhaps most compelling advocate.

9 D Preface 5; M Vorrede 5; KSA 3:17.

10 NB: *Menschliches, Allzumenschliches* alone actually consists of three books, including *Vermischte Meinungen und Sprüche* (Assorted Opinions and Maxims, 1879) and *Der Wanderer und sein Schatten*

not alone in this assumption.[11] But to assume such coherence is to assume a lot. Even if one agrees with Franco's take on the preface to *Morgenröte*, one must not forget that this preface was prefixed to the collection in 1887, that is, several years after the volume's initial publication in 1881. And the intervening years were pivotal for Nietzsche's development. Though Nietzsche's perhaps most notorious declaration – that God is dead – first appeared in the original edition of *Die fröhliche Wissenschaft* (GS 108; FW 108), the aphorism collections of the *Freigeist*-trilogy largely lack the key concepts that underlie Nietzsche's mature philosophy: particularly the will to power and the eternal recurrence of the same.[12] Only with the publication of *Also sprach Zarathustra* (Thus Spoke Zarathustra, 1883–1885) did these terms emerge as gravitational centers of Nietzsche's writings. The aphorism collections, lacking clear argumentative structure, are particularly susceptible to such gravitational shifts.

While scholars have frequently noted the lack of apparent order in the aphorism books,[13] there are those who recognize a change after *Also sprach Zarathustra*. Eva Strobel, for instance, notes that the aphorism collections published after *Zarathustra*, namely Book V of *Die fröhliche Wissenschaft* and *Jenseits von Gut und Böse* (Beyond Good and Evil), are more coherent and refined.[14] Likewise Werner Stegmaier's comprehensive study of Book V of *Die fröhliche Wissenschaft* argues that while there may be little structure to Books I–IV,[15] in Book V Nietzsche allows himself no digressions or trivialities; here his art of the aphorism achieves full maturity.[16] This is also the time when Nietzsche would provide his most lucid and sustained discussions of aphoristic writing. After the publication of *Also sprach Zarathustra* Nietzsche developed guidelines for reading the *Freigeist*-trilogy that reflected the emerging coalescence of his thought, returning to his earlier aphoristic works and supplementing

---

(The Wanderer and his Shadow, 1880), but because Nietzsche describes these latter two as supplements to *Menschliches* (and indeed, Nietzsche would later combine them under the title, *Menschliches, Allzumenschliches II*), Franco treats them as a single work.

11 Peter Heller, for instance, sets out to demonstrate the unity of Nietzsche's works, even if it is "the unity of dynamic antithesis" (Heller, Von den ersten und letzten Dingen, xi–xii); despite Heller's insistence on unity, his formulation nevertheless smacks of what Werner Stegmaier has recently criticized as the "dogma of ambivalence and contradictoriness" pervasive in Nietzsche scholarship; see Stegmaier, Nietzsches Befreiung der Philosophie, 77. Stegmaier himself operates on the hermeneutic principle that contradictions are not in Nietzsche's text, but result from interpretation, and the interpreter should seek to neutralize such contradictions along with ambivalences (Stegmaier, Nietzsches Befreiung der Philosophie, 86). Like Franco, Stegmaier gives Nietzsche the benefit of the doubt with regard to the coherence of his at times formally disjointed philosophy.

12 The eternal recurrence of the same does make a brief appearance in the penultimate passage of *Die fröhliche Wissenschaft*'s first edition (GS 341; FW 341), but the volume does not develop the concept explicitly.

13 Most famously by Danto, Nietzsche as Philosopher; but even Richard Schacht has described Nietzsche's works as an "assemblage of ... rather loosely connected notes" (Schacht, Nietzsche, xi).

14 Strobel, Das Pathos der Distanz, 163.

15 Stegmaier, Nietzsches Befreiung der Philosophie, 85, fn. 148.

16 Stegmaier, Nietzsches Befreiung der Philosophie, 61.

them with prefaces. This includes the preface to *Daybreak*, which plays an important role in the approaches of both Franco and Stegmaier. In discussing his works as a whole, the prefaces hint at the unexpressed coherence of the respective aphorism collections. This impression is further reinforced by the "model" of interpretation Nietzsche claims to provide in 1887's *Zur Genealogie der Moral*, in the preface of which he claims:

> An aphorism, properly stamped and molded, has not been "deciphered" when it has simply been read; rather, one has then to begin its *exegesis*, for which is required an art of exegesis. I have offered in the third treatise of the present book a model of what I regard as "exegesis" in such a case – an aphorism is prefixed to this treatise, the treatise itself is a commentary on it. (GM Preface 8)[17]

That model attests to the underlying unity and coherence of all Nietzsche's works. Part Three of the current study, "Re-Reading the Aphorism," examines this model and argues that while the approach suggested by these guidelines may reflect the position of the mature, post-*Zarathustra* Nietzsche, they do not necessarily align with the writing strategy motivating the earlier aphorism collections themselves. As Nietzsche puts it elsewhere in *Zur Genealogie der Moral*: "The cause of the origin of a thing and its eventual utility, its actual employment and place in a system of purposes, lie worlds apart" (GM II 12).[18] In Nietzsche's case, part of the challenge is to distinguish what initially led him to aphoristic writing in his Middle Period from the role he assigned to it in his mature philosophy.

The fourth and final part of this study, "The Aphoristic Paradigm," seeks to account for Nietzsche's sustained interest in the form despite substantial developments in his philosophy. It locates this unifying thread in the dynamic of excess – of transgression through superabundance – which characterizes Nietzsche's writings throughout his career. Perhaps somewhat counterintuitively, the aphorism constitutes a formal manifestation of the Dionysian excess Nietzsche thematizes in *Die Geburt der Tragödie* (The Birth of Tragedy). The structure of Dionysian excess provides a framework for understanding the operations of the aphorism, which revels in the transgression of the tight bounds drawn around it. In the act of reading, we are constantly tempted to establish the boundaries of a text, to limit potential meanings in order to discern the text's meaning. We try to neutralize semantic multivalences by

---

17 "die aphoristische Form [macht] Schwierigkeit: sie liegt darin, dass man diese Form heute n i c h t s c h w e r g e n u g nimmt. Ein Aphorismus, rechtschaffen geprägt und ausgegossen, ist damit, dass er abgelesen ist, noch nicht 'entziffert'; vielmehr hat nun erst dessen A u s l e g u n g zu beginnen, zu der es einer Kunst der Auslegung bedarf. Ich habe in der dritten Abhandlung dieses Buchs ein Muster von dem dargeboten, was ich in einem solchen Falle 'Auslegung' nenne: – dieser Abhandlung ist ein Aphorismus vorangestellt, sie selbst ist dessen Commentar" (GM Vorrede 8; KSA 5:255–256).

18 "die Ursache der Entstehung eines Dings und dessen schliessliche Nützlichkeit, dessen thatsächliche Verwendung und Einordnung in ein System von Zwecken [liegen] toto coelo auseinander" (GM II 12; KSA 5:313).

making them explicit, or to restrict a text's freedom through categorization in terms of genre, style, theme, or authorship. Nietzsche's writing willfully resists such attempts, and the guises that this resistance repeatedly assumes can be unified under what this study calls "excess." Through the concept of excess we can begin to understand the motivations behind his sustained interest in the aphorism, situating his aphoristic writings within his greater oeuvre and determining the relationship that this form encourages between Nietzsche's work and his reader.

Nietzsche's choice of the aphorism as the object for his model of an "art of exegesis" is particularly apt, for the aphorism has long been situated at the intersection of systematic and non-systematic discourse. Anglo-American Nietzsche scholarship tends to bifurcate along precisely this fault line. On the one extreme are those who insist on the systematic coherence of Nietzsche's philosophy.[19] On the other end of the scholarly spectrum are those "postmodern" readings that render Nietzsche's writings somehow "beyond interpretation, by failing to have a determinate structure, form, or meaning."[20] Though there may indeed be many "beyonds" in Nietzsche's writing, moving "beyond interpretation" is not one of them. This notion is problematic not because the description of Nietzsche's writing as irreducible to a particular meaning is necessarily false, but rather because it relies upon a false appositive: to lack determinate meaning is not the same as being beyond interpretation. Reciprocally, just because a text can be subjected to interpretation does not imply that its definite meaning can therefore be determined. This false appositive gives rise to a false opposition that pits interpretation and meaning against one another, as though the former provided liberation and the latter chains, or from another perspective, the former chaos and the latter stability.

Werner Stegmaier's strategy of "contextual interpretation" offers a compelling alternative to these extreme positions. His method begins by reading the individual aphorism in isolation, then broadens the scope gradually to consider the aphorism's place within the context of the published collection in which it appears, and finally reads the text in light of Nietzsche's oeuvre as a whole.[21] Stegmaier's most comprehensive illustration of this strategy, *Nietzsches Befreiung der Philosophie* (2012), follows in the footsteps of Peter Heller's 1972 study of the first section of *Menschliches, Allzumenschliches* both in the general contours of its method and in its focus on a single contig-

---

19 Brian Leiter's portrayal of Nietzsche as a "speculative methodical naturalist" provides one of the strongest presentations of this approach; as the designation implies, Leiter sees Nietzsche as a philosopher whose methods are continuous with those of the natural sciences, including a degree of rigor that precludes contradiction (Leiter, Nietzsche on Morality). See also, e.g., Nehamas, Nietzsche: Life as Literature; Clark, Nietzsche on Truth and Philosophy; Richardson, Nietzsche's New Darwinism, and Richardson, Nietzsche's System.
20 Nehamas, Nietzsche: Life as Literature, 20; see, e.g., Kofman, Nietzsche and Metaphor; Jacques Derrida, Spurs/Éperons; Oliver, A Dagger through the Heart.
21 See Stegmaier, After Montinari, particularly 14–15. For similar strategies, see Heller, Von den ersten und letzten Dingen, and van Tongeren, Reinterpreting Modern Culture.

There would seem to be a problem of terminology here, and Nietzsche himself recognized that the designation "Aphorismus" was not entirely unproblematic. In a journal entry from 1880, he betrays a degree of exasperation with the term:

> They're aphorisms! Are they aphorisms? – may those who reproach me for it reflect for a moment and then apologize to themselves – I don't need a word for myself.[31]

Though this passage leaves the antecedent of the pronoun "they" (es) unspecified, clearly Nietzsche addresses the issue of his current writing style here. When he wrote these remarks he had already published three *Aphorismen-Sammlungen* and was in the process of writing *Morgenröte*, his fourth. Yet the statement can be read in different ways, depending upon where one places the emphasis. It might be a simple assertion: "They *are* [indeed] aphorisms!" Thus understood, the statement erases any doubt regarding the generic identity of Nietzsche's present undertaking. Then again, it might echo or anticipate an accusation: "They're [nothing but] *aphorisms!*" The exclamation point thereby conveys a sense of shock, presumably that of the critical reader, at the author's audacity in producing texts that don't comply to the formal standards of academic philosophy. But regardless of how one reads the opening sentence, one thing appears certain: "They're aphorisms!" This opening statement's tone of certainty – complete with exclamation point – is quickly undermined by the jarring question, "Are they aphorisms?" This could be a response to an accusation or simply a second thought of the writer's own; in either case, emphatic certainty regarding generic identity is immediately followed by a sign of indecision. The question of genre would be far more easily resolved if this statement and question were reversed, but no, the confidence with which the passage begins quickly turns to doubt.

In this note from 1880, Nietzsche recognizes aphoristic writing as a point of contention for which he might be reproached, though the cause for reproach remains unstated. Certainly he could expect the non-standard academic form to meet resistance, or he may also have been thinking of his publisher, Ernst Schmeitzner, who apparently discouraged Nietzsche from writing aphorisms, contending that his readers no longer wanted them.[32] But even when the aphorism does find a broad audience, its perceived lack of cultural or philosophical seriousness can render it suspect. That same year had seen the first publication of Marie von Ebner-Eschenbach's popular *Aphorismen*, a collection of didactic sayings reminiscent of La Rochefoucauld. François Duc de La Rochefoucauld's *Réflexions ou sentences et maximes morales* (1665) is the source of many

---

31 "Es sind Aphorismen! Sind es Aphorismen? – mögen die welche mir daraus einen Vorwurf machen, ein wenig nachdenken und dann sich vor sich selber entschuldigen – ich brauche kein Wort für mich" (NL 7[192], 1880; KSA 9:356).
32 In a letter to Heinrich Köselitz, Nietzsche would contend that, "in jedem seiner letzten Briefe betonte [Schmeitzner], daß 'meine Leser keine Aphorismen mehr von mir lesen wollten'" (KGB III/1, 121–123, no. 143); though Schmeitzner may well have been right, he nevertheless claimed to await the manuscript of *Die fröhliche Wissenschaft* with anticipation (see his letter to Nietzsche from 10 May 1882; KGB III/2, 253–254, no. 121). See Schaberg, The Nietzsche Canon, 80

pithy insights like "Self-love is the greatest of all flatterers."[33] Ebner-Eschenbach in turn offers such gems as: "Vanity rejects all healthy nourishment, living exclusively on the poison of flattery, and in doing so it thrives in luxuriant abundance."[34] But while Nietzsche held La Rochefoucauld in high regard (more on this below), the name Ebner-Eschenbach does not appear in his publications or notebooks. Still, her collection was well received (as early as 1906 the esteemed literary scholar Eduard Engel would proclaim it "already a classic work"[35]) and did much to disseminate the term "Aphorismus" in the German-speaking world. It did little, however, to shake the association of the aphorism with trivial literature. In the period 1860–1880, the aphorism was often seen as a soporific manifestation of bourgeois mediocrity caught up in ideals of eternal truth and beauty that rendered not wit, but docile sophistication and blandness of thought.[36] Perhaps Nietzsche had this low estimation of the form in mind when wrestling with its generic designation. Bernard Greiner presumes that Nietzsche saw as the point of contention his choice to write aphorisms rather than a more systematic treatise à la Kant and Hegel.[37] According to this reading, Nietzsche anticipated the criticism that, were he a serious philosopher, he would not settle for a haphazard assortment of diverse assertions; rather, he would take the next step demanded by conventional philosophical discourse and arrange his claims into an integrated system of arguments. Greiner's explication nicely links the moment of reproach to the identification of the genre, reading the above text as an apologia for aphoristic writing. Nietzsche thereby seems to suggest that if these ignorant accusers took the time to think about it, they might actually recognize the error of their criticism.

But this reading, while elegant, fails to account for the doubt Nietzsche introduces with the question, "Are they aphorisms?" If this were an instance of unreserved advocacy for aphoristic writing, it would make more sense for Nietzsche to confirm the opening statement rather than undermine it through hesitation. Furthermore, the closing line, "I don't need a word for myself," exhibits a lingering misgiving that belies the confidence of the opening assertion. J. Hillis Miller reads this closing line as Nietzsche's refusal to waste words defending himself for his choice to write aphoristically.[38] Indeed, the fact that Nietzsche never bothered to publish this passage might be seen to reinforce this reading. But Miller unnecessarily stretches the meaning of the closing line, "Ich brauche kein Wort für mich." I say he does so unnecessarily because one can just as well read this closing as a return to the generic uncertainty raised by the question, "Are they aphorisms?"

---

33 "L'amour-propre est le plus grand de tous les flatteurs" (La Rochefoucauld, The Maxims, 2, no. 2).
34 "Die Eitelkeit weist jede gesunde Nahrung von sich, lebt ausschließlich von dem Gifte der Schmeichelei und gedeiht dabei in üppigster Fülle" (Ebner-Eschenbach, Aphorismen, 14; my translation).
35 Quoted in Spicker, Kurze Geschichte des deutschen Aphorismus, 106–107.
36 See Spicker, Kurze Geschichte des deutschen Aphorismus, 97.
37 Greiner, Friedrich Nietzsche, 9.
38 Miller, Aphorism as Instrument of Political Action in Nietzsche, 78.

The fact is, Nietzsche does not actually *need* the simple generic designation "Aphorismen." Many of those who have contributed to the aphoristic tradition in German letters have coined their own terms for their kinds of writing. Alongside more widespread terms like *Fragment, Maxime,* and *Sentenz,* we find highly idiosyncratic nomenclature: *Splitter* (splinters), *Brocken* (snatches), *Funken* (sparks), and many more.[39] But Nietzsche refrains from this particular kind of neologizing, and instead on several occasions uses the term *Aphorismus* to describe his own writing. This generic designation is of particular interest, because the notion of genre offers a means to approach these texts that do not conform to the convention of sustained argumentative discourse.

The actual term "aphorism" is frequently traced to Hippocrates (460 – 377 BCE). It comes from the Greek "aphorismos" (ἀφορίσμός), which itself derives from "aphorizein" (ἀφορίζειν), meaning "to mark off boundaries," or "to define."[40] The genre of the aphorism originally referred to a theorem or axiom, often from the realm of medicine. The text is typically portrayed as brief, precise, and in prose (distinguishing it from, say, the epigram).[41] But there is little consensus regarding the specific attributes of the aphorism. In Nietzsche scholarship, the meanings of "aphoristic" and "aphorism" have a tendency to fluctuate, not because there is serious debate regarding the genre, but rather for quite the opposite reason: because scholars tend to gloss over them or treat the terms as self-evident. The first study dedicated to Nietzsche's aphoristic mode, Heinz Krüger's dissertation, "Über den Aphorismus als philosophische Form" (On the Aphorism as Philosophical Form, 1956), offers little guidance, for it avoids discussing generic particularities by portraying the aphorism as a cognitive form (*Denkform*) rather than a linguistic one (*Sprachform*); this effectively neutralizes any formal examination of the genre. More commonly, however, scholars tend to promote generic definitions that are either too broad to be useful or so narrow that they raise more questions than they answer. There are those, for instance, who refer to just about everything Nietzsche wrote as an "aphorism," as though the "Maxims and Arrows" (Sprüche und Pfeile) that open *Götzen-Dämmerung* were generically indistinguishable from the twenty-five sections of *Die Geburt der Tragödie.*[42] To call every text an aphorism, however, diffuses the genre to such a degree as to erase any kind of generic distinction whatsoever, rendering the term effectively meaningless. On the other hand are those who bristle at any broad use of the term "aphorism," claiming

---

39 In the introduction to his collection of essays on the aphorism, Gerhard Neumann mentions two from Johann Georg Hamann: *Brocken* (snatches) and *Grillen* (crickets); three from Novalis: *Blütenstaub* (pollen), *Senker* (countersinks) and *Fermente* (enzymes); two from Adorno: *minima moralia* and *Monogramme* (monograms); and a slew of others, including *Funken* (sparks, Johann Wilhelm Ritter); *Späne* (shavings; Goethe), and others; Neumann, Einleitung, 3.

40 Liddel/Scott, A Greek-English Lexicon, 292.

41 See for example Schalk, Aphorismus; Schmidt/Gessmann, Philosophisches Wörterbuch, s.v. "Aphorismus," 43–44.

42 See, for example, Behler, Confrontations, 96; also Foster, Heirs to Dionysus, xi and 438, n. 11.

in frequently-repeated caveats that not all of Nietzsche's writings, even those in his aphorism collections, are aphorisms "in the strict sense."[43] We might include in this category Karl Jaspers' claim that Nietzsche's writing is not "*aphoristic* in the sense of the famous aphorists."[44] In 1934 Johannes Klein questioned the applicability of the term: "A very large part of the so-called 'aphorisms' [Aphorismen] are just very short treatises [Abhandlungen]," which Klein likens to Schopenhauer's "Aphorisms on the Wisdom of Life"; he notes further that while these "little treatises" often contain aphorisms, "that in no way makes them aphorisms themselves."[45] Continuing in this vein, Alexander Nehamas contends many decades later that because only a limited number of Nietzsche's statements reflect the terse, pithy witticisms commonly associated with the genre, that the value of the generic understanding is correspondingly limited, and that paying too much attention to the aphorism is therefore more of a detour than a useful avenue of approach to understanding Nietzsche.[46] Narrowing the genre to include only those texts which display brevity and wit, however, misapprehends the German aphoristic tradition. As I demonstrate below, such an approach applies a model of the genre that both defies Nietzsche's understanding of the form "Aphorismus" and ignores the tradition in which he consciously participates.

This narrow understanding of the aphoristic form "to denote a short expression of a general truth or pointed assertion,"[47] as Jill Marsden puts it, poses a further hazard. It not only excludes many of the texts that Nietzsche himself refers to as aphorisms, but it encourages the reader to include texts under the rubric of "aphorism" that perhaps do not belong there. Marsden's understanding of the genre enables her to write confidently of the "aphorisms" to be found in *Also sprach Zarathustra*, despite Nietzsche's insistence that the work is *not* a collection of aphorisms. Though this assertion may not entail that the work contains no aphorisms, at least one influential scholar considers it misleading to apply the generic designation "Aphorismus" to excerpts from longer passages.[48] The danger of such leniency in classification has

---

43 Häntzschel-Schlotke, Der Aphorismus als Stilform bei Nietzsche, 40; Greiner, Friedrich Nietzsche: Versuch und Versuchung in seinen Aphorismen, 78. Unlike Häntzschel-Schlotke, however, Greiner at least does not treat the generic identity of the aphorism as unproblematically self-evident. He situates "real aphorisms" somewhere between, "essay-like shorter treatises" and "psychological sketches," on the one hand, and, "anecdotes, metaphors, parables, illustrations, and the like," on the other (Greiner, Friedrich Nietzsche, 44). The aphorism must be short, but not too short. Still, his emphasis is on "brevity and concision" (Greiner, Friedrich Nietzsche, 29); my translations.
44 Jaspers, Nietzsche, 9; my translation.
45 Klein, Wesen und Bau des deutschen Aphorismus, 365; my translation.
46 Nehamas, Nietzsche: Life as Literature, 19; see also Abbey, Nietzsche's Middle Period, 158.
47 Marsden, Nietzsche and the Art of the Aphorism, 23.
48 NB: the pioneer of aphorism studies Franz H. Mautner discourages readers from confusing the aphorisms with aphorism-like texts removed from their original context. See Mautner, Der Aphorismus als literarische Gattung, 52. In his edition of collected German aphorisms, Gerhard Fieguth rarely truncates or otherwise edits any of the texts from Nietzsche that he includes (Fieguth, Deutsche Aphorismen, 148–161). He selects those texts that are brief, that fall under the layman's under-

been highlighted by recent developments in Nietzsche scholarship. Until not so long ago, it was widely held that Nietzsche himself had excerpted an aphorism from *Zarathustra* in the Third Treatise of *Zur Genealogie der Moral*. In the preface to the *Genealogie*, Nietzsche claims that "an aphorism is prefixed to this treatise [the Third], the treatise itself is a commentary on it" (GM Preface 8).[49] The Third Treatise, in turn, begins with an epigraph culled from *Also sprach Zarathustra:* "Unconcerned, mocking, violent – thus wisdom wants *us:* she is a woman and always loves only a warrior" (GM III; BWN 533).[50] Brief, provocative, and eminently quotable, the text adheres to the common understanding of what constitutes an aphorism.

How exactly Nietzsche gets from these particular words to the analysis of the ascetic ideal that is the focus of the treatise has long tested and perplexed his readers, particularly since he presents this *Commentar* as a "model" (Muster) of what he considers his "art of exegesis" (Kunst der Auslegung). The loose relationship between the opening "aphorism" and the treatise to follow has led some to suggest that Nietzsche's model of hermeneutic acumen amounts virtually to a philological free-for-all, if not a renunciation of interpretability itself.[51] If this is the paradigm of interpretation Nietzsche would have his reader follow, then it would seem that anything is possible, for while one may certainly link this passage from *Zarathustra* to the issues explored in the Third Treatise, the associative moves that enable Nietzsche to get from one text to the other require such interpretive acrobatics that they rule out all but the loosest exegetical restrictions. Nietzsche's "model" would seem offer a radical departure from the rigors of the nineteenth-century philology in which he was trained, allowing for a degree of exegetical freedom and interpretive play that effectively anticipates so-called "postmodern" readings of his work.

Scholars less inclined to celebrate such unbounded liberty in interpretation question whether the excerpt from *Zarathustra* prefixed to the Third Treatise is in fact the aphorism to which Nietzsche refers in the preface of the *Genealogie*, but this reassessment itself relies upon a greatly relaxed understanding of what qualifies as an aphorism. Following the epigraph, the Third Treatise unfolds in twenty-eight

---

standing of the aphorism, but he does not extract statements from longer passages to present them as aphorisms – that is, except once: he includes the first portion of the passage from the first book of *Also sprach Zarathustra*, "On Little Old and Young Women" (Von alten und jungen Weiblein; KSA 4:84–86). As mentioned earlier, Nietzsche specifically stated that *Zarathustra* was "not an aphorism-collection," and yet Fieguth has no trouble mining it this once for an aphoristic statement. Remarkably, however, he pares the passage down, and in doing so omits one of Nietzsche's most memorable, some might say aphoristic, statements: "Du gehst zu Frauen? Vergiss die Peitsche nicht!"
49 "dieser Abhandlung ist ein Aphorismus vorangestellt, sie selbst ist dessen Commentar" (GM Vorrede 8; KSA 5:255–256).
50 "Unbekümmert, spöttisch, gewaltthätig – so will uns die Weisheit: sie ist ein Weib, sie liebt immer nur einen Kriegsmann" (GM III; KSA 5:339); the passage comes from Z I Reading (PN 153); Z I Lesen (KSA 4:49).
51 See, for example, Nehamas, Nietzsche: Life as Literature, 114–115; Oliver, A Dagger Through the Heart; Shapiro, Nietzschean Aphorism as Art and Act, 409.

sections that vary in length from a single page to several pages. John T. Wilcox[52] and Christopher Janaway[53] have compellingly argued that not the epigraph, but Section 1 of the treatise itself constitutes the object of explication. Both the epigraph from *Zarathustra* and Section 1 can be seen to be "prefixed" (vorangestellt), for as Janaway notes, the first section of the treatise was literally "prefixed" to the essay, insofar as the printer's manuscript originally began with Section 2; the first section was only added later (see KSA 14:380). Maudemarie Clark, with reference to Wilcox's research into the issue, further buttresses this claim by investigating the manuscript itself in the Nietzsche-Archiv in Weimar.[54] She concludes that Section 1 was added after Nietzsche had completed Sections 2 through 23 of the *Genealogie* (which had originally been numbered 1–22).

This reading is persuasive in that one no longer needs to perform radical interpretive maneuvers to see how the opening section anticipates the structure of the treatise that follows. The price for this convenience, however, is an expanded understanding of the term "Aphorismus." Unlike the epigraph, which enjoys the pithy concision commonly associated with the aphorism,[55] Section 1 of the Third Treatise hardly rolls off the tongue. In full, this "aphorism" reads:

> What is the meaning of ascetic ideals? – In the case of artists they mean nothing or too many things; in the case of philosophers and scholars something like a sense and instinct for the most favorable preconditions of higher spirituality; in the case of women at best one *more* seductive charm, a touch of *morbidezza* in fair flesh, the angelic look of a plump pretty animal; in the case of the physiologically deformed and deranged (the *majority* of mortals) an attempt to see themselves as "too good" for this world, a saintly form of debauch, their chief weapon in the struggle against slow pain and boredom; in the case of priests the distinctive priestly faith, their best instrument of power, also the "supreme" license for power; in the case of saints, finally, a pretext for hibernation, their *novissima gloriae cupido*, their repose in nothingness ("God"), their form of madness. *That* the ascetic ideal has meant so many things to man, however, is an expression of the basic fact of the human will, its *horror vacui: it needs a goal* – and it will rather will *nothingness* than *not* will. – Am I understood? ... Have I been understood? ... *"Not at all, my dear sir!"* – Then let us start again, from the beginning. (GM III 1)[56]

---

52 Wilcox, What Aphorism Does Nietzsche Explicate in GM III; see also, Wilcox, That Exegesis of an Aphorism in Genealogy III.

53 Janaway, Nietzsche's Illustration of the Art of Exegesis.

54 Clark, From the Nietzsche Archive.

55 NB: Wilcox even questions the applicability of the term "aphorism" for the epigraph, for although it enjoys the pithy concision often associated with the genre (and called into question in the first chapter of the current study), it is not an independent text, but an excerpt extracted from one of Zarathustra's speeches; Franz Mautner would not call it an aphorism for precisely this reason.

56 "Was bedeuten asketische Ideale? – Bei Künstlern Nichts oder zu Vielerlei; bei Philosophen und Gelehrten Etwas wie Witterung und Instinkt für die günstigsten Vorbedingungen hoher Geistigkeit; bei Frauen, besten Falls, eine Liebenswürdigkeit der Verführung m e h r, ein wenig morbidezza auf schönem Fleische, die Engelhaftigkeit eines hübschen fetten Thiers; bei physiologisch Verunglückten und Verstimmten (bei der M e h r z a h l der Sterblichen) einen Versuch, sich 'zu gut' für diese Welt vorzukommen, eine heilige Form der Ausschweifung, ihr Hauptmittel im Kampf mit dem langsamen

Leaving out the moment of dialogue at the end, both Wilcox and Janaway demonstrate how the subsequent twenty-seven sections of the Third Treatise closely adhere to the structure outlined in Section 1, and how they protract the aphorism's self-assured bullet points into a sustained argument. Following Nietzsche's closing suggestion, Section 2 literally returns to the question that opens Section 1, "What is the meaning of ascetic ideals?" And the final section, Section 28, closes with the same conclusion reached in the opening aphorism: "man would rather will *nothingness* than *not* will." In between, the treatise unfolds largely along the same lines as the aphorism itself. It begins with a discussion of "artists," as embodied in the figure of Wagner, which then transitions in the fifth section into a discussion of "philosophers and scholars," as represented by Schopenhauer, the discussion of whose ascetic practices occupies the next five sections. After the tenth section, the structural parallel becomes less vivid, as discussion of the philosopher is increasingly interwoven with discussion of the ascetic "priest," which in turn develops into discussion of the unfortunate "majority." Janaway and Wilcox may not entirely agree on every detail,[57] but the thrust of their arguments – that the structure of the treatise follows the outline of the aphorism – is plausible.

This reading, of course, requires an understanding of the genre that allows for an aphorism closer to 200 words than twenty, or rather, the very plausibility of this reading encourages readers to expand their conception of the genre beyond simply the "short expression of a general truth or pointed assertion." Jaspers was right when he claimed that Nietzsche's writing is not "*aphoristic* in the sense of the famous aphorists," if by the "famous aphorists" he means the likes of Ebner-Eschenbach or La Rochefoucauld. But when Nietzsche presents the Third Treatise as a reading of an aphorism that bears little resemblance to the works of such authors, and when he describes *Menschliches, Allzumenschliches* as an *Aphorismen-Sammlung*, he seems to have a different sense in mind. "They're aphorisms! Are they aphorisms?" Apparently they are, and while this terminology may irk those who insist on a narrow understanding of the genre, Nietzsche's broader understanding is not without precedent in the German aphoristic tradition.

Schmerz und der Langenweile; bei Priestern den eigentlichen Priesterglauben, ihr bestes Werkzeug der Macht, auch die 'allerhöchste' Erlaubniss zur Macht; bei Heiligen endlich einen Vorwand zum Winterschlaf, ihre novissima gloriae cupido, ihre Ruhe im Nichts ('Gott'), ihre Form des Irrsinns. D a s s aber überhaupt das asketische Ideal dem Menschen so viel bedeutet hat, darin drückt sich die Grundthatsache des menschlichen Willens aus, sein horror vacui: e r b r a u c h t e i n Z i e l – und eher will er noch d a s N i c h t s wollen, als n i c h t wollen. – Versteht man mich? ... Hat man mich verstanden? ... 'S c h l e c h t e r d i n g s n i c h t! m e i n H e r r!' – Fangen wir also von vorne an" (GM III 1; KSA 5:339).

57 For instance, Janaway, Nietzsche's Illustration of the Art of Exegesis, sees the discussion of "saints" in GM III 17; Wilcox, What Aphorism Does Nietzsche Explicate in GM III, contends Nietzsche skips this point.

Sentenz and *Aphorismus*

Nietzsche himself sows the seeds of generic confusion in his first aphorism collection, *Menschliches, Allzumenschliches,* by aligning his project thematically, methodological-ly, and at least in part stylistically with that of the great French aphorists, "La Roche-foucauld and his spiritual and artistic relatives" (HH I 35).[58] Toward the end of his pro-ductive life, Nietzsche would provide a tidy clarification of the book's title : "where you see ideal things, I see – human, alas only all too human" (EH HH 1; BWN 738).[59] But in *Menschliches, Allzumenschliches* itself, he introduces the title phrase in a passage that emphasizes the object and method of his analysis rather than its findings. The passage "*Advantages of psychological observation*" was originally intended as part of a preface to the book (KSA 13:127), but instead it opens the book's second section. It does so by directly equating "reflection upon what is human, all too human" with "psychological observation" (HH I 35).[60] The term "psychological observation" (psychologische Beo-bachtung) clearly refers to a recent work by his friend Paul Rée (1849 – 1901), whose own collection of aphorisms appeared in 1875 under that very title, *Psychological Ob-servations.*[61] Any doubt that Nietzsche had Rée in mind is quickly dispelled by the pas-sage that follows, in which Nietzsche directly mentions the "writer of the 'Psycholog-ical Observations'" (Verfasser der "Psychologischen Beobachtungen"; HH I 36; MA I 36). Nietzsche's interest in what he dubbed *Réealismus* would eventually sour,[62] but at the time Rée's book appeared anonymously, Nietzsche claims to have recognized the author immediately and his reception of the work was openly – Lou Salomé would say "overly"[63] – enthusiastic.[64] Salomé accurately describes Rée's book as "max-ims in the spirit and style of La Rochefoucauld" (Sentenzen im Geist und Stil Laroche-foucaulds).[65] And indeed, it was likely Rée who first aroused Nietzsche's real interest in the French *moralistes* (i.e., psychologists). What characterizes these "moralists," it should be noted, is not a tendency to moralize, but rather a preoccupation with mor-ality and customs. As Nietzsche puts it, they "dissect morality" (die Moral seciren; WS

---

58 "La Rochefoucauld und seine Geistes- und Kunstverwandten" (MA I 35).

59 "wo i h r ideale Dinge seht, sehe i c h – Menschliches, ach nur Allzumenschliches!" (EH MAM 1; KSA 6:322).

60 "Vo r t h e i l e   d e r   p s y c h o l o g i s c h e n   B e o b a c h t u n g. – Dass das Nachdenken über Menschliches, Allzumenschliches – oder wie der gelehrtere Ausdruck lautet: die psychologische Beobachtung [...]" (MA I 35).

61 Rée, Psychologische Beobachtungen.

62 Robin Small has done much to illuminate this relationship; see Small, Nietzsche and Rée, and his edition and translation of Rée, Basic Writings. See also Donnellan, Friedrich Nietzsche and Paul Rée.

63 Andreas-Salomé, Friedrich Nietzsche in seinen Werken, 132. Nietzsche's own later remarks on his early enthusiasm for Réealismus come to the same conclusion; see EH HH 6, EH MAM 6; GM Preface 4, GM Vorrede 4.

64 See, e.g., KSB 5:122 f.

65 Andreas-Salomé, Friedrich Nietzsche in seinen Werken, 132; my translation. For a comprehensive list of intertextual references, see Treiber, Erläuterungen, 385 – 409.

19), emphasizing psychological rather than metaphysical explanations. Like Nietzsche after them, they scrutinized with merciless wit psychological phenomena like vanity, self-love, self-deception, and love of others, along with social customs such as marriage, friendship, law, and of course morality. With their shared suspicion of the human, all-too-human in mind, Robert B. Pippin has declared Nietzsche himself "one of the great 'French moralists.'"[66] Though Nietzsche likely already knew the names of some *moralistes* from his reading of Schopenhauer,[67] they do not appear in his own notebooks until after his friendship with Rée develops in 1875.[68] Rée's favorite authors became Nietzsche's, Salomé recalls, "the French aphorists: La Rochefoucauld, La Bruyère, Vauvenargues, Chamfort, influenced Nietzsche style and thought extraordinarily at this time."[69] Thus it should come as no surprise that Nietzsche uses Rée's expression of "psychological observation" in the same breath as he mentions "La Rochefoucauld and his spiritual and artistic relatives," for Rée himself is one.

This is not to say that Nietzsche spared the *moralistes* from his critical gaze. In his notes he would come to criticize La Rochefoucauld's critique of morality for ultimately reinforcing the very morality it took to task:

> La Rochefoucauld went half-way: he denied the 'good' characteristics of man – he should have denied the 'evil' too.

> When the moral skeptic has achieved distrust of morality, there still remains one step yet to take – skepticism of his own distrust. *Denial* and *Trust* – they shake each other's hand.[70]

---

66 Pippin, Nietzsche, Psychology, and First Philosophy, 9. The original French title of the book is *Nietzsche, moraliste français*.

67 At the close of the first chapter of *Parerga und Paralipomena II*, "Über Philosophie und ihre Methode," Schopenhauer praises the "feine Beobachtung und geistreiche Auffassung" in the "den Schriften bevorzugter Geister, wie da waren Theophrastus, Montaigne, Larochefoucauld, Labruyère, Helvetius, Chamfort, Addison, Shaftsbury, Shenstone, Lichtenberg u.a.m." (Schopenhauer, Über Philosophie und ihre Methode, 20–21). Rée himself was clearly influenced by Schopenhauer, and as Treiber points out, the motto of Rée's book – "l'homme est l'animal méchant par excellence," from Arthur, Count of Gobineau (1816–1882) – also appears in Schopenhauer (Treiber, Erläuterungen, 385).

68 Nietzsche was aware of these writers earlier; in his lecture notes on Democritus in 1867 he quotes Vauvenargues, most likely acquired through his reading of Albert Lange's *Geschichte des Materialismus* (History of Materialism, 1866); see Donnellan, Nietzsche and the French Moralists, 1–3. But the first mention in his philosophical notebooks of the names "Leopardi – Chamfort – Larouchefoucauld – Vauvenargues – Coleridge" occurs in Spring 1876 (NL 16[5] 1876; KSA 8:287).

69 "Rées Lieblingsautoren wurden nun auch die seinigen (Nietzsches): die französischen Aphoristiker, die La Rochefoucauld, La Bruyère, Vauvenargues, Chamfort, beeinflussten um diese Zeit außerordentlich Nietzsches Stil und Denken" (Andreas-Salomé, Friedrich Nietzsche in seinen Werken, 132; my translation). See also Brobjer, Nietzsche's Philosophical Context, 62–63.

70 "120. La Rochefoucauld blieb auf halbem Wege stehen: er leugnete die 'guten' Eigenschaften des Menschen – er hätte auch die 'bösen' leugnen sollen. / Wenn der moralische Skeptiker beim Mißtrauen gegen die Moral angelangt ist, so bleibt ihm noch ein Schritt zu thun – die Skepsis gegen sein Mißtrauen. Leugnen und Vertrauen – das giebt einander die Hände" (NL 3[1] 1882; KSA 10:67–68).

As Thönges points out, the willingness to take that extra step, to turn one's skepticism against oneself and engage in what Gerhard Neumann describes as "transcendental moralism," distinguishes the German aphoristic tradition (Thönges, Das Genie des Herzens, 102). Nevertheless, Nietzsche's praise for the French *moralistes'* powers of perception and expression is unreserved in *Menschliches* 35 "*Advantages of psychological observation.*"

It should be mentioned that the French *moralistes* did not limit themselves to writing maxims; La Rochefoucauld wrote many longer *Réflexions*; La Bruyère's psychological observations frequently reached close to a page in length; and Montaigne was a great popularizer of the essay as a literary-philosophical form. But it is the form of the maxim that Nietzsche identifies explicitly here. And his simultaneous praise of both their method and this form, the *Sentenz*, can lead to some generic confusion, for it closely associates the whole of *Menschliches, Allzumenschliches* with the *Sentenz*, although elsewhere Nietzsche describes the book unequivocally as a collection of "Aphorismen." In equating "reflection on the human, all-too-human" with "psychological observation," Nietzsche appears to present *Menschliches, Allzumenschliches* under the sign of the French *moralistes*, whose privileged form (at least according to this passage) is the *Sentenz*; they are "the great masters of the psychological maxim" (die großen Meister der psychologischen Sentenz). Had *Menschliches* 35 appeared as the opening of the book's preface, as Nietzsche originally intended, this would have further strengthened the book's association not only with these writers, but with this specific mode of their discourse as well. Even so, this pivotal aphorism, strategically positioned at the opening of the second *Hauptstück*, aligns the book's entire project thematically with that of the *moralistes*, who likewise meditate on the human, all too human, while also implying a degree of formal affiliation. Praising the refined skills of his French forerunners, he invites his reader to consider his style as akin to theirs:

> [E]ven the subtlest mind is not capable of properly appreciating the art of polishing maxims [*Sentenzen-Schleiferei*] if he has not himself been brought up for it and competed at it. Without such practical instruction, we take this creating and forming to be easier than it is; we do not have a keen enough feel for what is successful and attractive. (HH I 35)[71]

The author's own appreciation for such writing implies that he himself is in fact one who has been brought up for it and has competed at it, thus not only reinforcing his association with the great masters of the *Sentenz*, but suggesting that he, too, is a composer of such texts. So the texts in Nietzsche's first collection of aphorisms appear under a sign influenced by the French *moralistes*; these *moralistes* are masters of the maxim; Nietzsche positions himself as one, as well; and thus his collection of

---

71 "selbst der feinste Kopf ist nicht vermögend, die Kunst der Sentenzen-Schleiferei gebührend zu würdigen, wenn er nicht selber zu ihr erzogen ist, in ihr gewetteifert hat. Man nimmt, ohne solche practische Belehrung, dieses Schaffen und Formen für leichter als es ist, man fühlt das Gelungene und Reizvolle nicht scharf genug heraus" (MA I 35).

aphorisms invites comparison with those of La Rochefoucauld and company. The influence is undeniable, but the question remains: just how much does this association tell us about Nietzsche's own practice of writing *Aphorismen?*

He openly acknowledges in this passage the thematic and formal influence of the *moralistes* on his first *Aphorismen-Sammlung*, but this does not mean that he embraces their mode of writing across the board, as becomes clear when we parse the different levels of self-reference that emerge in this passage. On one level, Nietzsche discusses the overall project of *Menschliches, Allzumenschliches*, elucidating the volume's title in a manner that situates it within a tradition of critical thought. On another level, his discussion of "Sentenzen-Schleiferei" appears to continue this play of self-reference: Nietzsche implies that he himself has "competed at it," and large sections of Chapters 6, 7 and 9 in *Menschliches* bear this out. Each of these moments of self-reference, however, actually points to a different "self." Whereas the first refers to the volume itself, inviting the reader to consider the *Menschliches, Allzumenschliches* as a whole, the latter moment of self-reference suggests no such breadth of applicability. The book in its entirety may be concerned with psychological observations comparable to those of Rée and the French *moralistes*, but there is no reason to assume that its form in all aspects is intended to mimic theirs.

Nietzsche provides generic cues to guide his reader, but the reader must be alert to the signals they send. The particular word he associates with the Rée and the French masters of the maxim is not *Aphorismus*, but *Sentenz*. As scholars of Nietzsche and of the aphorism occasionally point out but rarely heed with any kind of consistency, the terms are only "partially synonymous."[72] In his English translation of *Menschliches, Allzumenschliches*, Gary Handwerk prudently opts to translate *Sentenz* with "maxim," which underscores the connection to the French tradition under discussion, as well as reflecting the German understanding of the term.[73] A *Sentenz*, akin to the French *sentence*, is precisely the kind of short, poignant, easily remembered statement that pretends to universal validity (English retains this sense in the term "sententious"). *Sentenz* is, for instance, the term Paul Rée used to describe his own *Psychologische Beobachtungen*, which largely limit themselves to brief texts and lack the variety to be found in Nietzsche's aphoristic works. In other words, a *Sentenz* is what in English we commonly call an aphorism.

This identification, however, is also somewhat misleading and has contributed to the contested status of the term "aphorism" in Nietzsche studies. Seemingly benign observations, such as "the most common word for aphorism [in Nietzsche's writings] is 'Sentenz,'"[74] legitimately suggest that we might translate *Sentenz* with the term "aphorism." But German also has the word *Aphorismus*. If that, too, is to

---

72 See, e.g., Nietzsche Research Group (Nijmegen), Nietzsche-Wörterbuch, s.v. "Aphorismus," 76.
73 NB: "Maxim" is also commonly used to translate the term "Spruch," or saying, as in *Assorted Opinions and Maxims* (Vermischte Meinungen und *Sprüche*) or "Maxims and Arrows" (*Sprüche* und Pfeile) from *Götzen-Dämmerung*.
74 Nietzsche Research Group (Nijmegen), Nietzsche-Wörterbuch, 73; my translation.

be translated with the word "aphorism," then we have unintentionally established an illegitimate identification of the two terms. This association of the *Sentenz* with the "aphorism" leads many scholars to treat *Sentenz* and *Aphorismus* as synonymous, and thus to assume that Nietzsche does so as well. As we have seen, however, this tendency to identify *Aphorismus* and *Sentenz* is not purely a matter of translation, and not entirely absent from German scholarly readings.

Once the distinction between *Aphorismus* and *Sentenz* is mentioned by scholars, it is most often promptly forgotten. This is the case even in the *Nietzsche-Wörterbuch*, which notes in the entry for "Aphorismus" that *Aphorismus* and *Sentenz* are only "partially synonymous," and yet it liberally cites passages by Nietzsche that do not contain the word "Aphorismus" or any derivation thereof, but only *Sentenz*. It provides, for instance, the following statement from Nietzsche's notebooks as a reference to the aphorism: "A maxim [*Sentenz*] is a link in a chain of thought; it demands that the reader reconstruct this chain on his own; that means it demands a lot."[75] Now this image of the chain has precedence with regard to the aphorism: Marie von Ebner-Eschenbach introduces her own collection of aphorisms in 1880 with the epigraph, "An aphorism is the last ring in a long chain of thought."[76] Still, Nietzsche, unlike Ebner-Eschenbach, does not actually use the term *Aphorismus* here, and to gloss over this fact is to perpetuate the assumption that the terms *Aphorismus* and *Sentenz* are simply interchangeable in his works.

This is not to say that Nietzsche sees the two forms as completely unrelated to one another. In *Götzen-Dämmerung*, he writes: "The aphorism [*Aphorismus*], the maxim [*Sentenz*], in which I am the first among the Germans to be master, are the forms of 'eternity'" (TI Skirmishes 51; PN 555–556).[77] This passage and the surrounding text will be discussed later in greater detail, but we can see from this brief excerpt the close proximity in which Nietzsche situates the two forms. Initially it appears that they are presented as identical, that *Sentenz* is introduced as an appositive of *Aphorismus*. This identification, however, is quickly called into question by what follows. The singular *Aphorismus* and the singular *Sentenz* combine to form a plural antecedent for the relative pronoun "denen" (which), though this is unavoidably lost in the English translation. That the two combine to form a plurality is, however, apparent in the predicate "are" (sind), which indicates a plural subject, suggesting that "the aphorism, the maxim" be read as "the aphorism AND the maxim," not "the aphorism, OR maxim." This differentiation is then emphasized by their description not

---

75 "Eine Sentenz ist ein Glied aus einer Gedankenkette; sie verlangt, dass der Leser diese Kette aus eigenen Mitteln wiederherstelle: dies heisst sehr viel verlangen" (NL 20[3], 1876–77; KSA 8:361; quoted in Nietzsche Research Group (Nijmegen), Nietzsche-Wörterbuch, 79; my translation).

76 "Ein Aphorismus ist der letzte Ring einer langen Gedankenkette" (Ebner-Eschenbach, Aphorismen, 3; my translation).

77 "Der Aphorismus, die Sentenz, in denen ich als der Erste unter Deutschen Meister bin, sind die Formen der 'Ewigkeit'" (GD Streifzüge 51; KSA 6:153). NB: Kaufmann here translates "Sentenz" with "apophthegm").

as the form of eternity, but as the "forms" (Formen) of eternity, allowing for the possibility that the forms, though intimately related, are distinct. How exactly they are to be distinguished from one another this passage does not say.

Nietzsche's phrasing here is particularly odd, considering that elsewhere he consistently situates the *Sentenz* as a subset of the *Aphorismus*. The passage "Und nochmals gesagt," for instance, which closes the penultimate section of *Menschliches, Allzumenschliches*, has all the trappings of a pithy *Sentenz*: "Public opinions – private laziness" (Oeffentliche Meinungen – private Faulheiten; HH I 282; MA I 482). Yet Nietzsche has no problem calling this an *Aphorismus*.[78] This inclusive understanding of the aphorism accords entirely with his later description of *Menschliches* in all its formal diversity as an *Aphorismen-Sammlung*. A collection of *Sentenzen*, on the other hand, does not allow quite as broad a formal spectrum, as can be seen in Nietzsche's unpublished *Sentenzen-Buch*. This collection of roughly 450 maxims bore multiple titles, including *Auf hoher See*, *Schweigsame Reden*, and *Jenseits von gut und böse*, each with the clearly-stated generic designation, "Sentenzen-Buch."[79] Unlike the book that would eventually appear under the latter title, this collection is comprised of short texts averaging approximately twenty-five words, with none over seventy.[80] Werner Stegmaier describes the *Sentenz* as an aphorism that consists of a single sentence or phrase,[81] and though this definition is too narrow to take literally, the basic understanding of the *Sentenz* as a subset of the *Aphorismus* that includes shorter variations is sound.

Lichtenberg's *Aphorismen*

Nietzsche's esteem for certain French writers frequently comes at the cost of German authors. In an aphorism from *Der Wanderer und sein Schatten* entitled "European Books" (Europäische Bücher), he imagines that the ancient Greeks would likewise prefer the style and ideas of the French *moralistes* to those of even the best German writers:

> When reading Montaigne, La Rochefoucauld, La Bruyère, Fontenelle (especially the *Dialogues des Morts*), Vauvenargues and Chamfort we are closer to antiquity than in the case of any other group of six authors of any other nation. [...]. [T]hey contain more *real ideas* than all the books of German philosophers put together [...]. How much, on the other hand, would even a Plato have understood of the writings of our best German thinkers – Goethe and Schopenhauer, for instance – to say nothing of the repugnance that he would have felt to their style [...]. [W]hat clearness and graceful precision there is in these Frenchmen! The Greeks, whose ears were most refined, could not but have approved of this art, and one quality they

---

78 Letter to Schmeitzner, 30 Mar 1878, KSB II.5:313, no. 702.
79 NL 3[1], 1882; KSA 10:53–108.
80 See Westerdale, Zur Ausdifferenzierung von Sentenz und Aphorismus.
81 Stegmaier, Nietzsches Befreiung der Philosophie, 11.

would even have admired and reverenced – the French verbal wit: they *loved* this quality greatly, without being particularly strong in it themselves. (WS 214)[82]

French writing frequently appears as a model for Germans (see also HH I 203 and 221; MA I 203 and 221), while German prose is ruled ugly or clumsy (WS 90 and 95). And yet the latter also has its treasures, which reveal much about Nietzsche's understanding of the genre *Aphorismus*.

In a passage entitled "The treasure of German prose" (Der Schatz der deutschen Prosa; WS 109), Nietzsche lists those rare German works that to him, besides Goethe's writings and conversations with Eckermann, warrant repeated reading. There are only four: "Lichtenberg's aphorisms, the first book of Jung-Stilling's autobiography, Adalbert Stifter's *Indian Summer*, and Gottfried Keller's *People of Seldwyla*" (WS 109).[83] In his early works, Nietzsche writes more often of the *Sentenz* than the *Aphorismus*. Indeed, though he extols the critical potential of the *Sentenz* throughout his early *Aphorismen-Sammlungen*,[84] and though some variation of the word *Sentenz* appears some sixteen times in *Menschliches, Allzumenschliches I* and *II*, the term *Aphorismus* itself appears only this once. This one appearance, however, is telling. The one time Nietzsche uses the term *Aphorismen*, he refers not to the writings of the French *moralistes*, but to those of Georg Christoph Lichtenberg (1742–1799), the writer commonly credited with introducing the aphorism into German letters. This association provides a valuable glimpse into Nietzsche's understanding of the generic tradition in which he situates himself when he describes his own works as *Aphorismen*.

At the same time when Nietzsche was poring over La Rochefoucauld and company, he was also beginning to read Lichtenberg intensively (Brobjer, Nietzsche's Philosophical Context, 63). A familiar figure in the German-speaking world, Lichtenberg was a professor of mathematics, astronomy, and physics in Göttingen, where his innovative use of experiments in his lectures at times drew a hundred students, a remarkable feat considering there were only around 400 at the entire university.[85] He was also well known in academic and literary circles as both a natural scientist and

---

82 "Europäische Bücher. – Man ist beim Lesen von Montaigne, Larochefoucauld, Labruyère, Fontenelle (namentlich der dialogues des morts) Vauvenargues, Champfort dem Alterthum näher, als bei irgend welcher Gruppe von sechs Autoren anderer Völker [...]. [S]ie enthalten mehr wirkliche Gedanken, als alle Bücher deutscher Philosophen zusammengenommen [...]. Wie viel hätte dagegen selbst ein Plato von den Schriften unserer besten deutschen Denker, zum Beispiel Goethe's, Schopenhauer's, überhaupt verstehen können, von dem Widerwillen zu schweigen, welchen ihre Schreibart ihm erregt haben würde [...]. Dagegen, welche Helligkeit und zierliche Bestimmtheit bei jenen Franzosen! Diese Kunst hätten auch die feinohrigsten Griechen gutheissen müssen, und Eines würden sie sogar bewundert und angebetet haben, den französischen Witz des Ausdrucks: so Etwas liebten sie sehr, ohne gerade darin besonders stark zu sein" (WS 214).
83 "Lichtenberg's Aphorismen, das erste Buch von Jung-Stilling's Lebensgeschichte, Adalbert Stifter's Nachsommer und Gottfried Keller's Leute von Seldwyla" (WS 109).
84 See, e.g., "In praise of the maxim" (Lob der Sentenz, AOM 186; VM 168).
85 See Teichmann, Georg Christoph Lichtenberg.

The body, Lichtenberg contends, has a role to play in what are conventionally considered cognitive processes. Nietzsche would perpetuate this notion in Zarathustra's elevation of the body to "the great reason" (die große Vernunft): "You say 'I' and are proud of this word," says Zarathustra, "But what is greater, what you don't want to believe, – your body and its great reason: it doesn't say I, but does I" (Z I Despisers).[101] Lichtenberg entertains the possibility that the body has a role to play in operations long attributed to the mind or soul. Nietzsche takes this to heart and maintains that the identity of the individual, however tenuous and fabricated, can never be divorced from the body. What Lichtenberg proposes as a thought experiment, Zarathustra presents as a given. Both of them call into question the repression of the corporeal commonly perceived as integral to Idealist philosophy. Such a passage is clearly aligned with Nietzsche's thought, and may have even influenced it, but clearly it does not accord with what most consider to be an "aphorism."

Again and again, Nietzsche expands upon thoughts proposed by Lichtenberg in texts that only loosely fall under the rubric "Aphorismen." Given such stylistic, thematic and argumentative affinities, it is not hard to understand how Nietzsche could emphatically recommend "Lichtenberg's aphorisms" to his readers and students. The conceptual kinship is not difficult to recognize, and indeed, Lichtenberg would be one of the few figures whom Nietzsche would consistently treasure throughout the length of his entire productive life. But pertinent to the current discussion is the way in which Lichtenberg resonates not simply in Nietzsche's thought and imagery, but also in the form of his writing. How Nietzsche describes Lichtenberg's writings illuminates how he situates his own generically. When Nietzsche recommends "Lichtenberg's aphorisms," he refers presumably to the volumes of Lichtenberg he owned and read repeatedly.[102] In this edition, the portions commonly called "aphoristic" today, however, do not appear under the heading "aphorisms," but rather simply as "Bemerkungen vermischten Inhalts" (Remarks of Assorted Content). As noted above, Lichtenberg himself never intended these notebooks for publication nor did he ever refer to their contents as aphorisms. Not until the Leitzmann edition of 1902–1908, that is, shortly after Nietzsche's death, did they appear under the title "Aphorismen," and even these would continue to demonstrate precisely the kind of formal diversity apparent in the passages from Lichtenberg cited above.[103]

So what does Nietzsche refer to when he deliberately (and preemptively) refers to Lichtenberg's writings as aphorisms? The excerpts above provide a glimpse of not

---

beträchtlichen, aber in manchen Menschen lebhaft genug, daß er ihnen bei Berührung einer Sache einfällt oder [sie] im Traum oder einem Fieber glauben der Satz sei weiter nichts als ein Stückgen Leinwand" (Sudel-E 32; quoted Stingelin, Unsere ganze Philosophie ist Berichtigung des Sprachgebrauchs, 28).

101 "'Ich' sagst du und bist stolz auf dieses Wort. Aber das Grössere ist, woran du nicht glauben willst, – dein Leib und seine grosse Vernunft: die sagt nicht Ich, aber thut Ich" (Z I Verächtern).

102 Lichtenberg, Vermischte Schriften.

103 Lichtenberg, Georg Christoph Lichtenbergs Aphorismen.

only the thematic, but also the formal affinity between Lichtenberg's and Nietzsche's writings. Though certainly at times Lichtenberg's writings approach the pith and concision of the *maxime*, most of his notes are hardly suitable for the salon. Indeed, the formal diversity of his writings is as impressive as their thematic range. Some texts cover several pages, while others consist of but two words. On the one hand are lengthier discourses on, say, suicide (Sudel-A 126), and on the other, simply a few words, like "An Amen-face" (Ein Amen-Gesicht; Sudel-F 939). If this is what Nietzsche means by the term aphorism, then his understanding of the term is much broader than the narrow sense of the *Sentenz*. It also stands to reason that Nietzsche could refer to both Lichtenberg's *Sudelbücher*, the first section of the *Genealogie's* Third Treatise, and his own *Menschliches, Allzumenschliches* as "Aphorismen." Though they all have their more conventionally "aphoristic" moments, more striking is their formal flexibility. In calling these writings "Aphorismen," Nietzsche aligns his work with a tradition that in German letters begins with Lichtenberg, a tradition distinguishable from that of the French *moralistes*.

Scholars of the aphorism have long distinguished between German and French traditions of aphoristic writing, differentiating them in terms of both form and attitude.[104] As one of the first to note the distinction, Walter Wehe asserts that whereas the French aphorism, with its closed and considered form, presents its knowledge as a definitive certainty, the German aphorism offers a provocation to further discussion and dispute.[105] This latter attitude is certainly evident in Lichtenberg's writings, which maintain the scientist's experimental approach both formally and thematically: "*To doubt things that are now believed without further investigation,*" he writes, "*that is always the most important thing.*"[106] Richard T. Gray builds on Wehe's distinction, suggesting that the difference between the two traditions reflects differing attitudes regarding society; whereas the French *maxime* or *sentence*, designed for consumption in social exchange, actually serves to reinforce prevailing values of the culture, the German *Aphorismus* assumes a more critical stance: where the former "integrates," the latter "antagonizes."[107] It could be argued that this critical stance also contributes to the formal variety displayed by the German aphorism, since the isolated writer is not compelled by the same criteria that dictate the efficacy of salon repartee. As a written rather than uttered statement, the German aphorism need not be committed to memory nor be deliverable with rapier precision. Though arguably still concise, the German aphorism enjoys a greater degree of formal freedom.

---

104 These modifiers refer not to any inherent national temperament, but rather to the historical origin of the two different aphoristic traditions; see Gray, Constructive Destruction, 44. NB: The opening chapter of Gray's book provides one of the most useful and insightful introductions to the European aphoristic tradition available in English.

105 See Wehe, Geist und Form des deutschen Aphorismus, 142.

106 "*Dinge zu bezweifeln, die ganz ohne weitere Untersuchung jetzt geglaubt werden, das ist die Hauptsache überall*" (Sudel-J$_{\text{II}}$ 1276; italics original).

107 Gray, Constructive Destruction, 43.

Nietzsche positions himself as heir to both the French and German aphoristic traditions. His project in *Menschliches, Allzumenschliches* adopts its method of "psychological observation" from "the great masters of the psychological maxim [Sentenz]," the French *moralistes*, and at times even "competes" at their *Sentenzen-Schleiferei*. And indeed, he would come to characterize himself in *Götzen-Dämmerung* as the first *Meister* of the *Sentenz* among Germans. But his claim to mastery does not limit itself to the *Sentenz*. He crowns himself the first German master of the *Aphorismus* as well, and in doing so incorporates all the textual possibilities that entails. Formally, his own "aphorism collection," *Menschliches, Allzumenschliches*, bears less of a resemblance to La Rochefoucauld's *Réflexions ou Sentences et maximes morales* than to Lichtenberg's *Sudelbücher*, which likewise inform the content of Nietzsche's writing. Formally and conceptually, Nietzsche profits from both traditions, but when speaking of the "Aphorismus," it is the German tradition, the tradition of Lichtenberg with all its formal diversity, that warrants primary consideration.

Acknowledging that Nietzsche's use of the term "Aphorismus" has precedent in the German aphoristic tradition is, of course, just the first step. It helps us to understand how he might call Section 1 of the Third Treatise of *Zur Genealogie der Moral* an aphorism, and how *Menschliches, Allzumenschliches* qualifies as an "Aphorismen-Sammlung." With this broader understanding, we can expand discussion of Nietzsche's aphoristic writing to include *Morgenröte*, *Die fröhliche Wissenschaft*, and later *Jenseits von Gut und Böse*. But we have yet to explore the value and function of the textual diversity that falls under the rubric "Aphorismus." The reasoning behind Nietzsche's turn to aphoristic writing has yet to be explained. And the interpretive means by which to answer the challenge of Nietzsche's *Aphorismen-Sammlungen* has yet to be addressed. These issues will be discussed in the chapters to follow.

Chapter Two. Aphoristic Pluralism

The previous chapter argued for a broader understanding of the term "aphorism," one that has precedent both in the German literary and philosophical tradition and in contemporary Nietzsche scholarship. Collections like *Menschliches, Allzumenschliches, Morgenröte,* and *Die fröhliche Wissenschaft* can thus employ a wide variety of textual forms without necessarily compromising their status as *Aphorismen-Sammlungen.* And indeed they do. With such textual diversity evident in Nietzsche's aphorisms, one must question Alexander Nehamas's dismissal of the form as "one style among many"[108] in Nietzsche's writings. Nehamas claims that it is rather the multiplicity of styles, that is, Nietzsche's "stylistic pluralism," that most thoroughly characterizes his writing. The "one style" Nehamas has in mind is clearly that of the *Sentenz,* and thus his skepticism would be justified if one were to understand the aphorism to be limited to this particular form. But Nehamas overestimates the stylistic unity of the aphorism. The kind of "stylistic pluralism" he discusses is already present in the very genre of the aphorism itself, as employed by Nietzsche and as represented by the German aphoristic tradition. The current chapter explores the formal diversity apparent in Nietzsche's aphorism collections, first by describing the multifarious forms that comprise them, and then by accounting for the critical role of this diversity itself in the German aphoristic tradition.

Diverse Forms

Nietzsche's turn to aphoristic writing in *Menschliches, Allzumenschliches* constitutes a radical stylistic break from the works that immediately precede it, *Die unzeitgemässen Betrachtungen* and *Die Geburt der Tragödie.* Such a break is then reiterated repeatedly within the volume itself. Topics leap from metaphysics to morality, religion to art, or gender, or child-rearing, or politics. Terse *bon mots* appear alongside lengthier discourses. Rhetorical word-plays and objective observations, bold assertions and pointed arguments emerge, sometimes in clusters, sometimes unpredictably. But even within this diversity there are recognizable trends. Certain forms arise frequently enough to warrant individual attention, so that even as we speak of the stylistic pluralism inherent in Nietzsche's aphorisms, we can also establish a taxonomy to aid in both the interpretation of individual aphorisms and our examination of the aphorism collection itself as a mode of discourse. While each of the subgroups discussed below is worthy of more comprehensive examination, the current study keeps discussion to a minimum in order to focus on the *diversity* of forms rather than their individual traditions and challenges.

---

108 Nehamas, Nietzsche: Life as Literature, 18.

Maxims (Sentenzen, Sprüche)

Scholars repeatedly claim that many of Nietzsche's aphorisms are not aphorisms "in the strict sense." But some of them actually are. In spite of the expanded understanding of the aphorism expounded in the previous chapter, some nevertheless do indeed present, as Marsden puts it, "a short expression of a general truth or pointed assertion." These are the texts that Nietzsche refers to as *Sentenzen* (maxims) or *Sprüche* (literally sayings or proverbs, often likewise translated as "maxims"). While the former reflects Nietzsche's alignment with his French predecessors, the latter emphasizes the proverbial tradition. Such texts frequently engage in what Gray describes as an "interchange between abstract law and specific case" that prompts the reader to hermeneutic activity: some present a general rule for which the reader must deduce individual examples; others invite the reader to induce a general rule from a particular example.[109] Acknowledging these reciprocal tendencies, Neumann describes such aphorisms as the "portrayal of the conflict" between that which is particular, observed and perceived through the senses on the one hand, and general, reflected and abstracted through the mind on the other (Neumann, Einleitung, 5). Nietzsche's *Sentenzen* and *Sprüche* exhibit a similar dynamic.[110]

Occasionally, Nietzsche's pithy aphorisms describe a particular instance that demands inductive reasoning on the part of the reader to make sense of the text, or, as is often the case with such inductive aphorisms, to raise the text above the level of a banality. On the surface, an aphorism like "*In danger*" (In Gefahr), from the final section of *Menschliches, Allzumenschliches*, presents an utterly quotidian observation: "*In danger.* – We are in the most danger of being run over when we have just gotten out of the way of some vehicle" (In Gefahr. – Man ist am Meisten in Gefahr, überfahren zu werden, wenn man eben einem Wagen ausgewichen ist; HH I 564; MA I 564). Because this passage appears in the context of a volume professing philosophical import, its very inanity spurs the reader to interpret the statement as indicative of some broader truth. Here Nietzsche invites the reader to participate in his project of psychological observation and to unlock the hidden value of this human, all-too-human situation. Outside the context of the collection, the name "Nietzsche" serves a similar function, inviting the reader's interpretive engagement with the promise of deeper insight; if Nietzsche said it, there must be more to it than is apparent at first glance.[111]

---

109 Gray, Constructive Destruction, 26.

110 See Faber, The Metamorphosis of the French Aphorism; Donnellan, Nietzsche and the French Moralists, 141–144.

111 This is perhaps why the note "'I have forgotten my umbrella'" ("Ich habe meinen Regenschirm vergessen"; NL 12[62], 1881; KSA 9:587) is so incredibly frustrating – precisely because it is unremarkable one assumes Nietzsche recorded the statement because it held some deeper insight; the use of quotation marks is both provocative and discouraging, drawing attention to the statement as utterance, while divorcing the statement from any identifiable context or source. Derrida discusses the insurmountable interpretive challenge presented by this passage in Derrida, Spurs/Éperons, 123.

The subject *man* (translated above as *we*, though it could just as well be translated as *you*, *they*, or *one*) further suggests the broad applicability of a universal rule, and is typical of the *Sentenz* and the *Spruch*.[112] The aphoristic subject, even in this very specific situation, is often general, appearing as *man* (see, e. g., HH I 300, 301, 303, 308, 312; MA I 300, 301, 303, 308, 312), but also frequently as *wir* (we; HH I 302, 309; MA I 302, 309), *Leute* (people; HH I 310, 311; MA I 310, 311), and *der Mensch* (the person; HH I 313; MA I 313). Widely employed aphoristic subjects also include *einer* (one who) and *wer* (whoever), though Nietzsche often elaborates upon these in order to narrow their scope; for instance, to "whoever thinks a lot" (wer viel denkt; HH I 526; MA I 526) or "whoever thinks more deeply" (wer tiefer denkt; HH I 518; MA I 518). The use of *types* as subjects, such as *sympathetic people* (die Mitleidigen; HH I 321; MA I 321) or *the vain man* (der Eitele; HH I 545; MA I 545), serves a similar function.

Even with its general subject, however, the situation described in the aphorism "*In danger*" is quite specific. The reader is driven to reason inductively and to ask what it is about this moment that warrants our attention. To be run down in traffic, in its passive construction, suggests an error on the part of the pedestrian; in the process of avoiding one error, however, we expose ourselves to further peril by focusing our attention on the harm recently averted. In training our gaze on that which might have been, we expose ourselves to future disaster. Or perhaps we do so by growing overconfident ruminating on our recent accomplishment. No matter how one reads it, the maxim only elicits our attention because, despite its highly restricted denotational meaning, it points to some greater wisdom that the reader must induce.

In a manner typical of the aphorism collection, Nietzsche also offers a countervailing position that problematizes precisely such inductive reasoning. The maxim "*Miraculous vanity*" (Wunderliche Eitelkeit) states:

> Anyone who boldly prophesies the weather three times and does so successfully believes a little bit, deep down in his soul, in his prophetic gift. We give credit to miraculous and irrational things when it flatters our self-esteem. (HH I 574)[113]

This bipartite maxim provides two accounts of inductive reasoning. On the one hand, we have the would-be prophet's misplaced faith in his own precognitive abilities based on the inadequate evidence of three bold and accurate predictions. On the other, we have the general lesson that Nietzsche himself draws from the behavior he describes without identifying any actual source for his own observation. Nietzsche inadvertently implicates himself in this passage. He may not lay claim to miraculous powers, but he extrapolates a general rule from questionable data all the same. May one not draw a different lesson from the very situation he describes?

---

112 See Donnellan, Nietzsche and the French Moralists, 142.
113 "Wunderliche Eitelkeit. – Wer dreimal mit Dreistigkeit das Wetter prophezeit hat und Erfolg hatte, der glaubt im Grunde seiner Seele ein Wenig an seine Prophetengabe. Wir lassen das Wunderliche, Irrationelle gelten, wenn es unserer Selbstschätzung schmeichelt" (MA I 574).

Perhaps a desire for the miraculous itself compromises our judgment, or a penchant for the irrational that defies reason. The possibility of alternative interpretations may not actually undermine Nietzsche's point; rather, it points to the inextricability of the aphorism's two parts. This individual aphorism does not merely present a particular instance from which the reader is to induce a general rule; nor is it simply a general rule for which the reader is to provide particular instances. Rather, it provides both, but as a warning regarding the dangers of inductive reasoning, which may be subject to less rational drives.

The majority of Nietzsche's maxims require deductive rather than inductive reasoning, providing a general rule for which the reader must then supply particular instances. The persuasiveness of such statements is often based not on argumentation (which would hamper swift delivery), but on imagery and word-play. Indeed, at times one wonders whether rhetoric does not itself form one of the less rational drives behind these statements. In the maxim *"The index of the scale"* (Das Zünglein an der Wage; HH I 86; MA I 86), Nietzsche asserts that less-than-noble priorities can determine the claims we choose to make: "One praises or criticizes according to which position will best allow our power of judgment to shine" (Man lobt oder tadelt, je nachdem das Eine oder das Andere mehr Gelegenheit giebt, unsere Urtheilskraft leuchten zu lassen). At times, Nietzsche's rhetorical flourishes are so pronounced that the language seems to drive the thought expressed.

Rhetorical Figures

Just as one can distinguish the maxim as a particular form of the Nietzschean aphorism, for taxonomic precision one may further subdivide the Nietzschean maxim according to the rhetorical figure it features. These include metaphor, metonymy, synecdoche, allegory, personification, hyperbole, understatement, parody, paradox, parallelism, inversion, objection, rhetorical question, and others. One apparent favorite of Nietzsche's, the *polyptotonic* maxim, exploits – and draws attention to – relationships sustained in language through repetition of words with the same root. For instance:

> *Thinkers as stylists.* – Most thinkers write badly because they tell us not only their thoughts but also the thinking of the thoughts. (HH I 188)[114]

Another instance of a pithy aphorism that draws its rhetorical heft from polyptoton is *Menschliches* 486:

---

114 "Denker als Stilisten. – Die meisten Denker schreiben schlecht, weil sie uns nicht nur ihre Gedanken, sondern auch das Denken der Gedanken mittheilen" (MA I 188).

> *The one thing that is necessary.* – A person must have one of these two things: either a naturally light-hearted disposition or a disposition lightened by art and knowledge. (HH I 486)[115]

Menschliches 84, *Refinement of Shame* (Feinheit der Scham), and 128, *Against the short-sighted* (Gegen die Kurzsichtigen), furnish further examples. Each of these derive both their persuasive power and their critical import from the repetition of related yet non-identical terms, which invites the reader to investigate the maxim's key terms as verbal constructs. Nietzsche may not provide "the thinking of his thoughts," but the polyptoton furnishes both the structure and the point of critique. The process of thinking and the resulting thought, like the light-hearted and the lightened disposition, may be related, but they must also be distinguished.

The *antanaclastic* maxim employs a structure and mode of critique akin to the polyptotonic. Rather than repeating words with the same root, antanaclasis involves the repetition of the same actual word, but with different meanings. To see how these figures are both similar and distinct, we can look at one maxim from *Menschliches, Allzumenschliches* which employs both: "The 'rich in spirit.' – Someone who seeks spirit has no spirit" (HH I 547).[116] The English translation here seeks to maintain the connecting term "spirit" (Geist) throughout, though clearly at a price. While "geistreich" means literally "rich in spirit," more commonly it simply means "witty," which this maxim seeks to be, even as it parses this descriptor. Furthermore, the "spirit" that the "rich in spirit" ironically lack may well be the intellect (Geist), or equally the (holy) spirit. Read as an antanaclastic aphorism, the maxim issues an indictment of the intellectual capacity of those who pursue the mystery of the holy spirit. A polyptoton (*geistreich/Geist*) links the maxim's title to its body, but the notoriously polysemic potential of *Geist* alone furnishes the passage with both its antanaclastic structure and its critical charge.

A kindred maxim employing antanaclasis to criticize potentially metaphysical terminology appears in *Vermischte Meinungen und Sprüche:*

> *Truth wants no gods beside it.* – Belief in the truth begins with the doubt of all hitherto believed "truths." (AOM 20)[117]

What conventionally serves as the ultimate locus of self-identity proves here non-self-identical. The appearance of the word *truth* (Wahrheit) in the title and twice in the body of this highly focused maxim invites diverse interpretations, drawing into question the self-identity of the key term, truth. Through antanaclastic repetition, the maxim performs the very criticism it describes. The maxim further emphasizes

---

115 "Das Eine, was Noth thut. – Eins muss man haben: entweder einen von Natur leichten Sinn oder einen durch Kunst und Wissen erleichterten Sinn" (MA I 486).
116 "Die 'Geistreichen'. – Der hat keinen Geist, welcher den Geist sucht" (MA I 547).
117 "Wahrheit will keine Götter neben sich. – Der Glaube an die Wahrheit beginnt mit dem Zweifel an allen bis dahin geglaubten 'Wahrheiten'" (VM 20).

the validity of such terminology through the use of quotation marks, which draw attention to the notion of truth as a verbal designation as well as compromising the absolute validity associated with the word. Through such rhetorical figures – and others, including *chiasmus* (e.g, HH I 519; MA I 519), *personification* (HH I 52, 83, 179; MA I 52, 83, 179), and *analogy* (HH I 492, 556, 570, 585; MA I 492, 556, 570, 585) – Nietzsche's *Sentenzen* perform their critical function with maximum concision.

Dull Maxims

Not all of Nietzsche's maxims are successful. While Nietzsche praises his French intellectual and stylistic forebears for their mastery of *Sentenzen-Schleiferei* (maxim-polishing or -sharpening; HH I 35; MA I 35), there are nevertheless occasions where his own maxims could benefit from additional honing. He frequently ignores his own advice from *Menschliches* 188, "Thinkers as stylists," providing the thinking of his thoughts and thereby sacrificing the concision he admires in La Rochefoucauld and company. One example comes from the section of *Menschliches, Allzumenschliches* called "Woman and Child" (Weib und Kind):

> *Match of love.* – Marriages made for love (the so-called love-matches) have error as a father and penury (need) as a mother. (HH I 389)[118]

The parenthetical intrusions may clarify Nietzsche's intent, but these moments of clarification diminish the maxim's effect. Given the maxim's title, the first parenthetical explanation seems superfluous; it provides some cultural context by introducing the modifier "so-called," but at the high cost of concision. This clumsiness is then reiterated by the second parenthesis. If Nietzsche intended "Noth" (necessity, here translated as *penury*) to mean "Bedürfnis" (need) and not the meaning it normally has when combined with the image of the mother (that is, necessity), then why did he not simply use the term "Bedürfniss"? The desire to have his rhetorical cake and eat it too dulls rather than sharpens the maxim.

While the maxim as a genre often seems to say too little, relying on the reader to supply the missing information, frequently Nietzsche's maxims say too much. At times he simply goes one step too far. For instance:

---

118 "Liebesheirathen. – Die Ehen, welche aus Liebe geschlossen werden (die sogenannten Liebesheirathen), haben den Irrthum zum Vater und die Noth (das Bedürfniss) zur Mutter" (MA I 389).

> *A model for others.* – Anyone who wants to give a good example must mix a grain of folly into his virtue: then others will imitate him and at the same time raise themselves above the person they are imitating – which people love to do. (HH I 561)[119]

The final phrase, "which people love to do," lands with a thud. The affect named is exceptionally vague, in that it seems to imply merely that people have a positive response when they exceed those whom they emulate. Nietzsche's later formulations of the will to power could perhaps offer a more focused account, but here we are left with the indistinct notion of "lieben" as the operative motivator. This text falls short both as an exercise in "psychological observation" and as a product of *Sentenzen-Schleiferei.*

Pseudo-Definitions

Another conventional aphoristic form of which Nietzsche avails himself is the *pseudo-definition*, a well-established form in both the French and German aphoristic traditions.[120] With its etymological root in the Greek *aphorizein* (akin to the Latin *definitio*), aphorisms frequently appear in the form of an unconventional and surprising definition. La Rochefoucauld provides multiple cynical copulae, such as, "Hypocrisy is a form of homage that vice pays to virtue"; "Honors won are down payments for those still to be won"; or "Flattery is a false coin given currency only by our vanity."[121] In Lichtenberg's *Sudelbücher* we find a version in which the statement's character as definition is merely implied – "The small penny prejudices, (virtues) (truths)."[122] Nietzsche presents a similar such identification sans copula: "*And to say it again.* – Public opinion – private laziness" (HH I 482).[123] Nietzsche's pseudo-definitions, however, tend to be of the overt variety, with the title operating as the lemma that the body of the aphorism goes on to define. These definitions are at times surprising, such as, "Joke. – A joke is the epigram on the death of a feeling" (AOM 202),[124] while others appear somewhat more conservative, like "Profession. – A profession is the backbone of life" (HH I 575).[125] Such definitions, in any case, serve less to define than to re-define, not so much clarifying as inciting the reader to reconsider the meaning of the term under consideration.

---

119 "Den Andern zum Vorbild. – Wer ein gutes Beispiel geben will, muss seiner Tugend einen Gran Narrheit zusetzen: dann ahmt man nach und erhebt sich zugleich über den Nachgeahmten, – was die Menschen lieben" (MA I 561).
120 See Donnellan, Nietzsche and the French Moralists, 141; Gray, Constructive Destruction, 49.
121 La Rochefoucauld, Réflexions ou Sentences et Maximes morales; 63 (V:218); 76 (V:270); 45 (V:158), respectively.
122 "Die kleinen Pfennigs Vorurtheile, (Tugenden) (Wahrheiten)" (Sudel-B 116).
123 "Und nochmals gesagt. – Oeffentliche Meinungen – private Faulheiten" (MA I 482).
124 "Witz. – Der Witz ist das Epigramm auf den Tod eines Gefühls" (VM 202).
125 "Beruf. – Ein Beruf ist das Rückgrat des Lebens" (MA I 575).

Modified Commonplaces

When Nietzsche twists a proverb to his own purposes, he is again availing himself of a form with a long and rich tradition in aphoristic writing.[126] For instance, he concisely criticizes asceticism by demonstrating its inversion of the practical impulse to "make a virtue of necessity": "*The ascetic.* – The ascetic makes a necessity out of virtue" (HH I 76).[127] Elsewhere he investigates Hölderlin's notion of "iron necessity" – "Iron necessity is a thing that people perceive in the course of history to be neither iron nor necessary" (HH I 514)[128] – though it is not immediately apparent whether he sides with Hölderlin or the people. This often cynical aphoristic tradition extends beyond commonplaces to include the modification of Biblical passages, as when Lichtenberg reinterprets Genesis, claiming, "God made man in his own image – that means likely that man made God in his."[129] Nietzsche, in his turn, would "improve" Luke 18:14: "He who humbles himself wants to be exalted" (HH I 87).[130] Such statements establish a dialogue with proverbial and Biblical traditions that provide a necessary component of the aphoristic statement's critical content. Lichtenberg's reinterpretation of Genesis is not simply an attempt to clarify the text, but to take issue with a dogmatic stance. Nietzsche does not simply refine Luke 18:14, but modifies it to reveal hidden motivation. The original text, reading "He who humbles himself will be exalted," is often understood as an expression of God's ultimate justice. Even at this early stage in his development, Nietzsche anticipates his later formulation of slave-morality by suggesting that at the heart of humility lies what he would later describe as the *ressentiment* of the impotent who desire power and respect. Both the text's title and its wording include the original biblical passage as an integral part of the aphorism, the dialogue between the two providing the aphorism with its critical import.

---

126 Wolfgang Mieder has published several studies on the proverbial sources for many German aphorists; see, e.g., Mieder, Sprichwörtliche Aphorismen. His preferred term for this practice is *Sprichworterweiterung.*
127 "Der Asket. – Der Asket macht aus der Tugend eine Noth" (MA I 76).
128 "Die eherne Nothwendigkeit. – Die eherne Nothwendigkeit ist ein Ding, von dem die Menschen im Verlauf der Geschichte einsehen, dass es weder ehern noch nothwendig ist" (MA I 514).
129 "Gott schuf den Menschen nach seinem Bilde, das heißt vermuthlich der Mensch schuf Gott nach dem seinigen" (Sudel-D 201; see also Sudel-D 274).
130 "Lucas 18,14 verbessert. – Wer sich selbst erniedrigt, will erhöht werden" (MA I 87). NB: Rée had also addressed this passage, writing, "Man erniedrigt sich, weil man denkt: Wer sich erniedrigt, wird erhöht werden" (75). Introducing *wollen* into his own reading allows Nietzsche to produce a much tighter text that is not simply an observation, but a modification of the original language itself. Perhaps he could have called it "Paul Rée verbessert."

Mini-Dialogues

Beginning with the opening of *Der Wanderer und sein Schatten*, Nietzsche composes actual *mini-dialogues* in his aphorism collections. The dialogue, of course, has been part of philosophical discourse since antiquity, and the mini-dialogue, a brief exchange of only a couple of lines, also enjoys a long history in aphoristic writing. The *Petits dialogues philosophiques* of Nicolas Chamfort (1741–1794), whom Nietzsche read closely (see GS 95; FW 95), often feature unnamed interlocutors, A and B, much as one finds in *Morgenröte* 491–493. They often read as two voices confirming or expanding upon a single thought:

> *On one's own tree.* – A: The thoughts of no thinker give me so much pleasure as my own do: that, of course, says nothing as to their value, but I would be a fool to refuse the fruit I find most tasty simply because it happens to grow on *my* tree! And I was such a fool at one time. – B: With others it is the reverse: but this too says nothing as to the value of their thoughts, and especially nothing against their value. (D 493)[131]

Such a dialogue is hardly dialogic, insofar as it does not represent the confrontation of thesis and antithesis. Rather, the two thoughts appear to reinforce one another. In this case, they perform the affirmation described in the dialogue, which is only fitting. This is, after all, only a *pseudo*-dialogue.

The passage that immediately follows offers a different structure. Not only does it forego designating the speakers by initial, but the two also appear to represent different perspectives:

> *Final argument of the brave.* – "There are snakes in these bushes." – Good, I shall go into the bushes and kill them. – "But perhaps you will be their victim, and not they yours!" – What do I matter! (D 494)[132]

Which of these interlocutors represents the brave man mentioned in the passage's title is clear, but despite the title, what this dialogue portrays is perhaps less argument than deliberation. With Nietzsche as the monological source of this dialogue, the text can be seen to offer an internal debate with oneself, despite its dialogic structure. As though to unify the speakers into a single voice, Nietzsche eliminates the quotation marks from the final statement, allowing them to stand for the voice of the aphorism itself.

---

131 "Auf dem eigenen Baume. – A: 'Ich habe bei den Gedanken keines Denkers so viel Vergnügen, wie bei den eigenen: das sagt freilich Nichts über ihren Werth, aber ich müsste ein Narr sein, um die für mich schmackhaftesten Früchte zurückzusetzen, weil sie zufällig auf meinem Baume wachsen! – Und ich war einmal dieser Narr.' – B: 'Andern geht es umgekehrt: und auch diess sagt Nichts über den Werth ihrer Gedanken, namentlich noch Nichts gegen ihren Werth'" (M 493).
132 "Letztes Argument des Tapferen. – 'In diesem Gebüsche sind Schlangen.' – Gut, ich werde in das Gebüsch gehen und sie tödten. – 'Aber vielleicht wirst du dabei das Opfer, und sie werden nicht einmal das deine!' – Was liegt an mir!" (M 494).

Along with Chamfort, Lichtenberg also provides Nietzsche with a predecessor in this form. At times Lichtenberg composes lengthy conversations such as Sudel-C 317, which imagines a discussion between author and reader as a conversation between barkeeper and patron, but he also avails himself of the shorter dialogue. One such example reads simply: "Who's there? Only me. Oh, that is superfluous enough" (Wer ist da? Nur ich. O das ist überflüssig genug; Sudel-B 240). Even one person proves too much for the speaker, but as is so often the case with Nietzsche's mini-dialogues, the question remains: does he speak to another person, thus implying that one *other* person is too much and suggesting that the speaker is self-sufficient, or does he speak to himself, which leads to the conclusion that he himself is (or aspects of him are) already gratuitous? When Nietzsche splits the authorial voice – whether into two concurring or two conflicting voices – he participates in a tradition of aphoristic writing that has its roots in both the French and German traditions.

Thought-Experiments

The *Sentenz* in all its rhetorical diversity, the pseudo-definition, the twisted common-place, and the mini-dialogue all have precedence in the aphoristic tradition, and furthermore, they are readily recognized as "aphoristic," even by those who insist upon the brevity of the form. But from Lichtenberg Nietzsche also inherited a particularly German form of aphoristic writing that opens up the formal possibilities of the aphorism, namely the *Gedankenexperiment*, or thought-experiment. Though the Germans did not invent the process – Lucretius and Galileo employed these forms as well – Lichtenberg did coin the term.[133] He posed questions like:

> What kind of effect would it have on me if I had to sit by candlelight in a large room draped in black, where the ceiling was also covered in black cloth, with black carpeting, black chairs, and a black canapé, while dressed in black and waited upon by servants dressed in black?[134]

This is not general truth or biting critique or pithy bon mot aimed to persuade or impress or even to document. Lichtenberg's musings begin with himself: the natural scientist who corresponded with Goethe regarding the perception of colors wonders what the effect on himself would be, but his reader cannot help but wonder along with him. He frequently poses such questions in the subjunctive, for the question is not ironic, but genuine; he has no answer. No stranger to the subjunctive,[135] Lich-

---

133 Schildknecht, Philosophische Masken.
134 "Was für einen Effekt würde es nicht auf mich haben, wenn ich einmal in einer ganz schwarz behangenen großen Stube, wo auch die Decke mit schwarzem Tuch beschlagen wäre, und bei schwarzen Fußteppichen, schwarzen Stühlen und schwarzem Canapee, in einem schwarzen Kleide bei einigen wenigen Wachskerzen sitzen müßte und von schwarz gekleideten Leuten bedient würde?" (Sudel-F 325).
135 See Schöne, Aufklärung aus dem Geist der Experimentalphysik.

tenberg also poses the following query: "Question: Could a man be brought up in such a way that, without losing his mind, his concepts were so strangely interconnected, that he would be useless in society, an artificial fool."[136] Grammatically, the question requires a yes-or-no answer, but the value of the text itself lies in its provocation; one is led to consider precisely the kinds of conceptual networks that this artificial fool would problematize. This seemingly simple question invites a flurry of further inquiries regarding the integration of education, society, wisdom, and authenticity. Such a question promotes thinking rather than simply conveying a thought or arguing a position or celebrating the aphorist's wit.

Following in this tradition, Nietzsche likewise proposes vividly illustrated thought experiments. In a passage entitled "A scene from comedy that occurs in life," he offers the following hypothetical situation:

> Someone thinks up a clever opinion on some topic in order to deliver it in some social setting. Now in a comedy, we would listen and observe how he tries to set full sail for a certain point and to steer the conversation toward a place where he can make his remark: how he continually pushes the conversation toward a single destination, occasionally losing his direction, then regaining it, finally reaching the right moment: his breath almost fails him – and then someone else in the group takes the remark right out of his mouth. What will he do? Oppose his own opinion? (HH I 345)[137]

Nietzsche's text builds precisely the kind of drama it describes, accelerating up to that pivotal moment, the dash providing a brief caesura, before deflating. Despite the fact that Nietzsche situates the scene "in a comedy," the title insists that it "occurs in life." Thus the questions at the end are less dramaturgical than psychological. Nietzsche compels his reader to consider the relationship between not only the form and content of our opinions, but the context of their delivery and the manner in which their (potential) reception reflects upon the speaker, and how these considerations influence the speaker's own adherence to a particular opinion. If one "thinks up a clever opinion… in order to deliver it in some social setting," one subjects one's thought to the contingencies of society, inviting a potentially ridiculous outcome.[138]

---

136 "Frage: Könnte ein Mensch so erzogen werden, dass er, ohne eigentlich von Sinnen zu kommen, seine Begriffe so seltsam verbände, daß er in der Gesellschaft nicht zu gebrauchen wäre, ein artifizieller Narr" (Sudel-F 549).
137 "Eine Lustspiel-Scene, welche im Leben vorkommt. – Jemand denkt sich eine geistreiche Meinung über ein Thema aus, um sie in einer Gesellschaft vorzutragen. Nun würde man im Lustspiel anhören und ansehen, wie er mit allen Segeln an den Punct zu kommen und die Gesellschaft dort einzuschiffen sucht, wo er seine Bemerkung machen kann: wie er fortwährend die Unterhaltung nach Einem Ziele schiebt, gelegentlich die Richtung verliert, sie wiedergewinnt, endlich den Augenblick erreicht: fast versagt ihm der Athem – und da nimmt ihm Einer aus der Gesellschaft die Bemerkung vom Munde weg. Was wird er thun? Seiner eigenen Meinung opponiren?" (MA I 345)
138 This aligns with another maxim from *Menschliches*: "*Advocate of truth.* – Truth is least likely to find advocates not when it is dangerous to speak the truth, but when it is boring to do so" (Ver-

ard, for not only do they threaten to falsify data by giving priority to the system rather than the observation, but in doing so, they also stifle rather than stimulate further investigation. Rather than spurring the scientist on to further discovery, "[m]ethods [as opposed to aphorisms], carrying the shew of a total, do secure men, as if they were at furthest."[150] In Bacon's estimation, the method of writing isolated aphorisms that are beholden to no particular interpretive system offers a twofold response to these dangers: it allows for combinatorial freedom and invites continued contemplation. Bacon claims that "this delivering of knowledge in distinct and disjointed aphorisms doth leave the wit of man more free to turn and to toss, and to make use of that which is delivered to more several purposes and applications."[151] Unlike closed systematic arrangements, combinatorial freedom stimulates further thought.

The isolated aphorism contributes to this stimulation. As Bacon puts it: "antiquity used to deliver the knowledge which the mind of man had gathered in observations, aphorisms, or short and dispersed sentences [...] which did invite men, both to ponder that which was invented, and to add and supply further."[152] In isolation, the aphorism is thus "open" in a twofold sense: in that it invites recombination and recontextualization of the aphoristic text, and in that it invites the reader to continued contemplation. Bacon opposes the stimulative *traditio per aphorismos* to the stifling *traditio methodica* of the Scholastics:[153]

> knowledge, while it is in aphorisms and observations, [...] is in growth; but when it once is comprehended in exact methods, it may perchance be further polished and illustrated, and accommodated for use and practice, but it increaseth no more in bulk and substance.[154]

With their invitation to continue thinking and their freedom from any particular systematic context, aphorisms prove dynamic. They challenge any injudicious reduction of the aphoristic observation to premature organization. Therein lies the aphorism's virtue for empirical science: the observation, as encapsulated in the aphorism, precedes the system that would interpret it.

For Nietzsche, the regular gaps between aphoristic texts are integral for the effectiveness of the form. In a letter to his publisher Ernst Schmeitzner regarding the format of *Morgenröte*, he writes: "I consider 'Menschliches Allzumenschliches' the standard for spatial distribution. Don't print too cramped! The fault of the book is that the essential thoughts follow one another too *closely*."[155] The aphorism collection promotes further thought by literally providing spaces for the reader to fill. Nietzsche

---

150 Bacon, Works, vol. 3, 405.
151 Bacon, Works, vol. 7, 321.
152 Bacon, Works, vol. 3, 498.
153 See Mautner, Der Aphorismus, 8.
154 Bacon, Works, vol. 3, 292.
155 "Als Norm für die Raum-Eintheilung betrachte ich 'Menschliches Allzumenschliches'. Ja nicht eng zusammen drucken! Der Fehler des Buches ist so schon, daß die wesentlichsten Gedanken zu dicht sich folgen" (Letter to Schmeitzner, 13 Mar 1881, KGB III/1:69, no. 89).

shares Bacon's objective of stimulating further thought in his readers by providing less than the reader wants or requires. In a passage from *Menschliches, Allzumensch-liches* called "The incomplete as what is effective" (Das Unvollständige als das Wirksame; HH I 178; MA I 178), Nietzsche's praise for perceived incompleteness is remarkably reminiscent of Bacon:

> the relief-like, incomplete representation of a thought or of a whole philosophy sometimes has more effect than working it out thoroughly does: we leave more for the viewer to do, he is roused to continue shaping and to think through to the end what has set itself before him in such strong light and shadow, and to overcome by himself the obstacle that hindered it from fully emerging before. (HH I 178)[156]

Although Nietzsche does not mention the aphoristic form explicitly in this passage, it is difficult when reading it not to think of the very form and context of the passage itself. After one hundred seventy-seven aphorisms, Nietzsche finally deigns to remark upon the ostensibly fragmentary or incomplete nature of the work *Menschliches, All-zumenschliches*. His earlier works – the academic philological articles, *Die Geburt der Tragödie*, his *Unzeitgemäße Betrachtungen* – had been, at least formally, somewhat more conventional. At least they gave the impression of coherent, linear development and ostensible resolution. *Menschliches, Allzumenschliches*, on the other hand, does not provide even the pretense of systematic design (beyond general thematic group-ings); Nietzsche opts rather to perforate the volume with discernible gaps, even within this individual text itself. But this particular aphorism praising incompleteness does not openly refer to the volume in which it appears. And indeed, precisely this lack of direct self-reference in this passage contributes to its persuasiveness, for the reader experiences the effect of which Nietzsche speaks by recognizing with little effort at least one element without which the thought could be seen as "in-complete." By *not* mentioning *Menschliches, Allzumenschliches*, but allowing the reader to complete the thought, this passage itself presents an incomplete passage on the nature of incompletion that provides the reader a taste of the resolution that the book has hitherto withheld. Such resolution remains withheld, however, for while we may have begun to account for the incompleteness of this thought by recognizing its self-reflexive attitude, the totality of *Menschliches, Allzumenschliches* remains obscure.

The perceived incompletion of this particular aphorism derives from the absence of a particular element, but the perception of incompletion that accompanies the aphorism in general, as a genre, has its basis not in the individual text, but in the text's independence from any particular argumentative structure, or, as scholars of

---

156 "Die reliefartig unvollständige Darstellung eines Gedankens, einer ganzen Philosophie [ist mitunter] wirksamer, als die erschöpfende Ausführung: man überlässt der Arbeit des Beschauers mehr, er wird aufgeregt, das, was in so starkem Licht und Dunkel vor ihm sich abhebt, fortzubilden, zu Ende zu denken und jenes Hemmniss selber zu überwinden, welches ihrem völligen Heraustreten bis dahin hinderlich war" (MA I 178).

the aphorism tend to say, from any particular system. Central to Bacon's understanding of the aphorism is his skepticism vis-à-vis overly-hasty systematization, and indeed, scholars tend to emphasize the anti-systematic attitude of the German aphorism over anything else, including brevity and wit. As Gray puts it, "traditionally the [German] aphorism is a symptom of the express lack of, or protest against [...] systematic ideology."[157] Spicker asserts that it is not brevity or pithiness or wit that characterizes the aphorism, but rather the stance against dogmatism and system.[158] Recognizing the important role of the notion of system in aphorism studies, he insists that the "anti-systematic" is at the core of the concept of the aphorism.[159]

In turning to the aphorism, Nietzsche avails himself of a form that stands at odds with the dominant philosophical conventions of his day. Descartes had emphasized method as the means to guarantee the truth of knowledge, and Kant further intensified the demand for a systematic approach to philosophical issues. Systematic philosophy as we understand it today derives its character largely from Kant, who insisted on the architectonic, systematic structure of human reason. As Tilman Borsche points out, aphoristic writing challenges such an approach by affirming the isolated statement which need not recognize itself as a "moment within a rational whole."[160] Even if an aphorism itself may be systematic, it need not yield a comprehensive system or have a place within one. Such a stance is anathema to an understanding of philosophy that places ultimate value in the systematic totality rather than the isolated finding. Truth in systematic philosophy is a function of the whole, and thus systematic philosophy would have the aphoristic statement ultimately integrated into its larger totality.

Nietzsche's own critical approach to systematic discourse aligns itself well with the skeptical attitude at the heart of the German aphoristic tradition, for he identifies in the tendency toward systematic discourse a willing suppression of doubt that undermines its claim to value truth. "Beware of systematizers!" Nietzsche warns in *Morgenröte*;

> Systematizers practice a kind of play-acting: in as much as they want to fill out a system and round off its horizon, they have to try to present their weaker qualities in the same style as their stronger – they try to impersonate whole and uniformly strong natures. (D 318)[161]

They treat their weaker beliefs as they would their stronger ones. Such a lack of integrity is but a short step from forming convictions, which, as Nietzsche notes in

---

157 Gray, Constructive Destruction, 10.
158 Spicker, Der Aphorismus, 354.
159 Spicker, Der Aphorismus, 352.
160 Borsche, System und Aphorismus, 48–64; my translation.
161 "Vorsicht vor den Systematikern! – Es giebt eine Schauspielerei der Systematiker: indem sie ein System ausfüllen wollen und den Horizont darum rund machen, müssen sie versuchen, ihre schwächeren Eigenschaften im Stile ihrer stärkeren auftreten zu lassen, – sie wollen vollständige und einartig starke Naturen darstellen" (M 318).

Menschliches, Allzumenschliches, "are more dangerous enemies of truth than are lies." The dogmatism that threatens to arise in the development of system and the formation of convictions is anathema to him.

In a note reminiscent of Bacon, Nietzsche identifies the development of convictions as antithetical to freedom of spirit:

> Opinions grow out of *passions; inertia of the spirit* lets them stiffen into *convictions.* – He, however, whose spirit is *free* and restlessly alive can prevent this stiffening through continual change .... we advance from opinion to opinion, through one party after another, as noble *traitors* to all things that can in any way be betrayed – and yet we feel no sense of guilt. (HH I 637)[162]

A healthy skepticism is more appropriate for the aphorist, and here, in the penultimate aphorism of *Menschliches, Allzumenschliches*, Nietzsche invites his reader to consider all that has come before as something that need not be defended dogmatically. "Doubt everything at least once," Lichtenberg advises, "even if it's the claim two times two is four,"[163] and Nietzsche echoes this sentiment with the claim, "Belief in the truth begins with doubting all hitherto believed 'truths'" (AOM 20; VM 20). To cease the pursuit of knowledge in the belief that one has achieved truth is less a goal than a danger. It mocks the "intellectual conscience" (das intellectuale Gewissen) that Nietzsche discusses in the second aphorism of *Die fröhliche Wissenschaft*, where he writes, "to stand in the midst [...] of this whole marvelous uncertainty and interpretive multiplicity of existence *and not question*, not tremble with craving and the rapture of such questioning [...] – that is what I feel to be *contemptible*" (GS 2).[164]

To renounce systematization in favor of the perpetual pursuit of knowledge is an integral part of the German aphoristic tradition, and this skepticism vis-à-vis systematic discourse is manifested in the very genre itself. The generic term "aphorism" warrants the same skeptical approach as any other systematizing designation. "What Bacon says about the harmfulness of systems could be said about every word," Lichtenberg writes; "Many words that express entire classes, or all the steps of a stepladder, are used by one step as an *individual*. That means again undefining the

---

162 "Aus den Leidenschaften wachsen die Meinungen; die Trägheit des Geistes lässt diese zu Ueberzeugungen erstarren. – Wer sich aber freien, rastlos lebendigen Geistes fühlt, kann durch beständigen Wechsel diese Erstarrung verhindern; [...] [wir] schreiten ... dann, durch den Geist getrieben von Meinung zu Meinung, durch den Wechsel der Parteien, als edle Verräther aller Dinge, die überhaupt verrathen werden können – und dennoch ohne ein Gefühl von Schuld" (MA I 637).
163 "Zweifle an allem wenigstens Einmal, und wäre es auch der Satz: zweimal 2 ist 4" (Sudel-K$_{II}$ 303).
164 "inmitten [...] der ganzen wundervollen Ungewissheit und Vieldeutigkeit des Daseins stehen und nicht fragen, nicht zittern vor Begierde und Lust des Fragens [...] – das ist es, was ich als verächtlich empfinde" (FW 2).

words."[165] In a sense, this is exactly what the aphorism, in all its multifarious guises, does: it perpetually undefines itself.

The notion of genre conventionally seeks to describe and define its constituents, to distinguish those texts that are a part of a given genre from those that are not. Such a codification is, however, at odds with the motivation ascribed by scholars to aphoristic writing. In Bacon's presentation of the aphorism, it is the disconnectedness of the individual texts that endows this form with the capacity to avoid dogmatic systematizations; in its later manifestations, this disconnectedness can be seen to emerge on thematic, formal, and taxonomic levels. Not only does the statement of the individual aphorism resist dogmatic systematization through its "distinct and disjointed" presentation, but the aphorism itself resists such systematization by assuming diverse guises: it addresses diverse topics, takes diverse shapes, and adopts diverse designations. By taking on an excess of identities, the aphorism can be seen to continue its critique of system on the level of genre. In this sense, the failure of scholars to come to a consensus on the generic identity of the aphorism is in fact consistent with their depiction of the genre as critical of system, here system as manifested by a traditional notion of genre.

This does not require that we do away with the genre of the aphorism altogether. In Gerhard Neumann's analysis, Bacon's portrayal of the genre attempts to synthesize systematic thinking with pure observation. Neumann describes Bacon's aphoristic enterprise as an attempt to coordinate the interpretive system and unadulterated observation;[166] he calls it an "open" order that mediates between system and individual experience, between theoretical and empirical knowledge.[167] Elsewhere, in a passage notably reminiscent of Bacon, Neumann himself describes the aphorism as the "portrayal of the conflict" between that which is particular, observed, and perceived through the senses on the one hand, and that which is general, reflected, and abstracted through the mind on the other.[168] In Neumann's analysis, this strategy informs the aphoristic writings of Lichtenberg, Novalis, Friedrich Schlegel and Goethe, which do not so much deny systematic discourse as mediate between system and the individual experience, between theoretical and empirical knowledge. Bacon's stance is thus not so much anti-system as simply critical of its unreflected, dogmatic application. The "experimental attitude" that Gray would later ascribe to the aphorism, "a subtle dialectical interchange between working hypothesis and derived facts,"[169] openly acknowledges the influence of both Neumann and Bacon. In each of these

---

165 "Was Baco von der Schädlichkeit der Systeme sagt, könnte man von jedem Wort sagen. Viele Wörter, die ganze Klassen ausdrücken, oder alle Stufen einer ganzen Leiter, werden wie von einer Stufe als individua gebraucht. Das heißt die Wörter wieder indefinieren" (Sudel-C 278); Gerhard Neumann discusses this passage in Neumann, Ideenparadiese, 191.
166 Neumann, Ideenparadiese, 72.
167 Neumann, Ideenparadiese, 46.
168 Neumann, Einleitung, 5.
169 Gray, Constructive Destruction, 28.

cases, the tension that emerges between the aphorism and systematic knowledge does not so much negate the validity of systematic discourse as simply emphasize its lack of absolute authority.

If we follow Neumann's approach that the aphorism is not so much *anti*-system as suspicious or critical of systematic discourse, then this understanding of the tradition does not imply that we do away with the genre of the aphorism. The notion of genre need not be discarded as a dogmatic system, but it should be acknowledged as heuristic and therefore provisional, capable of revision with the introduction of new texts and the conscious development of new criteria. Given this understanding, the aphorism in a way stands both inside and outside genre: inside, in that we can speak of an aphoristic tradition; outside, in that it refuses the kind of definitive categorization that would settle the issue of generic identity decisively. Repeatedly transgressing the bounds that seek to define it as a genre, the aphorism irritates the comfortable sense of closure that a clearly defined genre provides by revealing and magnifying the constructed nature of genre itself. In this sense, the aphorism exemplifies Nietzsche's claim in *Zur Genealogie der Moral* that "all concepts in which an entire process is semiotically concentrated elude definition; only that which has no history is definable" (GM II 13).[170] The aphorism has a long and rich history, and, perhaps counterintuitively, it is precisely because of this that it resists the confines of any stable notion of genre. While recognizing the aphorism's generic excesses may not exonerate Nietzsche scholars of their tendency to use the term haphazardly, it does help to account for this practice.

Despite its identifiable tradition and the critical potential of its pluralism, the aphorism's generic elasticity still presents difficulty. Neumann suggests one way to neutralize the generic excesses of the form in order to come to grips with the genre: due to the diversity of forms to be found under the rubric "aphorism," one cannot simply insert the aphoristic writings of any author into a preconceived formula, but must analyze the way that the particular author employs the form. Approaching the issue dialectically, Neumann proposes that rather than seeking to determine a universal conception of the genre that accounts for all aphorisms by all aphorists, we take into account the individual nature of each author of aphorisms in all its particularity, bringing it into dialogue with a broader, flexible concept of the genre in a way that opens up the play of genre rather than closing it down.[171] In other words, he suggests that we approach the genre with the same skepticism that Bacon – and Nietzsche – would have us approach any system. The author is itself an integral part of the context through by means of which we not only interpret individual aphorisms, but also recognize them as such.

---

170 "alle Begriffe, in denen sich ein ganzer Prozess semiotisch zusammenfasst, entziehen sich der Definition; definirbar ist nur Das, was keine Geschichte hat" (GM II 13).
171 See Neumann, Einleitung, 1.

Nietzsche embraces the German aphoristic tradition in all its formal diversity, giving rise to a "stylistic pluralism" even within those volumes that qualify as "aphorism collections." The last chapter argued that the answer to Nietzsche's question, "Are they aphorisms?" is "Yes" when one allows for a broader understanding of the aphorism. But in that same passage in which Nietzsche poses this question, he refrains from saying whether or not his writings are in fact aphorisms, and thereby refuses to reduce the form to a single, unified generic designation. And yet, remarkably enough, this can also be seen as typical of the aphoristic tradition in German letters. Scholars of literature have been frustrated by the form's protean quality. This lack of unified formal character, however, can itself be seen as a formal manifestation of the aphoristic attitude. Much as Bacon's aphoristic method encourages a healthy suspicion of preemptive interpretive systems, the aphorism *as a genre* adopts a critical stance toward the system that is generic classification.

When Nietzsche asserts, "They're aphorisms!" and then immediately follows with the question, "Are they aphorisms?," he continues in the tradition of Bacon and Lichtenberg, emphasizing rhetorically the uncertainty and incompleteness that inhere in the genre. It forces us beyond the question "Are they aphorisms?" and urges us to ask what it would mean to call them such, to consider what do we do when we assign a text to a particular genre. At times such classification describes a form, or a theme, but always some kind of tradition. And the reader hopes that the designation brings with it a clue as to how one can approach the text. Though Nietzsche may have continually sought bold new forms of expression, his uncertainty regarding the appropriate generic designation combined with his admonition that we take the form seriously, situates him well within the German tradition of aphoristic writing. What leads Nietzsche to that tradition, and what he then does with it, is the subject of the coming chapters.

Part Two. **The Turn to the Aphorism**

Gegen die Kurzsichtigen. – Meint ihr denn, es müsse Stückwerk sein, weil man es euch in Stücken giebt (und geben muss)?

Vermischte Meinungen und Sprüche
Aphorismus 127

Against the short-sighted. – Do you think it must be piecemeal because one gives it to you (and must give it to you) in pieces?

Assorted Opinions and Maxims
Aphorism 127

Chapter Three. The Aphoristic Option

The first edition of *Menschliches, Allzumenschliches* begins with a dedication that signals a transformation in Nietzsche's thinking: "Dedicated to the memory of Voltaire on the anniversary of his death, 30 May 1778" (Dem Andenken Voltaire's geweiht zur Gedächtniss-Feier seines Todestages, des 30. Mai 1778; KSA 14:115). Opening the work with a dedication to this French thinker, rather than to Wagner or Schopenhauer, who had been the subjects of his two most recent publications,[172] suggests a weakening of the Romantic influence and the ascension of Enlightenment thought in Nietzsche's deliberations. The excerpt on method from Descartes that accompanied the first edition of *Menschliches* "In Place of a Preface"[173] reinforces this impression, as do the positive words he later devotes to "La Rochefoucauld and his spiritual and artistic relatives" (HH I 35; MA I 35). Even before confronting the formal transformation Nietzsche's writing has undergone, the dedication and the epigraph, "In Place of a Preface," give the reader reason to expect something radically different from Nietzsche's earlier works.

But on the following page, Nietzsche immediately recasts his dedication to Voltaire as a disclaimer:

> This monological book, which came into being during a winter residence in Sorrento (1876 to 1877), would not have been given to the public at this time if the proximity of the 30th of May 1878 had not aroused all too intensely the wish to offer a timely personal tribute to the greatest liberator of the human spirit. (HH I, p. 2)[174]

This clarification effectively transforms the dedicatory utterance from an expression of homage into a gesture of disavowal. Nietzsche claims to publish the book not because it is complete and ready for public consumption, but because of an accident of the calendar. Were it not for the centennial of Voltaire's death, the book "would not have been given to the public at this time." Why that is the case he leaves unstated.[175] Such a concession may have its rhetorical charm, but it is hardly the most effective

---

172 SE, "Schopenhauer as Educator" (UB III, Schopenhauer als Erzieher) and RWB, "Richard Wagner in Bayreuth" (UB IV, Richard Wagner in Bayreuth).

173 "An Stelle einer Vorrede" (KSA 2:11).

174 "Dieses monologische Buch, welches in Sorrent während eines Winterauftenthaltes (1876 auf 1877) entstand, würde jetzt der Oeffentlichkeit nicht übergeben werden, wenn nicht die Nähe des 30. Mai 1878 den Wunsch allzu lebhaft erregt hatte, einem der grössten Befreier des Geistes zur rechten Stunde eine persönliche Huldigung darzubringen" (KSA 2:10).

175 Probably he would have continued to revise the text – the copies of *Menschliches* from Nietzsche's personal library are rife with emendations – though the second edition (1886) makes no revisions to the volume's aphorisms themselves. But this is largely because the second edition consisted primarily of unsold copies of the first edition that had been rebound, so no editorial intervention was possible at that time. Nietzsche does, however, add a preface and an epilogue (the poem, "Among Friends"/Unter Freunden) and removes the dedication to Voltaire and the epigraph from Descartes.

way for a philosopher to introduce his turn to aphoristic writing, given that the form is already often maligned for its apparent lack of systematic completion. Nietzsche exposes his first collection of aphorisms to the accusation that its form, like the publication of the book as a whole, is simply an accident of history, like Lichtenberg's *Sudelbücher*, Pascal's *Pensées*, or indeed, Nietzsche's own *Nachlass*. Introducing *Menschliches* with such a disclaimer potentially discourages those who would see its aphoristic form as a reflection of Nietzsche's philosophical priorities. It paints the aphorism as a form of incompletion, if not failure.

In the preceding chapters I argued that despite their formal diversity, Nietzsche did indeed write aphorisms after the German aphoristic tradition, and that this formal diversity itself performs a critical role in that tradition. The current chapter looks more directly at Nietzsche's actual turn to the aphorism in *Menschliches, Allzumenschliches*. Though many influential scholars portray Nietzsche's use of the aphorism as a distressing liability, one cannot overlook his sustained advocacy of the form. After considering the main criticisms of Nietzsche's aphoristic method, I investigate its appeal in terms of the genre's origins not only in literature and philosophy, but also in the natural sciences. Standing at the crossroads of these three disciplines, the aphorism provides Nietzsche with a strategic means of navigating the often-conflicting impulses that run through his writings, particularly what some have come to call the "naturalist" and "postmodern" aspects of his philosophy.

An Opportunity

Scholars otherwise sympathetic to Nietzsche's thought frequently portray his turn to the aphorism as more than simply a challenge, but as a shortcoming that must be surmounted. And such a reproach is not limited to any particular side of analytic-continental or naturalist-postmodernist divides. Martin Heidegger depicts Nietzsche's writing itself as structurally compromised by its aphoristic quality. Heidegger develops his reading strategy through analysis of *Der Wille zur Macht*, which he considers representative of Nietzsche's "actual philosophy,"[176] though he readily acknowledges that it is comprised of "preliminary works and piecemeal drafts."[177] For Heidegger, the two concepts of the will to power and the eternal recurrence of the same conflate to form Nietzsche's "*sole* thought"[178]; this thought, though not overtly present in Nietzsche's writings, equips them with a center of orientation from which the reader can navigate Nietzsche's fragmented text and establish its "real meaning." While the general strategy of orienting Nietzsche's philosophy around a particular concept or pair of concepts is not unusual, Heidegger's influential emphasis on *Der Wille zur*

---

176 Heidegger, Nietzsche, vol. 1, 17; my translation.
177 Heidegger, Nietzsche, vol. 1, 15; my translation.
178 Heidegger, Nietzsche, vol. 1, 481; my translation.

Macht reinforces a problematic understanding of Nietzsche's aphoristic writing as itself likewise incomplete. The fact that this truly incomplete yet widely influential later "work" bears a superficial structural resemblance to Nietzsche's earlier aphoristic works in its division into relatively brief, not necessarily connected texts has a retroactive effect on the reception of those earlier, intentionally aphoristic works. If *Der Wille zur Macht* resembles Nietzsche's aphoristic works and *Der Wille zur Macht* represents a never-completed project, then those aphoristic works, by association, also represent uncompleted projects. By this logic, large swaths of Nietzsche's published corpus are open to the criticism that they are merely fragmentary attempts at a complete philosophy.

Jacques Derrida's response to Heidegger questions his predecessor's emphasis on the wholeness to be sought in Nietzsche's fragmented texts, but not without himself viewing the fragmentary quality of Nietzsche's writings askance. Though otherwise well disposed to Nietzsche's stylistic eccentricities and their performative critique of conventional philosophical discourse, Derrida sounds a note of criticism when he suggests that Nietzsche writes in aphorisms because he is not up to his philosophical task. In *Spurs: Nietzsche's Styles*, he claims that "[t]his inability to assimilate – even among themselves – the aphorisms on woman and the rest – perhaps it must simply be admitted that Nietzsche himself did not see his way too clearly there." [179] Such a statement reinforces the impression that Nietzsche's use of the aphorism exposes a deficiency rather than a conscious strategy.

This impression echoes the position of an otherwise very different reader of Nietzsche, namely Arthur Danto. Danto's influential study ascribes the aphoristic quality of Nietzsche's works to his "singular lack of architectonic talent."[180] In this analysis, aphoristic writing represents a piecemeal approach that seeks to establish a philosophical system by accretion, or, more precisely, through the accumulation of aphorisms. The aphoristic element in Nietzsche's writing is for Danto a shortcoming of that writing, an indication of the writer's project left undone. Danto sees it as his duty to correct this flaw and bring Nietzsche into the fold of academic philosophy, an objective already evident in the title of his study, *Nietzsche as Philosopher*.[181] To this end, Danto pursues a common strategy: establish a central thought that orients Nietzsche's philosophy and build from there. He aims "to show the connections, altogether systematic, among those exotic doctrines that otherwise loom so blankly out of the surrounding aphorisms and frantic obiter dicta,"[182] and at the center of this philosophical system is the notion of nihilism. This centralizing notion enables Danto to overcome the formal disarray of the aphoristic collections by providing a single issue that orients all of Nietzsche's positions. Other scholars have placed

---

179 Derrida, Spur/Éperons, 101; oddly, the translation leaves out the modifier, "on woman."
180 Danto, Nietzsche as Philosopher, 22.
181 NB: Such a title would be redundant, indeed ridiculous, in the case of Kant or Hegel, and yet Nietzsche is granted it twice; see Vaihinger, Nietzsche als Philosoph.
182 Danto, Nietzsche as Philosopher, 22.

other issues at the center of Nietzsche's thought – the will to power, eternal recurrence, sublimation, etc. – though not all contend that providing such thematic orientation results in the kind of proto-analytic philosophical system Danto seeks to unveil in Nietzsche's works.

Though very different in their philosophical approaches, Heidegger, Derrida, and Danto all provide precedents for critics who would contend that the aphorism is not a viable mode of philosophical discourse. They each portray the form as indicative of something lacking: a lack of clarity (Derrida) or a lack of completion (Heidegger, Danto). For Heidegger, the lack of completion results from the intrusion of history and the sudden termination of Nietzsche's productivity; for Danto, this perceived lack results simply from Nietzsche's lack of ability. Despite the differences in their intellectual orientations, each paints the aphorism as a liability for Nietzsche's philosophical ambitions.

Though more sympathetic to Nietzsche's aphoristic method early on,[183] Lou Salomé comes to promote the view that his aphoristic writing results from his poor health and lifestyle rather than any philosophical priorities.[184] More recently this negative assessment has been perpetuated by Edmund Heller's study with the telling title, *Nietzsches Scheitern am Werk*, which grants the entirety of Nietzsche's aphoristic production the character of his literary estate.[185] In this account, Nietzsche is a systematic thinker who is simply not up to the task of producing a systematic philosophy and thus must settle for what isolated contributions he can make.

Nietzsche himself, however, provides a different view of the aphorism. Unlike Lichtenberg, whose *Sudelbücher* were never intended for publication, Nietzsche actually moves on to the next stage of revision that Lichtenberg's method of intellectual account-keeping describes: he actually refines and transfers his thoughts into proper "leidgers," that is, his published aphoristic volumes. The choice to publish his writings in such a fragmented form is thus not an accident of history, as in the case of his *Nachlass*, but of intent, even if the dedication to *Menschliches, Allzumenschliches* does arouse a modicum of uncertainty.

What many critics see as a liability that warrants their suspicion, Nietzsche invariably touts as a strength. As discussed in the introduction to the current study, throughout his career he lauds the advantages of the aphorism, criticizing philosophies that are overly eager to provide a systematic account of everything. In a note from the summer of 1885, he directly admits, and indeed celebrates, the fact that the aphorism does not present ideas the way more systematic philosophy does, opposing it directly to the more conventional treatise. He writes:

---

183 Andreas-Salomé, Friedrich Nietzsche in seinen Werken, 185 ff.
184 Andreas-Salomé, Looking Back, 49.
185 Heller, Nietzsches Scheitern am Werk.

> In books of aphorisms like mine there are plenty of forbidden, long things and chains of thought between and behind short aphorisms, some of which would be questionable enough for Oedipus and his sphinx. I don't write treatises: they're for jack-asses and magazine-readers.[186]

If treatises are for "jack-asses and magazine-readers," presumably the aphorism is not. In this note Nietzsche draws a sharp distinction between his own method and that of more traditional philosophers, berating the more conventional, systematic form of the treatise as unfit for serious readers.

Nevertheless, Nietzsche himself does provide fodder for accusations of incompletion. In *Vermischte Meinungen und Sprüche*, in a passage called "Against the shortsighted," he asks, "Do you think it must be piecemeal because one gives it to you (and must give it to you) in pieces?" (AOM 127).[187] Presumably the "it" (es) of which Nietzsche speaks here is that which he himself is "giving," namely his own writing. This statement on the form of his discourse cuts in two different directions. On the one hand, it provides an apologia for aphoristic writing, suggesting that only the short-sighted see his writing as "piecemeal" (Stückwerk); for the clear-sighted reader, his writings are not. On the other hand, the passage suggests that these writings are presented in pieces by necessity – they "must" be presented thus – even if this demand is mentioned only as a parenthetical afterthought. Nietzsche leaves it to the reader to determine just why he considers himself compelled to render his thought in pieces rather than as a coherent whole.

Early accounts located the source of this imperative in Nietzsche's ailing health.[188] Janz's biography perpetuates this position, claiming that "Only reluctantly does Nietzsche bow under pressure to the short form of the aphorism,"[189] though one is left to wonder why he did not continue to employ the aphorism as his health deteriorated. Studies dedicated specifically to Nietzsche's aphoristic writing tend to portray his turn to the form as a response to demands dictated by the findings of his philosophy. Krüger describes it as the "necessary form of his thought,"[190] though he insists that the aphorism is a *Denkform* rather than a *Sprachform*. Following Krüger's lead, Häntzschel-Schlotke begins with the assumption that "thoughts determine the form of thought" and from this infers that the "manner of his thinking, the direction of inquiry, and the results gained … demand [fordern] a particular linguistic

---

186 "In Aphorismenbüchern gleich den meinigen stehen zwischen und hinter kurzen Aphorismen lauter verbotene lange Dinge und Gedanken-Ketten; und Manches darunter, das für Oedipus und sein Sphinx fragwürdig genug sein mag. Abhandlungen schreibe ich nicht: die sind für Esel und Zeitschriften-Leser" (NL 37[5], 1885; KSA 11:579).

187 "Gegen die Kurzsichtigen. – Meint ihr denn, es müsse Stückwerk sein, weil man es euch in Stücken giebt (und geben muss)?" (VM 127)

188 Riehl, Friedrich Nietzsche: Der Künstler und der Denker, 16; Besser, Die Problematik der aphoristischen Form, 120 f.; see also the account of Arthur Egidi in Gilman/Parent, Conversations with Nietzsche, 129.

189 Janz, Friedrich Nietzsche, vol. 2, 32; my translation.

190 Krüger, Über den Aphorismus als philosophische Form, 105; my translation.

Nietzsche's own position, Nietzsche does not condemn the notion of truth outright, nor does he present a devaluation of "human truth,"[213] but rather he redefines the notion of truth in a way that simply acknowledges its lack of universal validity. This actually reinforces the value of human truths by rejecting the notion that there is a greater perspective compared to which non-absolute human truths would have to be considered secondary. Without some divine, universal point of comparison, human truths are not devalued, but rather they become the value. This value is simply not absolute. This realization, however, need not lead to crisis.

That Nietzsche does not condemn truths for being non-absolute in "Wahrheit und Lüge" becomes evident when we compare two versions of the fable with which it opens. Recall that the essay begins:

> In some remote corner of the universe that is poured out in countless flickering solar systems, there once was a star on which clever animals invented knowledge. That was the most arrogant and the most untruthful moment in "world history" – yet indeed only a moment. After nature had taken a few breaths, the star froze over and the clever animals had to die. (TL 246)[214]

Nietzsche here describes knowledge as anthropocentric, a centralizing of the human that is inconsistent with its actual position in the universe. This spatial critique of human knowledge is compounded by a temporal one: humankind is terminable, and therefore so is knowledge. But even if this moment is untruthful, the passage does not suggest that we, the "clever animals," reject our knowledge as false.

Nietzsche does, however, demand such a rejection in the earlier version of the fable that appears in the posthumously published text, "Ueber das Pathos der Wahrheit" (On the Pathos of Truth), the first of the *Fünf Vorreden zu fünf ungeschriebenen Büchern* (Five Prefaces to Five Unwritten Books; KSA 1:753 ff.) which Nietzsche presented to Cosima Wagner for Christmas in 1872. In "Pathos," the fable appears almost exactly as it we find it in "Wahrheit und Lüge," but an additional three sentences go on to suggest the existence of absolute truth. Whereas the opening passage of "Wahrheit und Lüge" concludes with the line, "After nature had taken a few breaths, the star froze over and the clever animals had to die," the fable in "Pathos" continues:

> And it was time for this to happen: for although they boasted of having gained much knowledge, in the end they had discovered to their great chagrin that all their knowledge was false. They

---

213 Pace Clark, Nietzsche on Truth and Philosophy, 93

214 "In irgend einem abgelegenen Winkel des in zahllosen Sonnensystemen flimmernd ausgegossenen Weltalls gab es einmal ein Gestirn, auf dem kluge Tiere das Erkennen erfanden. Es war die hochmüthigste und verlogenste Minute der 'Weltgeschichte': aber doch nur eine Minute. Nach wenigen Athemzügen der Natur erstarrte das Gestirn, und die klugen Thiere mussten sterben" (KSA 1:875).

died, and in dying they cursed the truth. That was the nature of these desperate animals that had invented knowledge. (PT 86–87)[215]

In this version, the clever creatures came to realize that the knowledge they had gained was actually *false*. This implies that they somehow recognized a truth compared to which their knowledge was somehow illegitimate. Were Nietzsche to maintain the position that human knowledge and the truths developed thereby were in fact false, as he does in this earlier version of the fable, then one would have to admit that some supra-human, perhaps metaphysical, notion of truth is at play. But comparison of the two versions of the fable reveals that Nietzsche strategically removes from "Wahrheit und Lüge" the condemnation of truth that marks the animals' demise in the earlier version. In the later version, then, the animals do not curse the truth, they simply die, and their knowledge along with them. Thus Nietzsche specifically eliminates the suggestion that one might "get behind" appearances and achieve a truth compared to which all perspectival knowledge would be rendered false. In doing so, he also relieves himself of any *necessity* to compromise his own claims through the adoption of a particular form of discourse such as the aphorism.

Though Nietzsche may be critical of systematic discourse and of language as a vehicle of any kind of extra-linguistic truth, this does not in itself entail that he adopt a form of writing that somehow circumvents problems that he identifies as inherent in the system. "Wahrheit und Lüge," and likewise the passage "Language as a Supposed Science" from *Menschliches, Allzumenschliches*, do not so much devalue human truths as warn against endowing such conceptual truths with the unconditional privileges hitherto granted them. Such a position would constitute a devaluation only from a perspective which relies upon a standard of correspondence Nietzsche simply refuses to recognize. It is a mistake to leap from Nietzsche's claim that every view is an interpretation to the evaluation that every view is "merely" an interpretation. Nehamas rightly takes issue with this false inference, noting that "[t]o say that [a view] is 'merely' an interpretation is to take a further and unjustified step and to claim that there are in fact alternatives (of which we are aware) that rob it of its claim to being correct."[216] If there is no better form of understanding compared to which an interpretation must be considered second-rate, then it makes no sense to deride an interpretation as "merely" an interpretation. Nietzsche may continue to formulate statements; if he chooses to do so aphoristically, that is his prerogative. If he does so, that results from the liberating aspects of his critique, not from a sense of pending crisis.

---

215 "Es war auch an der Zeit: denn ob sie schon viel erkannt zu haben, sich brüsteten, waren sie doch zuletzt, zu großer Verdrossenheit, dahinter gekommen, daß sie alles falsch erkannt hatten. Sie starben und fluchten im Sterben der Wahrheit. Das war die Art dieser verzweifelten Thiere, die das Erkennen erfunden hatten" (KSA 1:759–760).
216 Nehamas, Nietzsche: Life as Literature, 66.

If there is a connection between Nietzsche's critiques of language and his turn to the aphorism, it is not one of necessity, but of opportunity. What for Chandos represents a crisis, for Nietzsche presents an opening: a chance to liberate himself from the yoke of an academic philosophical discourse that claims a privileged position with regard to truth. No longer bound by the pretense of correspondence, Nietzsche is free to determine which aspects of language and thought he finds most cogent and produce his texts accordingly. This not only enables a great plurality of textual possibilities, but also allows Nietzsche to traverse at will between what are conventionally considered distinct disciplines. Such formal and discursive diversity is operative in Nietzsche's turn to aphoristic writing, which often plays with multifarious forms as it straddles the realms of literature, philosophy, and, again like Lichtenberg's, the natural sciences.

Literature and Science

Even in its broadest definitions, the aphorism, like Nietzsche, straddles the border between literature and philosophy.[217] Historically the form has been associated with figures commonly held to be philosophers, from both Antiquity (Heraclitus, Democritus, Epicurus, Seneca, Marcus Aurelius) and more recent times (Leibniz, Kierkegaard, Schopenhauer, Wittgenstein). At the same time, it appears in the writings of many figures of a more explicitly literary bent, particularly in German (Goethe, Schlegel, Ebner-Eschenbach, Kafka, Canetti),[218] but also in other languages (Leopardi, Wilde, Stanisław Lec, Gómez de la Serna). In his voluminous histories of aphoristic writing, Friedemann Spicker links the intermediary position of the genre to its non-literary origins.[219] He traces the development of aphoristic writing from its roots in the sciences with Hippocrates and Bacon, through its applications in the diverse fields of philosophy, medicine, and anthropology, to its emergence in moralist-didactic literature and its initial treatment as a literary convention in the first half of the nineteenth century. At this latter point in the development of aphoristic writing, its hybrid history makes itself manifest, and the aphorism becomes, as Neumann demonstrates, the living expression of the conflict between logical-mathematical and aesthetic truth.[220] As the young Austrian poet-philosopher Emil Lucka described it in the early twentieth century, the genre draws its content from the realm of thoughts, while its form is that of an artwork, creating something of a centaur, a hybrid of philosophy and art.[221]

---

217 See, for example, Wehe, Geist und Form des deutschen Aphorismus, 130; Fedler, Der Aphorismus: Begriffsspiel zwischen Philosophie und Poesie.

218 See Fricke, Aphorismus, 40 ff.

219 Spicker, Der Aphorismus, 21; see also 380.

220 Neumann, Ideenparadiese, 84.

221 Lucka, Der Aphorismus, quoted in Krüger, Über den Aphorismus als philosophische Form, 19.

It is likely this much-invoked yet problematic position of the aphorism has contributed to the neglect that the form, as a form, has long suffered in scholarship. The writer Robert Musil accounts for the aphorism's infrequent treatment thus:

> Aphorism [Aphorismus]: Not fish and not fowl. Not epigram and not discovery. It apparently lacks completeness, catchiness, reducibility, or suchlike. Simply movement without experience, connection, etc. Hence the aversion to it.[222]

And Musil is not the only one to draw a connection between such aversion and the form's indeterminate disciplinary identity. Philosophers have paid the form little heed for its perceived lack of argumentative rigor, while scholars of literature have often ignored the form because they consigned it to the realm of philosophers.[223] This is a little odd, considering that philosophy has long indulged in a wide variety of forms, from poetry, fragments and dialogues, to meditations, maxims and critiques,[224] and yet the aphorism's fate parallels Nietzsche's own early reception, neglected as adrift somewhere between disciplines.[225] For neither Nietzsche nor the aphorism occupies a position that can be unequivocally designated exclusively philosophical or literary, or rather, each bears the earmarks of both philosophy and literature.

Nietzsche's penchant for hyperbole, vivid metaphors, and poetic turns of phrase and his proclivity for parable and rhetorical ingenuity add to the literary quality of his writing. What enables it is his critique of language and truth. This critique, as much as the more overtly "literary" aspects of Nietzsche's writing, helps to situate his writing, like the genre of the aphorism itself, simultaneously in the realms of literature and philosophy. Nietzsche's early accounts of language and truth, accounts crucial for postmodern readings of Nietzsche, already call for a serious reconsideration of philosophical discourse, and thereby for the actual distinction between these two realms. By compromising the convention that philosophy traffics in truths whereas literature maps the realm of the imagination, Nietzsche's reformulation of the concept of truth renders questionable any fundamental distinction between literary and philo-

---

222 Musil, Tagebücher, Aphorismen, Essays und Reden, 423; my translation.
223 See Gray, Constructive Destruction, 16, citing Johnston, The Vienna School of Aphorists, 277.
224 Arthur C. Danto provides an admittedly incomplete list of literary forms employed in philosophy: "dialogues, lecture notes, fragments, poems, examinations, essays, aphorisms, meditations, discourses, hymns, critiques, letters, summae, encyclopedias, testaments, commentaries, investigations, tractatuses, Vorlesungen, Aufbauen, prolegomena, parerga, pensees, sermons, supplements, confessions, sententiae, inquiries, diaries, outlines, sketches, commonplace books, and [...] addresses" (Danto, Philosophy as/and/of Literature, 8).
225 Looking back years later, Nietzsche claimed that the literary quality of his writings were a liability in the eyes of his academic colleagues: "Still in my 45th year, my colleagues kindly inferred that the literary form of my writings was the reason no one read them, (that) I should do it differently" (Noch in meinem 45ten Jahre geben mir Gelehrte der Basler Universität in aller Gutmüthigkeit zu verstehen, die litterarische Form meiner Schriften sei der Grund, weshalb man mich nicht lese, ich sollte das anders machen; NL 22[28], 1888; KSA 13:597).

sophical language with regard to their relation to truth. This position opens up limitless possibilities for the philosopher, whose mode of expression is no longer inhibited by the pretense of correspondence. Among his poems and polemics, the aphorism, with its long history of skating between philosophy and literature, offers Nietzsche a multifarious tradition suitable for one whose philosophy thwarts conventional disciplinary boundaries on principle and explores the new freedoms enabled by his insights vis-à-vis conventional philosophical discourse. By collapsing this particular distinction between literary and philosophical language, Nietzsche situates his writings at the intersection of literature and philosophy without fear of contradiction.

Crucial for the aphorism's literary quality is its demand for supplementation; that is, its open appeal to the interpretive intervention of the reader in the formation of meaning that lends the text its eternal quality. In the final year of his productive life, in the passage that closes the longest section of *Götzen-Dämmerung*, Nietzsche ties this quality to the aphoristic form:

> To create things on which time tests its teeth in vain; in form, in *substance*, to strive for a little immortality – I have never yet been modest enough to demand less of myself. The aphorism [Aphorismus], the maxim [Sentenz], in which I am the first among the Germans to be the master, are the forms of "eternity"; it is my ambition to say in ten sentences what everyone else says in a book – what everyone else does *not* say in a book... (TI Skirmishes 51; PN 555–556)[226]

By associating aphoristic writing with this twofold ambition, Nietzsche suggests two particular qualities of the aphorism. First is the traditional understanding of the aphorism as concise; its succinctness presumably allows him to excise all superfluous elements from his discussion, covering as much ground in ten sentences as others do in a book. But the aphorism's concision is rarely as simple as that. As Fricke compellingly argues, aphorisms, though they may come in a variety of lengths, are always written concisely; writing concisely, however, does not mean "'to write little' or 'only to write what is necessary,' but rather: to write less than would actually be necessary, and leave the necessary supplementation to the reader."[227] The aphorist Erwin Chargaff appropriately puts it quite concisely, "Aphorisms are that which remains, when everything important isn't said."[228] What an aphorism says and what it does not say are intertwined.

This leads to the second, more elusive quality of the aphorism to be gleaned from Nietzsche's praise for the form in *Götzen-Dämmerung*. This second ambition, to say

---

226 "Dinge zu schaffen, an denen umsonst die Zeit ihre Zähne versucht; der Form nach, d e r S u b s t a n z n a c h um eine kleine Unsterblichkeit bemüht sein – ich war noch nie bescheiden genug, weniger von mir zu verlangen. Der Aphorismus, die Sentenz, in denen ich als der Erste unter Deutschen Meister bin, sind die Formen der 'Ewigkeit'; mein Ehrgeiz ist, in zehn Sätzen zu sagen, was jeder Andre in einem Buche sagt, – was jeder Andre in einem Buche n i c h t sagt . . . " (GD Streifzüge 51; KSA 6:153).

227 Fricke, Aphorismus, 16; my translation.

228 Quoted in Spicker, Aphorismen über Aphorismen, Fragen über Fragen, 173; my translation.

"what everyone else does *not* say in a book," is itself more puzzling. On the one hand, the reader wonders what exactly other books do not say and why they do not say it. On the other hand, what does Nietzsche himself want to say that they do not and how will he do that? To say "what everyone else does *not* say in a book" could mean simply to provide alternatives to those things that have been offered in books before. Nietzsche may also mean to say what others *dare not* say, the kind of thing for which he is notorious. The immediate conclusiveness of such interpretations, however, runs into resistance when one considers the inconclusiveness implied by the ellipsis with which he ends the statement.[229] Although the sentence is grammatically complete, Nietzsche concludes the passage with a mark of incompletion, suggesting that something is missing from the current text, that Nietzsche himself is not saying something in his book. Although he claims his ambition is to say what "everyone else" does not say in a book, he implicates himself in this by the immediate use of ellipsis to "conclude" his statement.

Nevertheless, according to a passage from Nietzsche's second aphorism collection, *Vermischte Meinungen und Sprüche*, even the excluded element is not entirely banished from the text. In an aphorism that illuminates the irony of "concluding" a text with an ellipsis, he suggests that it is possible to say something in a book that is not included in the writing itself:

> For the sake of the dull and malevolent it should for once be said that, here as so often in this book, the author is alive to this objection, and that there is much in it that does not appear on the printed page. (AOM 175)[230]

In this passage, Nietzsche claims his message exceeds the bounds of the printed page, residing both inside and outside his book. He admonishes his reader to consider that there are things in this book, a collection of aphorisms, that are not articulated, confirming the presence of more than simply the words of the text. What is left out, he seems to suggest, are precisely those things that can be read, but are not written, in the book, among them presumably the "forbidden, long things and chains of thought between and behind short aphorisms." This does not imply that Nietzsche's writings are fragmentary, but rather that they contain elements not present in the written text to be supplemented by the reader as part of the process of interpretation.

What Nietzsche says in his books, then, is also what he himself does not say, and thus one might aver that his further goal is to say in ten sentences what he himself does not say in his books. The ellipsis at the end of the statement from *Götzen-Dämmerung* invites a moment of contemplation on the part of the reader to consider

---

229 NB: Kaufmann fails to include the ellipsis in his translation, ending the sentence with a full stop (PN 556).

230 "Der Plumpen und Böswilligen halber soll es doch einmal gesagt werden, dass es hier, wie so oft in diesem Buche, dem Autor eben auf den Einwand ankommt, und dass Manches in ihm zu lesen ist, was nicht gerade darin geschrieben steht" (VM 175).

the possibilities of interpretation. The reader's continued contemplation, by the logic of *Vermischte Meinungen und Sprüche* 175, becomes part of the book. In its praise of aphoristic writing, this passage from *Götzen-Dämmerung* performs precisely the kind of operation that Nietzsche himself, and scholars as well, associate with the aphorism. Like the aphorism, the passage says more than is written, transgressing the limitations of its own formal presentation by openly demanding the active participation of the reader that scholars and theorists have long associated with the form, and that Nietzsche anticipates in his praise of the "relief-like incomplete representation of a thought" (HH I 178; MA I 178) discussed in the previous chapter.

To leave something unsaid is not, in Nietzsche's eyes, automatically an indictment. Nor is it a result of necessity. Rather, it can constitute a conscious stylistic choice. As mentioned, the polyptotonic passage "Thinkers as Stylists" from *Menschliches, Allzumenschliches* advocates for the stylistic superiority of such abridgement: "Most thinkers write poorly," he contends, "because they communicate to us not only their thoughts, but also the thinking of their thoughts" (HH I 188; MA I 188). Here we have a tightly packaged statement buttressed by rhetorical precision, further intensified by the text's performative quality. The aphorism leaves unstated precisely why communicating one's thinking results in bad writing. Nietzsche avoids poor style (as defined here) by not communicating the thinking of his thoughts, leaving it instead for the reader to determine. In many ways, aphoristic writing as a whole can be said to resist the stylistic blunder against which Nietzsche warns here. The above passage provides a concise, quotable formulation of a thought that appears in a less-polished form in Nietzsche's notebooks:

> One should not conceal and despoil the *facts* of how our thoughts have come to us. The most profound and inexhaustible books always have something of the aphoristic and sudden character of Pascal's *Pensées*.[231]

It is unclear how Nietzsche intends the term "aphoristic" in this excerpt: whether he refers to Pascal's original turns of phrase, his penetrating insights, or the fragmentary character of the *Pensées* (or some combination of these). Still, the message reinforces "Thinkers as Stylists" in its positive portrayal of judicious elision.

The demand for the creative involvement of the reader in the determination of meaning characterizes the experience of reading Nietzsche as well as the experience of reading literature, which consistently calls upon the reader to fill in textual gaps.[232] Thus promoting the literary quality of the text aligns Nietzsche's project with a common understanding of aphoristic writing as both literature and philosophy.

---

231 "Man muß nicht Wissenschaftlich affektiren, wo es noch nicht Zeit ist, wissenschaftlich zu sein; [...] Man soll die T h a t s a c h e, wie uns unsere Gedanken gekommen sind, nicht verhehlen und verderben. Die tiefsten und unerschöpftesten Bücher werden wohl immer etwas von dem aphoristischen und plötzlichen Charakter von Pascals Pensées haben" (NL 35[31], 1885; KSA 11:522).
232 Reader-response criticism, for instance, is predicated on this dynamic.

Yet when Nietzsche initially turns to the aphorism in *Menschliches, Allzumenschliches*, he does so not with the declared intent of melding literature and philosophy, but rather philosophy and the natural sciences, or at least to introduce the rigorous methods of the natural sciences into the project of philosophy. In the opening aphorism of his first collection of aphorisms, *Menschliches, Allzumenschliches*, Nietzsche proposes as an alternative to the Idealist tradition of which he disapproves a new project of "historical philosophy" (die historische Philosophie; HH I 1; MA I 1). This project, he writes, is "no longer to be thought of as separate from natural science" (gar nicht mehr getrennt von der Naturwissenschaft zu denken). The praise of science that emerges in the following cluster of passages concentrates largely on issues of method. Rejecting what he considers the metaphysician's practice of locating value and truth in some miraculous "thing in itself," he leaves no room in his historical philosophizing for "eternal facts" (ewige[] Tatsachen) or "absolute truths" (absolute[] Wahrheiten; HH I 2; MA I 2). Instead, he advocates the pursuit of "the small, unassuming truths" (die kleinen unscheinbaren Wahrheiten) that are found "through strict method" (mit strenger Methode; HH I 3; MA I 3); to value such unpretentious truths over metaphysical and artistic errors is "the distinguishing feature of a higher culture" (das Merkmal einer höhern Cultur). Such positive assessments of the methods of scientific discourse emerge repeatedly throughout Nietzsche's career, leading some to consider him as a "methodological naturalist," meaning that he advocates a method of philosophical inquiry that is "continuous with empirical inquiry in the sciences."[233] The simultaneity of Nietzsche's turn to this "historical philosophy" modeled on scientific inquiry and his turn to aphoristic writing suggests a correlation between these two developments.

Later in his career, in a passage from *Jenseits von Gut und Böse* that has become pivotal for the "naturalist" reading of Nietzsche, he would describe his project as translating man back into nature:

> To translate man back into nature; to become master over the many vain and overly enthusiastic interpretations and connotations that have so far been scrawled and painted over the eternal basic text of *homo natura*; to see to it that man henceforth stands before man as even today, hardened in the discipline of science, he stands before the *rest* of nature, with intrepid Oedipus eyes and sealed Odysseus ears, deaf to the siren songs of old metaphysical bird catchers who have been piping at him all too long, "you are more, you are higher, you are of different origin!" – that may be a strange and insane task, but it is a *task*. (BGE 230)[234]

---

233 Leiter, Nietzsche on Morality, 3.
234 "Den Menschen nämlich zurückübersetzen in die Natur; über die vielen eitlen und schwärmerischen Deutungen und Nebensinne Herr werden, welche bisher über jenen ewigen Grundtext h o m o n a t u r a gekritzelt und gemalt wurden; machen, dass der Mensch fürderhin vor dem Menschen steht, wie er heute schon, hart geworden in der Zucht der Wissenschaft, vor der a n d e r e n Natur steht, mit unerschrocknen Oedipus-Augen und verklebten Odysseus-Ohren, taub gegen die Lockweisen alter metaphysischer Vogelfänger, welche ihm allzulange zugeflötet haben: 'du bist mehr! du bist höher! du bist anderer Herkunft!' – das mag eine seltsame und tolle Aufgabe sein, aber es ist eine A u f g a b e" (JGB 230).

Through science, Nietzsche proposes we can break the spell of metaphysical sirens that lure humankind to mistakenly differentiate itself from nature, to define itself against nature. Precisely because man has been "hardened in the discipline of science," he can now recognize his place in rather than above nature. Nietzsche had already expressed a similar sentiment in the first edition of *Die fröhliche Wissenschaft*, asking:

> When will all these shadows of God cease to darken? When will we have completely de-deified nature? When will we be allowed to begin *naturalizing* us humans by means of a pure, newly discovered, newly redeemed nature? (GS 109).[235]

This line of inquiry comes on the heels of Nietzsche's initial declaration that "God is dead," in *Die fröhliche Wissenschaft* 108. The means by which to "de-deify" nature and "naturalize" humankind are to be found in the methods of science. In *Menschliches, Allzumenschliches*, this requires a mode of "historical philosophy" that considers the historical contingencies operative in what transcendental Idealist philosophy presents as eternal essences.

Above all, the advantage Nietzsche descries in the scientific approach lies in its methods. In one of his aphoristic volumes Nietzsche declares, "school has no task more important than teaching rigorous thinking, careful judging, and logical thinking" (HH I 265).[236] Everyone, he asserts, "should get to know a science fundamentally: then he will know what method means and how necessary extreme prudence is" (HH I 635).[237] This advocacy for the methods of science continues through Nietzsche's career, from *Menschliches, Allzumenschliches* to *Der Antichrist*, in which it receives its most vivid expression, but its emergence in the former is particularly crucial, considering that Nietzsche introduces this shift just as the method of his own writing has undergone a radical development. Through the methods of science, Nietzsche hopes to overcome the prejudices of metaphysics and at last erase the final traces of an imaginary transcendent world compared to which the physical world qualifies as only secondary. By turning to the aphorism when he turned to science, Nietzsche could thus be seen to follow in the footsteps of Francis Bacon, whose scientific priorities led him likewise to aphoristic writing.

Science itself, however, is by no means invisible to Nietzsche's critical gaze. Indeed, many of his most notorious statements take science to task (making it easy to understand how the "naturalist" Nietzsche who advocates scientific methods took so long to find a foothold in scholarship). This critique would intensify in his mature

---

235 "Wann werden uns alle diese Schatten Gottes nicht mehr verdunkeln? Wann werden wir die Natur ganz entgöttlicht haben! Wann werden wir anfangen dürfen, uns Menschen mit der reinen, neu gefundenen, neu erlösten Natur zu v e r n a t ü r l i c h e n !" (FW 109).

236 "Die Schule hat keine wichtigere Aufgabe, als strenges Denken, vorsichtiges Urtheilen, consequentes Schliessen zu lehren" (MA I 265).

237 "Jedermann [sollte] mindestens eine Wissenschaft von Grund aus kennen gelernt haben: dann weiss er doch, was Methode heisst und wie nöthig die äusserste Besonnenheit ist" (MA I 635).

work. In the second edition of *Die fröhliche Wissenschaft*, in a passage entitled "How we, too, are still pious," he contends,

> that it is still a metaphysical faith on which our faith in science rests, – that even we knowing ones of today, we godless ones and antimetaphysicians, take even our fire from the flame ignited by a millennia-old faith, that Christian's faith, which was also Plato's, that God is truth, that the truth is divine. (GS 344)[238]

He would pick up this line of reasoning directly in the third treatise of *Zur Genealogie der Moral*, which portrays the search for truth as culminating in the realization that the value of truth itself must be called into question (GM III 24). The scientific endeavor, in its own search for truth, is not an alternative to the ascetic ideal, but rather its natural heir; indeed, its "unconditional will to truth ... is *faith in the ascetic ideal itself*" (GM III 24). Insofar as science "still inspires passion, love, ardor, and *suffering at all*, it is not the opposite of the ascetic ideal but rather *the latest and noblest form of it*" (GM III 23). These are, of course, later works by Nietzsche, but even when he calls for a de-deification of nature and a naturalizing of humankind, in that same passage, *Die fröhliche Wissenschaft* 109, he warns against anthropomorphizing the universe through such scientific notions as "laws of nature" (Gesetze in der Natur). And even in the later works he would continue to advocate the rigorous methods of science. His position in *Der Antichrist* is unmistakable: "scientific *methods*... one must say it ten times, *are* what is essential, also what is most difficult, also what is for the longest time opposed by habits and laziness" (A 59).[239]

Though Nietzsche suggests in *Menschliches, Allzumenschliches* that he models his aphoristic "historical philosophizing" on the methods of natural science, he provides ample reason to evaluate the findings of science critically, but this does not in itself constitute an objection to science. As discussed above, in *Menschliches* 11, "Language as supposed science," Nietzsche chastises humans for believing that in language they have mastered *aeternae veritates* of the world. Despite this error, Nietzsche does not demand that humans therefore renounce language. Indeed, he identifies an important benefit derived from this mistaken conflation of language and knowledge of the world, namely, the possibility of science. "Language," he writes, "is the first step of the effort for science" (HH I 11).[240] The faith in truth as something discovered (gefunden) enables scientific inquiry and the development

---

238 "dass es immer noch ein metaphysischer Glaube ist, auf dem unser Glaube an die Wissenschaft ruht, – dass auch wir Erkennenden von heute, wir Gottlosen und Antimetaphysiker, auch unser Feuer noch von dem Brande nehmen, den ein Jahrtausende alter Glaube entzündet hat, jener Christen-Glaube, der auch der Glaube Plato's war, dass Gott die Wahrheit ist, dass die Wahrheit göttlich ist" (FW 344); see also FW 373: "'Wissenschaft' als Vorurtheil" ("Science" as Prejudice; GS 373).
239 "wissenschaftlichen Methoden, [...] man muss es zehnmal sagen, sind das Wesentliche, auch das Schwierigste, auch das, was am längsten die Gewohnheiten und Faulheiten gegen sich hat" (AC 59); see also A 13; AC 13.
240 "die Sprache [ist] die erste Stufe der Bemühung um die Wissenschaft" (MA I 11).

of reason (Vernunft). Though language gives rise to beliefs that Nietzsche considers erroneous – for example, the equality of distinct things and the self-identity of the same thing over time – science, and even mathematics, could only come about through the assertion of these errors as truths. "Fortunately," Nietzsche somewhat surprisingly concedes, "it is too late" (HH I 11).[241] Even in *Menschliches, Allzumenschliches*, the aphorism collection in which he turns to the model of natural science for his philosophical program, Nietzsche tempers his advocacy of scientific method by applying the same scrutiny it promotes to its own operations. Natural science may provide a model for his "historical philosophizing," but that by no means inoculates it against critical examination.

Nietzsche's own scientific endeavor, it would seem, is not at odds with his conflation of literature and philosophy, but rather it provides this configuration with yet a further dimension. The science he would come to advocate, it must not be forgotten, is a gay one. *La gaya scienza* is a designation he borrows not from a scientific or philosophical tradition, but from literature.[242] Furthermore, Nietzsche is a philologist; when he proposes that everyone "should get to know a science fundamentally," he does not exempt himself. Philology is his *Wissenschaft*, and thus it should come as no surprise that in his effort to translate man back into nature (BGE 230; JGB 230), he aims to do so by getting to the fundamental text, *der Grundtext*, of *homo natura*. Not the essence of man, not his eternal soul or being, but the text, the terrible text (der schreckliche Grundtext; BGE 230; JGB 230), provides an object for scientific inquiry, but not its end. *Homo natura*, too, is yet another text, and as such requires interpretive intervention.

As Christoph Cox has compellingly argued, Nietzsche's naturalist approach itself leads him to recognize the irreducibility of interpretation as an integral part of his philosophy. Just as the will to truth overcomes the notion of truth, so the scientific enterprise ultimately must bite itself in the tail and confront its own limitations. In Cox's words, "naturalism demands a rejection of both the epistemological ideal of a 'God's-eye view' and the ontological ideal of a 'pre-given world' leading Nietzsche to a holistic or hermeneutic position that accepts the primacy and irreducibility of interpretation."[243] Nietzsche's praise of the scientific method amounts thus to a praise of the "intellectual conscience" that undermines any pretense of access to or possession of dogmatic truth (see, e.g., HH I 633; MA I 633) and acknowledges the "interpretive multiplicity of existence" (Vieldeutigkeit des Daseins).[244] Nietzsche the naturalist is thus not scientistic, insofar as he does not propose that science leads to any form of final truth. Nevertheless, just because science cannot achieve this impossible goal, it is not without value. In Cox's reading, Nietzsche's philosophy ben-

---

241 "Glücklicherweise ist es zu spat" (MA I 11).
242 Nietzsche borrows the subtitle to *The Gay Science*, "la gaya scienza," from the late-medieval Provençal troubadours, for whom it referred not to science or philosophy, but to poetry.
243 Cox, Nietzsche: Naturalism and Interpretation, 70.
244 Here I borrow Cox's translation of *Vieldeutigkeit* as "interpretive multiplicity" over Kaufmann's "rich ambiguity"; see Cox, Nietzsche: Naturalism and Interpretation, 51, n. 51.

efits from precisely this tension between its scientific aspirations and the limitations placed upon those by the necessary operations of interpretation. On the one hand, Nietzsche's naturalism mitigates the subjectivity of interpretation, providing Nietzsche with a means to evaluate interpretations against one another, while on the other hand, recognizing the irreducibility of interpretation prevents Nietzsche's naturalist methodology from developing into a scientistic dogma.

The early Nietzsche portrays precisely this stance in the figure of the "liberated intellect" from "Wahrheit und Lüge." In the second section of the essay, Nietzsche distinguishes between the rational man and the intuitive man. The former he associates with the world of concepts and abstraction; he is unartistic, prudent, reasonable, and reliable, seeking honesty, truth, and freedom from delusion (TL 256; WL, KSA 1:889); he is the man of science who believes that language can contain truth. The latter is associated with the primitive metaphor-world, rejoicing in the "splendor of metaphorical intuitions" (Glanz der metaphorischen Anschauung; TL 256; WL, KSA 1:889); he is unreasonable, reveling in dissimulation, considering "as real only that life which has been disguised as illusion and beauty" (nur das zum Schein und zur Schönheit verstellte Leben als real; TL 256; WL, KSA 1:889). Given Nietzsche's discouraging remarks in the essay regarding the world of concepts,[245] one might be tempted to think that he must logically privilege the intuitive over the rational man (as Cox does).[246] But his depiction of the intuitive man does not sustain such a reading: due to the intuitive man's irrational attitude, he does not know how to learn from experience "and falls again and again into the same ditch" (und [fällt] immer wieder in dieselbe Grube; TL 256; WL, KSA 1:890). This cannot be the model to which Nietzsche would have his reader aspire, although the rational man, who at the close of the text wraps himself in his overcoat and walks away in the rain with slow strides, hardly offers a comforting alternative.

Nietzsche himself exhibits attributes of both these characters, and in so doing aligns himself with "the liberated intellect" (dem freigewordenen Intellekt; TL 255; WL, KSA 1:888), which offers a third alternative. Like the liberated intellect, when he employs language and terminology borrowed from metaphysics in order to articulate his critique of language and truth, he exploits the "immense framework and planking of concepts to which the needy man clings his whole life in order to preserve himself" (ungeheure Gebälk und Bretterwerk der Begriffe, an das sich klammernd der bedürftige Mensch sich durch das Leben rettet). But he treats these as "nothing but a scaffolding and toy for the audacious feats" (nur ein Gerüst und

---

245 For example: "In any case, the origin of language is not a logical process, and the whole material in and with which the man of truth, the scientist, the philosopher, works and builds, stems, if not from a never-never land, in any case not from the essence of things"; TL 249 (Logisch geht es [...] jedenfalls nicht bei der Entstehung der Sprache zu, und das ganze Material worin und womit später der Mensch der Wahrheit, der Forscher, der Philosoph arbeitet und baut, stammt, wenn nicht aus Wolkenkukuksheim, so doch nicht aus dem Wesen der Dinge; WL, KSA 1:879).
246 Cox, Nietzsche: Naturalism and Interpretation, 91.

ein Spielzeug für seine verwegensten Kunststücke). Not only does Nietzsche use notions like the "thing-in-itself," even as he denies the validity of such a notion, but he continues to employ language to make arguments and claims, although he contends that language cannot operate as a vehicle of truth.[247] Like the rational man, the liberated intellect employs the structure of concepts, but he also reserves the right to smash it apart, scattering it, and then ironically to put it together again, joining the most remote and separating what is closest (TL 255; WL, KSA 1:888). Having done so, he aligns himself with the intuitive man, in that without the conceptual framework, he is guided "now not by concepts but by intuitions" (jetzt nicht von Begriffen sondern von Intuitionen; TL 255; WL, KSA 1:889). Such intuitions fall outside the realm of language:

> There exists no word for these intuitions; when man sees them he grows dumb, or else he speaks only in forbidden metaphors and in unheard-of combinations of concepts. He does this so that by shattering and mocking the old conceptual barriers he may at least correspond creatively to the impression of the powerful present intuition. (TL 256)[248]

In writing "Wahrheit und Lüge," Nietzsche builds a scaffold of thought with the aid of both language and metaphysical concepts, however ironically utilized and subject

---

247 Clark relegates "Wahrheit und Lüge" to Nietzsche's juvenilia with the argument that the essay commits Nietzsche to the value of transcendent truth, a Kantian position that truth requires some correspondence to the thing-in-itself (Clark, Nietzsche on Truth and Philosophy, 65, 86, 93). She discerns this position in several key passages from the essay in which Nietzsche does indeed mention the "thing-in-itself" (Clark, Nietzsche on Truth and Philosophy, 85), or the impossibility of our anthropomorphic knowledge at any point being "true in itself." Such statements are, in Clark's estimation, evidence of Nietzsche's dependence upon metaphysical notions of truth (as correspondence) and thus she questions the value of reading "Wahrheit und Lüge" for understanding Nietzsche's attitude toward language and truth. Yet each of the statements she cites from the essay contains some kind of distancing gesture, such as parentheses or the subjunctive mood. When mentioning the "'thing in itself,'" for instance, Nietzsche frequently couches the term in quotations marks, but whether as apologetic or as indicative of an actual quotation, they hardly bear witness to Nietzsche's advocacy of the concept. And Nietzsche doesn't say that the "thing-in-itself" *is* the pure, disinterested truth, but that it *would be*, suggesting that in fact it isn't. Clark herself even recognizes the critical effect of such distancing gestures as the subjunctive in her discussion of the will to power (Clark, Nietzsche on Truth and Philosophy, 213). Nietzsche regularly includes some kind of disclaimer that invites a critical stance vis-à-vis terms suggestive of metaphysics. For example, when he mentions truth as the coherence of term and thing, or the possibility of language as "the adequate expression of all realities" (KSA 1:878), he quickly narrows these notions by soon referring to them as truths "to the degree just described," not simply as truth. Nietzsche reminds the reader that the term "truth" can be understood in many "senses" (as per the title of the essay) and that the reader must be careful not to fall prey to the connotations of the term before determining what sense is at play in a particular passage.

248 "für sie ist das Wort nicht gemacht, der Mensch verstummt, wenn er sie sieht, oder redet in lauter verbotenen Metaphern und unerhörten Begriffsfügungen, um wenigstens durch das Zertrümmern und Verhöhnen der alten Begriffsschranken dem Eindrücke der mächtigen gegenwärtigen Intuition schöpferisch zu entsprechen" (WL, KSA 1:889).

to destruction and revision. He further employs these methods, one might say, in refusing to publish the text.

The aphorism as a scientific method provides Nietzsche with a form that encourages the kind of audacious feats he associates with the liberated intellect, for it allows him to perform his philosophy without the safety net of systematic discourse. Nietzsche, of course, is not the first to turn to the aphorism in the name of science; nor is he the first to do so with a critical regard to systematic thinking. But while the Baconian aphorism, in stimulating further cogitation and combinatorial experimentation, seeks to avoid the undue influence of prejudicial systems of interpretation, it does not entirely disavow the value of systematization. As Vickers describes it, Bacon "seems to value the aphorism because it is 'open-ended', it does not predict or commit him to a definite, fully worked-out system: yet nevertheless he has a clear idea of the place of these aphorisms within his system [...], and he has already begun to organise within this section of it."[249] The virtue of the aphoristic method in this instance is that it enables the scientist to create a system inductively based on observations, rather than forcing observations to fit a predetermined system. That does not, however, demand that no systems be developed. Though in his classic study Walter Kaufmann acknowledges no connection between Nietzsche's and Bacon's aphoristic practices, his account of Nietzsche's "method" aligns itself closely with Vickers's description of Bacon: Kaufmann portrays Nietzsche as "not a system-thinker but a problem-thinker," who seeks to escape the prejudices of a pre-formed system of thought by addressing each problem individually; this he does through a constant reconfiguration of his aphoristic "monads."[250] For Kaufmann, aphoristic writing provides the key to Nietzsche's "method,"[251] with each aphoristic text constituting an "experiment" that does not lay claim to universal validity, but rather allows for the continued introduction of new evidence and the abandonment of old, superseded positions. The individual aphoristic text thus has priority over any necessarily prejudicial system that one might wish to establish. Though unmentioned, the traces of Bacon's characterization of the aphorism are unmistakable here.

Kaufmann's account of Nietzsche's aphoristic writing reflects the Baconian aphorism in its confidence that there is a systematic unity to be discerned within Nietzsche's aphoristic experiments. Thus Bacon's aphoristic writing is not so much anti-systematic as "presystematic"[252] – it may offer a defense against prematurely establishing an interpretive system, but it is still a stage in a process leading toward the development of such a system. For Kaufmann, systematization is inherent in the notion of the experiment, for "the experiment is stopped prematurely if systematization

---

249 Vickers, Francis Bacon and Renaissance Prose, 83.
250 Kaufmann, Nietzsche, 82 and 75.
251 Kaufmann, Nietzsche, 79. NB: It is statements such as this that lead scholars like Nehamas to question what he considers the disproportionate role the notion of the aphorism has hitherto played in Nietzsche scholarship.
252 Vickers, Francis Bacon and Renaissance Prose, 85.

mand upon the reader to actively fill in its gaps inhere not primarily in the structure of the individual aphorism itself, but rather in the transition to the neighboring expression.[263] By insisting on the isolation of the aphorism, Fricke assumes the presence of a surrounding text that enables and encourages the reader to recognize the statement's isolation. The aphoristic collection in particular emphasizes this isolation of the individual aphorism, for as Fricke says, "aphorisms isolate one another reciprocally."[264] Of course an aphorism could feasibly isolate itself from any kind of text, but the collection most effectively enables us to recognize the aphorism as aphorism, to settle upon this generic designation because it consists solely of mutually isolated and isolating aphoristic texts. The aphorism collection repeatedly emphasizes the isolation of the individual aphorisms by refusing to establish any single dominant text, narrative, or argument that centers the discourse upon which the aphoristic text comments or from which it deviates.

Due to the reciprocating isolation of the individual aphoristic texts, the aphorism collection allows for the author's easy addition of supplementary material. Goethe would take advantage of this aspect in the composition of his *Meister*. Wanting the combination of *Wilhelm Meisters Lehrjahre* and *Wilhelm Meisters Wanderjahre* to comprise three volumes, he padded the novel with the two aphorism clusters, "Betrachtungen im Sinne der Wanderer" and "Aus Makariens Archiv." He could do so not only because he had reams of such notes ready to hand, but because the aphoristic form does not require – indeed, it resists – narrative integration. Nietzsche would likewise avail himself of this characteristic, for instance by inserting the last aphorism of *Vermischte Meinungen und Sprüche* only at the last minute.[265] A more drastic example is the addition of an entire fifth book of forty-one aphorisms to the second edition of *Die fröhliche Wissenschaft* in 1886. Nietzsche further underscored the flexibility allowed by the aphorism collection when, frustrated by delays in the proofing and printing process, he demanded his publisher Fritzsch return the manuscript of this fifth book so that he might use it to expand a second edition of *Jenseits von Gut und Böse* (see letter from 13 Feb 1887, KGB III/5, 21–22, no. 799). There is no demand to incorporate the additional aphoristic material seamlessly because the aphorism collection is itself always riddled with seams.

---

263 Fricke, Aphorismus, 9.
264 Going beyond any negative definition based on more-or-less formal characteristics that an aphorism cannot display, Gerhard Neumann's exemplary study, *Ideenparadiese*, openly incorporates a positive notion of the collection into his portrayal of the aphorism. This notion takes on central importance in his account, foregrounding what he sees as the *dialectical* nature of aphoristic writings. The relationship of the individual aphoristic text to the collection parallels the conflict between the particular and the general that in his account characterizes the individual aphoristic statement. His study argues that such interplay between the aphorism and the aphorism-group is common among German aphorists of the late eighteenth and early nineteenth centuries (Neumann, Ideenparadiese, 829), who consistently publish their aphoristic writings in collections.
265 See Nietzsche's letter to Schmeitzner, beginning of March, KGB II/5, 390–391, no. 810.

More than simply reinforcing the generic identity of the aphorism, the collection constitutes a crucial aspect of the form's critical value. Francis Bacon incorporated the collection as an integral part of his pre-systematic aphoristic method. By bringing the "senses and particulars" [266] recorded by the aphorism into dialogue with one another, one can hope to induce the "system" to which they belong. Brian Vickers uses an organic image to describe the "system" that results from this application of "an 'anti-systematic' form": Bacon's aphoristic method is "cellular" because "very few of the aphorisms are really independent: they tend to go in groups, as one idea or attitude is developed across several of them, and [...] these little clusters of cells are given a definite place in the overall structure."[267] Behind this method lies the assumption that Bacon works with more than a single isolated aphorism. The aphoristic collection emerges early in the aphoristic tradition and constitutes an essential aspect of the form as promoted by the aphorism's first theorist.

Attempts to bring Nietzsche's diverse aphorisms together into a coherent reading abound in Nietzsche scholarship. Indeed, this is a crucial aspect of Nietzsche's aphoristic challenge – the impulse to shape his aphorism collections into a coherent system of thought. Sometimes this results in a highly concentrated, linear retelling, for instance in the *Nietzsche-Handbuch*'s account of the first chapters of *Menschliches, Allzumenschliches*:

> N[ietzsche] predicts the '*Alleged Victory of Skepticism*' (HH I 21); from this standpoint he lays out the arrangement of his writing, as he sketches a '*History of the Origins of Thought*' (HH I 16), through which the '*Fundamental Questions of Metaphysics*' (HH I 18) are proven to be illusory; the Kantian and Schopenhauerian concepts of the 'thing in itself' and 'appearance' (HH I 10) prove especially insubstantial, i.e., traceable to the effectiveness of a 'brain function' (HH I 12), which is also effective ... in the '*Logic of the Dream*' (HH I 13) and in the illusions of 'Language' (HH I 11).[268]

In keeping with the demands of its own genre, the *Nietzsche-Handbook* delivers as concisely as possible an overview of *Menschliches*, and it does so by linking together distinct aphoristic elements into a grammatically coherent linear narrative that does not necessarily reflect the sequence of the aphorisms as they appear in Nietzsche's own collection. This may be an extreme example, but the method emerges in just about any interpretation that seeks to interrogate Nietzsche's aphorism collections on their own terms rather than focusing on their relation to Nietzsche's later work. This includes the exemplary studies by Abbey (Abbey, Nietzsche's Middle Period, 2000) and Franco (Franco, Nietzsche's Enlightenment, 2011).

At first glance, Nietzsche's own presentation appears to promote a linear interpretive method in which the reader supplies the transitions between one text and the next. One

---

266 Bacon, Works, vol. 4, 50 (*Novum Organum*); quoted in Vickers, Francis Baron and Renaissance Prose, 82.
267 Vickers, Francis Bacon and Renaissance Prose, 82.
268 Ries/Kiesow, Von Menschliches, Allzumenschliches bis zur Fröhlichen Wissenschaft, 94; my translation. NB: the references to *Menschliches* have been altered to conform with the present study.

can easily recognize connections between the aphorisms that launch the first chapter, "Von den ersten und letzten Dingen" (Of the First and Last Things). The mode of historical philosophizing introduced in the first aphorism is fleshed out in the appeal for historical sensibility in the second; the concomitant denial of absolute truths in the second is taken up in the advocacy of unpretentious truths in the third; the overestimation of symbolic forms in the third is likened to astrology in the fourth; etc. Nietzsche does not, however, sustain this relay structure. He breaks between *Menschliches* 5 and *Menschliches* 6, returning in *Menschliches* 6 to larger questions of the relationship between philosophy and science, which is then taken up in *Menschliches* 7.

The impression of coherence recurs frequently in Nietzsche's aphorism collections, but sudden shifts from one topic to another remind the reader that the aphoristic structure preserves the possibility for sudden, unannounced turns and leaps. Volumes such as *Menschliches, Allzumenschliches* are largely arranged in thematically coherent chapters, but these too offer occasionally erratic constellations (particularly the sections that feature aphorisms of the maxim variety, such as "By oneself alone" and "On woman and child"[269]). Reciprocally, the collections *Morgenröte* and *Die fröhliche Wissenschaft*, with their five chapters each, present often unpredictable collections of sundry observations, though occasionally these, too, appear in coherent clusters that lead the reader to suspect that despite this aphoristic structure, there just might be an underlying order. Studies like Franco's take it as their task to illuminate this assumed underlying unity, but they do so through extensive supplementation (Franco relies heavily on the contemporaneous *Nachlass*) and elision (his analysis of *Menschliches*, for instance, ignores four of the book's nine chapters). The very structure of these volumes both elicits and resists such interpretive interventions.

Aphorisms and Fragments

As mentioned, Walter Kaufmann portrays Nietzsche as "not a system-thinker but a problem-thinker," who seeks to escape the prejudices of a pre-formed system of thought by addressing each problem individually; this he does through a constant reconfiguration of his aphoristic "monads." For Kaufmann, each aphoristic text constitutes an "experiment" that does not lay claim to universal validity, but rather allows for the continued introduction of new evidence and the abandonment of old, superseded positions. The individual aphoristic text thus has priority over any necessarily prejudicial system that one might wish to establish. On the other hand, the aphoristic experiment offers a kind of stability alien to systematic discourse: "while systems come and go, the experiment – perhaps variously interpreted – remains."[270] But while this notion of the aphorism may express a critical view of systematic discourse,

---

269 Perhaps this is why Franco elides these sections in his otherwise thorough study.
270 Kaufmann, Nietzsche, 87.

ultimately it reinforces faith in the priority of such discourse. For Kaufmann insists that systematization is the eventual goal of any experiment.[271] Beneath the critical stance towards systematic discourse is the deferred dream of systematization.

With such systematic unity in mind, Kaufmann can claim that Nietzsche strives "to transcend any mere 'anarchy of atoms' and to achieve a coherent philosophy."[272] Kaufmann draws this phrase "anarchy of atoms" from the seventh section of *Der Fall Wagner* (The Case of Wagner), which he considers to be the best criticism of Nietzsche's own style. In answer to the question, "What is the mark of every *literary* decadence?" (Womit kennzeichnet sich jede l i t t e r a r i s c h e décadence?), Nietzsche writes:

> That the life no longer resides in the whole. The word becomes sovereign and leaps out of the sentence, the sentence reaches out and obscures the meaning of the page, and the page comes to life at the expense of the whole – the whole is no longer a whole. This, however, is the simile of every style of decadence: every time there is an anarchy of atoms. (CW 7)[273]

Nietzsche's criticism of this style, Kaufmann insists, attests to the philosopher's intent to overcome any such disorder; despite appearances, Nietzsche's writings nevertheless "add up to a philosophy" (Kaufmann, Nietzsche, 79) in which unity is not absent, but "obscured" (Kaufmann, Nietzsche, 91). As with Bacon's aphorism, Nietzsche's "method" may be suspicious of systems, but it still aims toward one.

But Nietzsche's criticism of this "anarchy of atoms" appears very late in his career (1888). For the younger Nietzsche, the atomic structure holds much more appeal, at least when one considers Nietzsche's early fascination with the atomist, Democritus of Abdera (ca. 460 – 380 BCE). Early in his career, Nietzsche had developed a keen interest in the fragmentary writings of the ancient philosopher. In the extant fragments of his works, Democritus portrays the world as comprised of microscopic atoms that only cross the threshold into perceptibility through aggregation.[274] Through combination, clustering together, conglomerating, atoms become the diversity of things we register in the world. But while the atoms themselves may be eternal, they are always in motion, and thereby always carry the potential for dissolution and reconfiguration. Nietzsche found something attractive in this:

---

271 Kaufmann, Nietzsche, 94.

272 Kaufmann, Nietzsche, 77.

273 "Damit, daß das Leben nicht mehr im Ganzen wohnt. Das Wort wird souverän und springt aus dem Satz heraus, der Satz greift über und verdunkelt den Sinn der Seite, die Seite gewinnt Leben auf Unkosten des Ganzen – das Ganze ist kein Ganzes mehr. Aber das ist das Gleichnis für jeden Stil der décadence: jedes Mal Anarchie der Atome" (WA 7).

274 See Kirk/Raven, The Presocratic Philosophers, 402 – 433.

> In and of itself, there is a magnificent poetry to the atomistic conception. An eternal rain of diverse, minute bodies, which fall in manifold ways and in falling entwine with one another, creating a vortex.[275]

Such an understanding of the world opens up all identities to potential disruption, for as nothing more than aggregations of atoms in motion, the objects of perception, and indeed the perceiver, are inherently susceptible to and indeed destined for disaggregation. According to this view, all identities are necessarily contingent. Largely on the basis of this notion, James I. Porter has argued that Nietzsche's interest in atomism pervades his larger philosophical project. As Porter puts it:

> Atomism is a potent dissolvent of all naturalized illusions. Simply to think about the way the world appears to us in its *phantasmata* (the simulacral impression caused by atoms) is to think about the way meaning is made; and it is to unmake meaning, to grasp it as a phantasm.[276]

Inherent in Democritus' portrayal of the world and its relation to perception is a critique of the way in which meaning develops. The atomistic world-view emphasizes the disconnect between the eternal atoms and the contingent objects of perception, rendering the active role of the perceiver in the construction of meaning henceforward ineffaceable. Nietzsche himself would come to adopt this attitude in his critiques of culture and philosophy, which often hinge precisely on the constructedness and contingency of meaning. This awareness does not necessarily undermine the validity of Nietzsche's reading, just as an atomistic method need not result in an "anarchy of atoms." The condemnation to be gleaned from this phrase lies not necessarily in the "atoms," but in the "anarchy," with each atom seeking to tyrannize the rest. The atoms themselves, however, may cluster and form constellations, even systems, yielding "a magnificent poetry." Even if the "atomic" constellations that emerge are by necessity contingent and fleeting, subject not only to revision, but to complete disintegration, to dismiss them for their lack of absolute authority would be to court the nihilism against which Nietzsche warns in his depiction of the death of God.

The aphorism collection subjects itself to alternative approaches that resist one another: one that beckons to systematization and another that cultivates disintegration, one that decries the anarchy of atoms and another that enables it. We find the archetype for the former mode in Francis Bacon's theory of aphoristic writing, but Bacon's ambition of eventual systematization renders his example ill-suited for the latter; his faith in systematic understanding is incompatible with Nietzsche's conception of the world as "in all eternity chaos." With this in mind, we might seek Nietzsche's predecessor elsewhere, in a figure whose writings not only entertain the possibility that in-

---

275 "An und für sich liegt eine großartige Poesie in der Atomistik. Ein ewiger Regen von diversen Körperchen, die in mannichfalt. Bewegung fallen und im Fallen sich umschlingen, sodaß ein Wirbel entsteht" (BAW 3:332 and 4:44).
276 Porter, Nietzsche and the Philology of the Future, 90.

terpretation can yield chaos, but actually revel in it. This predecessor is not Bacon, but rather the Romantic writer and theorist Friedrich Schlegel (1772–1829).

Schlegel's practice of composing, collecting and publishing what he referred to as *Fragmente* continues to challenge his readers and critics. In their very form (and Schlegel's reflections upon their form) they provide an intervention into contemporary aesthetic debates, which grappled extensively with the relationship of the individual instance to the greater totality.[277] Like Nietzsche's aphoristic collections, these literary, critical, and often philosophical fragments compel their reader to consider their potential yet unarticulated relationship to a larger whole. Schlegel's fragments offer a point of comparison, for they confront the potential for dissolution that threatens Nietzsche's aphoristic writings in a way other works rarely dare.

Though Nietzsche never seriously engaged with Schlegel's work,[278] their writings share both thematic and formal qualities, including a tendency to blur the distinction between these two aspects. Ernst Behler figures Nietzsche as Schlegel's heir, positioning the two along the same trajectory of modernity that he charts in terms of irony and its development. Both Schlegel and Nietzsche recognize the inextricable embeddedness of our experience in language. Each acknowledges that he himself is not somehow exempt from this predicament, and their writings self-referentially thematize its implications.[279] The critique of philosophical discourse and its pretensions leads Nietzsche to disavow any fundamental distinction between philosophy and literature, and this aligns him well with his Romantic predecessor.[280]

Both the Schlegelian fragment and the Nietzschean aphorism exploit a certain productive or provocative lack that requires supplementation. The very generic designation of the fragment, of course, establishes its incompleteness; likewise, the apparent self-contained autonomy of the aphorism relies upon the interpretive participation of the reader. Manfred Frank opposes fragment and aphorism by arguing that the for-

---

277 See, e.g., Norman, Nietzsche and Early Romanticism.

278 See Behler, Nietzsches Auffassung der Ironie, 10; see also Del Caro, Nietzsche contra Nietzsche, 56.

279 Behler, Irony and the Discourse of Modernity, 112.

280 NB: While Nietzsche's frequent critiques of romanticism in many ways echo Goethe's disparaging characterization of the romantic as "sick" (Conversations with Eckermann, 2 April 1829), his remarks are clearly directed at Wagner and not at the theories emerging from Jena in the final decade of the eighteenth century. In fact, the writers making up the core of early romanticism – Friedrich Schlegel and his brother August Wilhelm, Novalis, Schleiermacher and Schelling – barely register in Nietzsche's writings (Though he does quote Novalis in HH I 42, MA I 142 and mention A. W. Schlegel's philological work on the Greek chorus in BT 7, GT 7). Nevertheless, the traces of early romantic thought are evident: the Schlegels and Schelling helped to launch the idea of Greek tragedy as drawn between the poles of the Dionysian and Apollinian, which, as Philippe Lacoue-Labarthe puts it, gives rise to "an entire tradition of academic philosophy (which, on his own initiative, Nietzsche had joined) revolv[ing] around precisely this opposition" (Lacoue-Labarthe, Apocryphal Nietzsche). More generally, Lacoue-Labarthe and Jean-Luc Nancy see the legacy of romanticism behind Nietzsche's assault on the division between art and philosophy, which, as maintained in Chapter Three, is operative in Nietzsche's turn to the aphorism (Lacoue-Labarthe/ Nancy, The Literary Absolute, 148, n.25).

mer is not "self-contained" (selbstgenügsam), whereas the latter is just that.[281] But while this distinction may resonate with scholars of the fragment,[282] it does not do justice to Nietzsche's aphorisms. As Stegmaier puts it, aphorisms "are never fully comprehensible, but in their reference to one another they become sufficiently comprehensible."[283] Like the fragment, the aphorism collection suggests the "incompletion" of the individual text, or rather, the reliance of the text on further texts to establish its own comprehensibility. The constituents of each form frequently point beyond themselves, often to the other texts with which they appear. This impression is reinforced by the formal presentation of Nietzsche's aphorisms, which, like Schlegel's fragments, always appear in groups. This structural multiplicity, defying the unified continuity of narrative or argument, intimates the structure of deferral, while at the same time opening the door to the possibility of conflicts, inconsistencies and contradictions.

There are those who discourage the comparison between Schlegel's fragments and Nietzsche's aphorisms. Often seen as simply an extension of Enlightenment thinking, the fragments produced by Schlegel and his Jena cohorts have been situated in a number of possible relationships to the whole from which they have presumably been severed, portrayed as providing, say, the seed from which this larger totality might emerge organically, or the particular which invites a dialectical rapport with the greater wholeness.[284] But more recent scholarship tends to read Schlegel's fragment-writing not as yet another extension of German idealism, but rather as a critique of philosophical systems based on first principle.[285] With no promise of resolution, Schlegel's fragments offer a non-redemptive, non-teleological form of writing that revels in experimentation. As Michel Chaouli describes it, Schlegel's fragments are best understood not in purely organic or mechanical terms, but in terms of eighteenth-century chemistry. Through the fragment, the writer participates in a project of "chemical" combinatorics in which texts, statements, words, syllables, even individual letters function as elements subject to their own rules of operation. Though the author may intervene, the elements of writing will continue to mix and divide independently of this author, allowing potentially for an infinite amount of permutations. The text, Chaouli argues, proves not so much "the *product* created by an intentional producer, [but] an open-ended *process* of combinatorial formation and deformation."[286] This results in the artwork's autonomy not only from society or from prejudice, but indeed from the artist himself.[287]

---

281 Frank, Über Stil und Bedeutung, 101.
282 See for instance Chaouli, The Laboratory of Poetry, 54–55.
283 Stegmaier, Nietzsches Befreiung der Philosophie, 12; my translation.
284 See, e.g., Neumann, Ideenparadiese, 567–569; Lacoue-Labarthe/Nancy, The Literary Absolute, 44–49.
285 Cf. Lacoue-Labarthe/Nancy, The Literary Absolute; Frank, Unendliche Annäherung; Menninghaus, Unendliche Verdopplung.
286 Chaouli, The Laboratory of Poetry, 5.
287 Chaouli, The Laboratory of Poetry, 12.

Both Nietzsche's aphorisms and Schlegel's fragments initiate a potentially infinite process of interpretation, both through their need for supplementation and the possibility of continual recombination. Such an account may be seen to echo the atomism of Democritus in its anti-teleological operations, but Schlegel's concern, like Nietzsche's, is with the verbal artifact. The readings that result from the interpretive process assume the status of literary experiments. As experiments, any narrative or argument derived from them likewise is unavoidably subject to reconfiguration, like the scaffold of concepts exploited by the "liberated intellect" of "Wahrheit und Lüge." But this in itself is no cause for despair, if one is willing to forego the demand for the absolute.

Schlegel's literary and aesthetic ambitions tolerate, and indeed celebrate, a degree of nonsense and incomprehensibility that is simply untenable for the aphoristic method proposed by Bacon. Chaouli accounts for the emergence of nonsense and incomprehensibility in Schlegel's writings as resulting from the same experimental impulse that leads him to laud chemistry and write fragments and encourage combinatorial exchange of all units of language: "Does not the genre of the experiment," he asks, "be it in writing or in material reality, not entail that one is prepared to end up not only with glorious novelties but also with bizarre unstable, oddly shaped contraptions?"[288] Schlegel can welcome even failed experiments as artistic accomplishments, since he pursues an aesthetic-artistic program which is not bound by the strictures of philosophical inquiry.

There is, however, an undeniable current in Nietzsche's writing that runs counter to Schlegel's at times anarchic artistic experimentation. Nietzsche may develop a philosophy that encourages experimentation and acknowledges the irreducibility of interpretive processes, but nevertheless he participates in what is in many ways a conventional philosophical project. While Nietzsche, like Schlegel, may revel in experimentation, encourage combinatorial diversity, and present a network of diverse and distinct texts for his reader to navigate in a potentially endless process of interpretation, the forces of chaos unleashed by Schlegel's radical intervention into the operations of language – and potentially by his own – pose a potential problem for Nietzsche's philosophical ambitions. Interventions, such as his condemnation of the "anarchy of atoms," tend to come late in his career, after the publication of *Also sprach Zarathustra*. For the works of the Middle Period, however, there is no such promise or even an identifiable aspiration of eventual order. The threat of dissolution persists.

A key feature distinguishing Schlegel's fragments from Nietzsche's aphorisms, when we consider the chemical, anti-teleological model of the former, is Schlegel's tolerance for the infelicitous results of the interpretive freedoms their works allow. The mature Nietzsche may acknowledge that incomprehensibility is at times a danger for the uninitiated, but internal discord is not ruled out as a possibility for the Nietzsche of the Middle Period. Indeed, he would come to indict his own earlier writ-

---

288 Chaouli, The Laboratory of Poetry, 196.

ings when later, in *Zur Genealogie der Moral*, he offers a "model" of interpretation (discussed at length in the following chapter). This "model" may not completely neutralize such threats, but it does brand them as such, pulling the reader away from the endless play of interpretive possibilities that Schlegel gladly promotes. Nevertheless, the threat of nonsense, of disintegration, of chaos and anarchy remains in the writings of Nietzsche's Middle Period. He may at times encourage his readers to chart a coherent narrative path through his aphoristic writings, to adopt a systematic approach to his works, but once again, the irreducibility of interpretation prevents any interpretation from assuming finality. Nihilism remains a threat after the death of God. Nietzsche makes this apparent not only through the statements he makes, but through the form of the aphorism collection itself.

Part Three. **Re-Reading the Aphorism**

Ein Aphorismus, rechtschaffen geprägt und ausgegossen, ist damit, dass er abgelesen ist, noch nicht "entziffert"; vielmehr hat nun erst dessen A u s l e g u n g zu beginnen, zu der es einer Kunst der Auslegung bedarf.

Zur Genealogie der Moral
Vorrede

An aphorism, properly stamped and molded, has not been "deciphered" when it has simply been read; rather, one has then to begin its *exegesis*, for which is required an art of exegesis.

On the Genealogy of Morals
Preface

Chapter Five. An Art of Exegesis

In the summer of 1885, shortly after completing the fourth and final part of *Also sprach Zarathustra*, Nietzsche penned a note that directly opposes aphoristic writing to the more conventional philosophical form of the *Abhandlung* or treatise:

> In books of aphorisms [*Aphorismenbüchern*] like mine there are plenty of forbidden, long things and chains of thought between and behind short aphorisms, some of which would be questionable enough for Oedipus and his sphinx. I don't write treatises [*Abhandlungen*]: they're for jackasses and magazine-readers. (NL 37[5], 1885; KSA 11:579).

The challenges of aphoristic writing make it unsuitable for "jack-asses and magazine-readers," who rely upon the author to tease out for them the "long things and chains of thought" that lie behind, connect and contextualize his remarks. And yet despite his disparaging evaluation of the *Abhandlung* here, Nietzsche would shortly thereafter write a few himself, and in the process of doing so would demonstrate that the relationship between the aphorism and the treatise need not be oppositional. Indeed, he comes to portray the two as complementary.

Only two years after writing down the above passage, Nietzsche published what is arguably his most systematic and cohesive book, *Zur Genealogie der Moral*, a book composed of a preface and three *Abhandlungen*. In these three treatises,[289] Nietzsche continues his assault on Western mores. Of particular interest for the current discussion is the Third Treatise, "What is the meaning of ascetic ideals?" Here Nietzsche questions the value of the pursuit of truth as an extension of the ascetic priest's misguided privileging of the metaphysical over the historical or corporeal. The Third Treatise bears particularly upon our understanding of Nietzsche's aphoristic writing, for it purportedly presents a model interpretation of an aphorism. As has been mentioned, Nietzsche writes in the preface of the *Genealogie* that "people find difficulty with the aphoristic form: this arises from the fact that today this form is *not* taken *seriously enough*." He then goes on to suggest just how one might remedy this situation:

> An aphorism, properly stamped and molded, has not been "deciphered" when it has simply been read; rather, one has then to begin its *exegesis* [*Auslegung*], for which is required an art of exegesis. I have offered in the third treatise of the present book a model [Muster] of what I regard as "exegesis" in such a case – an aphorism is prefixed [vorangestellt] to this treatise, the treatise itself is a commentary [Commentar] on it. (GM Preface 8)[290]

---

289 Though many scholars still write of the book's three "essays," for the sake of consistency, the more appropriate translation of *Abhandlung* as "treatise" will be used here. This designation is already in circulation; see for instance Janaway, Beyond Selflessness.

290 "Ein Aphorismus, rechtschaffen geprägt und ausgegossen, ist damit, dass er abgelesen ist, noch nicht 'entziffert'; vielmehr hat nun erst dessen A u s l e g u n g zu beginnen, zu der es einer Kunst der Auslegung bedarf. Ich habe in der dritten Abhandlung dieses Buchs ein Muster von dem dargeboten, was ich in einem solchen Falle 'Auslegung' nenne: – dieser Abhandlung ist ein Aphorismus vorangestellt, sie selbst ist dessen Commentar" (GM Vorrede 8; KSA 5:255 – 256).

With this appeal to exegetical diligence, Nietzsche once again betrays his academic background in philology and the bias toward textual analysis that accompanies such training. But he doesn't just call for the reader to employ his "art of exegesis" when seeking to "decipher" an aphorism, he claims to provide an example of what such an exegesis of an aphorism would look like. To put this in terms of the note from 1885, this *Abhandlung* promises to lay bare those many "forbidden, long things and chains of thought" evoked by the aphorism prefixed to it, and in doing so it affords a *Muster*, a model or paradigm, of how Nietzsche would have his other aphoristic texts read.

In the roughly two years from the completion of *Also sprach Zarathustra* in May 1885 to the publication *Zur Genealogie der Moral* in November 1887, Nietzsche displayed a renewed interest in aphoristic writing. In August 1886, he published *Jenseits von Gut und Böse*, and in June of 1887 he added Book V to the expanded edition of *Die fröhliche Wissenschaft*. In between he composed new introductions for each volume of *Menschliches, Allzumenschliches* and for *Morgenröte*. The discussion of the aphorism in the *Genealogie* is a continuation of this trend and is of a piece with *Jenseits von Gut und Böse* and Book V of *Die fröhliche Wissenschaft*. Yet one might question whether this model actually applies to the earlier aphoristic works as well. If the aphorism collections that Nietzsche composes after *Zarathustra* are indeed different, in that they are more tightly integrated[291] and present an art of the aphorism that is more disciplined, focused, and coherent,[292] then it should come as no surprise if the Third Treatise presents the aphorism as such. Doing so, however, may just reveal more about the mature, post-*Zarathustra* Nietzsche than it does about the works of his Middle Period. It reveals how Nietzsche at this later point in his career would have these earlier aphorism collections read. And thus we may well read this notion of a paradigmatic interpretation of an aphorism not so much as a guide for how best to read the aphoristic works of the Middle Period, but rather as a gesture that itself warrants contextual interpretation.

What Does an Art of Exegesis Mean?

Nietzsche composed the eighth and final section of the preface to the *Genealogie* – that is, the section in which he calls for an "art of exegesis" – shortly after completing Section 23 of the Third Treatise.[293] At this point, the notion of interpretive multiplicity was clearly on his mind, and the impulse to provide a model of interpretation would seem to respond to his ruminations on the ascetic ideal's exclusion of any alternative interpretive possibilities, for Section 23 highlights the danger of the mono-

---

291 Strobel, Das Pathos der Distanz, 163.
292 Stegmaier, Nietzsches Befreiung der Philosophie, 61.
293 See KSA 14:380; also Clark, From the Nietzsche Archive.

lithic interpretation of the world that issues from the ascetic ideal. Here Nietzsche writes that this ideal provides humankind with a universal objective, but in doing so,

> it permits no other interpretation, no other goal; it rejects, denies, affirms, and sanctions solely from the point of view of its interpretation (and has there ever been a system of interpretation more thoroughly thought through?). (GM III 23)[294]

The ascetic ideal suffers no rival accounts of the world. Confronted with its thoroughness, competing ideals fail to materialize. Even science (Wissenschaft), Nietzsche argues, proves "not the opposite of the ascetic ideal but rather *the latest and noblest form of it*" (GM III 23). In criticizing the ascetic ideal for its monopoly on interpretation and its exclusion of any alternative interpretive possibilities, Nietzsche implicitly advocates a plurality of interpretations. It is thus perhaps not surprising that he might seek to avoid unleashing an interpretive free-for-all by vehemently demanding exegetical rigor, as he would then do in his addendum to the preface.

The Third Treatise offers an exercise in interpreting interpretation. When Nietzsche invites the reader to recognize the treatise as an interpretation of an aphorism, he is urging his reader to determine the contours of that interpretation in order to elucidate what he means by an "art of exegesis." By portraying his reading as paradigmatic, he invites the reader to interpret his interpretation in order to establish a means to interpret further aphorisms. And this is all played out on the body of a text that presents itself as a discourse on meaning, for already the title of the Third Treatise presents itself as a hermeneutic puzzle: "What do ascetic ideals mean?" (Was bedeuten asketische Ideale?). The meaning of the expression "ascetic ideals" as it develops over the course of the treatise is not limited to the ambitions of the occasional religious extremist; it goes beyond the "three great slogans of the ascetic ideal" – "poverty, humility, chastity" (GM III 8)[295] – to indict art, science, philosophy, and the absolute value of truth itself. But of course the primary aim of the essay is not simply to define the ascetic ideal; it is "to bring to light, not what this ideal has *done*, but simply what it *means*; what it indicates; what lies hidden behind it, beneath it, in it" (GM III 23).[296] Nietzsche seeks to identify the source behind the great power and appeal of these ideals. In other words, "What do ascetic ideals mean?" asks a much more provocative question: whence the power of these ideals that have dominated Western culture despite their open denial of the value of power? And what does the near-ubiquity of these ideals tell us about human beings

---

294 "es lässt keine andere Auslegung, kein Andres Ziel gelten, es verwirft, verneint, bejaht, bestätigt allein im Sinne *seiner* Interpretation (– und gab es je ein zu Ende gedachteres System von Interpretation?)" (GM III 23).

295 "die drei großen Prunkworte des asketischen Ideals sind: Armuth, Demuth, Keuschheit" (GM III 8; KSA 5:352).

296 "Nicht was dies Ideal g e w i r k t hat, soll hier von mir an's Licht gestellt werden; vielmehr ganz allein nur, was es b e d e u t e t, worauf es rathen lässt, was hinter ihm, unter ihm, in ihm versteckt liegt" (GM III 23; KSA 5:581).

exegetical strategy that it allows. By demonstrating a strong tie between the aphorism and the interpretation, this reading has no need to extend exegetical liberties beyond conventional hermeneutic standards. If we assume that the aphorism Nietzsche interprets is indeed Section 1 of the Third Treatise, then there is no need to ascribe any kind of extraordinary interpretive strategy to Nietzsche; his moves are not all that radical, even for a nineteenth-century philologist.

Let us for the moment assume that Section 1 is in fact the aphorism Nietzsche reads in the Third Treatise. As a classical philologist who had taught courses in ancient rhetoric, Nietzsche could, of course, easily have offered a rhetorical-philological reading of the text. His "model" of an "art of exegesis" could have analyzed the passage's tropes or figures or rhythms, or the odd break into dialogue in the final lines of the aphorism. He could have examined how the passage threatens to fall victim to its own critique by depicting the ascetic ideals as "meaning nothing or too many things," but avoids this performative contradiction by distilling the various understandings into a single pithy – one might even say aphoristic – conclusion: that the human will "will rather will *nothingness* than *not* will." But even as a former instructor of rhetoric, Nietzsche evidently does not have this kind of interpretive strategy in mind when he demands an "art of exegesis," and indeed, such a reading would be all but impossible *avant la lettre*. The interpretive moves he does make, however, are in themselves hardly more dramatic. For instance, in the treatise he fleshes out the general terms of the aphorism, "artists" and "philosophers," with specifics, Wagner and Schopenhauer. Here Nietzsche inverts and yet continues a strategy employed in the final two *Unzeitgemäße Betrachtungen* (Unfashionable Observations): "Schopenhauer als Erzieher" (Schopenhauer as Educator, 1874) and "Richard Wagner in Bayreuth" (1876). Wagner and Schopenhauer interest Nietzsche insofar as they constitute archetypes representing larger trends in modern European culture.[312] The general term "artists," for instance, is replaced by the specific figure of Richard Wagner, who provides the face for the broader world of art. Moving into the realm of the specific, however, serves a simple explanatory function, as it elucidates what Nietzsche means by the term "artists" and how for them the ascetic ideal comes to mean so many things that it loses all meaning.

In the course of the Third Treatise, Nietzsche introduces a bevy of new concepts that, like the figures of Schopenhauer and Wagner, appear in the initial aphorism only in the most general terms. For instance, the pivotal notion of the will to power, which accounts for the apparent contradiction in the ascetic priest's empowering abnegation of this-worldly pursuits, goes unmentioned in the aphorism, even though in the body of the treatise this notion provides the unifying motif for all

---

312 Here he follows the logic he later describes in *Ecce homo:* "I never attack persons; I merely avail myself of a person as a strong magnifying glass that allows us to make visible a general but creeping calamity"; EH Wise 7; BWN 688 (ich greife nie Personen an, – ich bediene mich der Person nur wie eines starken Vergrösserungsglases, mit dem man einen allgemeinen, aber schleichenden, aber wenig greifbaren Nothstand sichtbar machen kann; EH weise 7; KSA 6:274).

forms of the ascetic ideal. The perspectivism that comes to play a crucial role in the treatise also has no counterpart in its opening aphorism, and appears to arise, if not from nowhere, then certainly not from the aphorism itself. But, of course, it is quite reasonable to expect the reader to recognize the telltale terminology from the Nietzschean arsenal: art, artist, philosopher, this world, power, priest, nothingness, will. It is not reckless to suggest that when Nietzsche speaks of "the artist" as a category, he is likely equating that figure with Wagner, who occupied his thought from the start of his philosophical career to its end. Furthermore, the notion of the will to power would be familiar to readers of Nietzsche's recent works, *Also sprach Zarathustra* and *Jenseits von Gut und Böse*. Though this requires a degree of familiarity with Nietzsche's other writings, that is hardly a radical exegetical strategy. And indeed, the indebtedness of Nietzsche's model reading on passages from *Jenseits von Gut und Böse* and Book V of *Die fröhliche Wissenschaft* aligns it well with Stegmaier's strategy of "contextual interpretation."

This kind of cross-textual self-referencing is not unique to the more conservative mode of reading that arises from the identification of Section 1 as the object of interpretation. Responding to Nietzsche's assumption in the preface to the *Genealogie* "that one has first read [his] earlier writings and has not spared some trouble doing so" (GM Preface 8),[313] Marsden also seeks to illuminate the epigraph through reference to Nietzsche's other publications, returning naturally to the passage in *Also sprach Zarathustra* from which Nietzsche draws the text:

> Who among you can at the same time laugh and be exalted?
> He who climbs upon the highest mountains laughs at all tragedies, real or imaginary.
> Courageous, unconcerned, mocking, violent – thus wisdom wants us: she is a woman and always loves only a warrior. (Z I Reading; PN 153)[314]

By providing the source at the end of the epigraph, Nietzsche provides a channel for Marsden to introduce the concept of laughter into her discussion. Laughter, she notes, plays a key role in the Third Treatise, for not only does Nietzsche declare that the tragedian must learn to laugh at himself (GM III 3), but his analysis ultimately calls upon "comedians of this [ascetic] ideal" (GM III 27)[315] as its most effective opposition.[316] Awareness of this cross-textual context enables the reader to make this leap between the aphorism and the treatise. One could then expand this understanding to read the epigraph as a critique of the priestly psychology, or, as Kelly Oliver

---

313 "dass man zuerst meine früheren Schriften gelesen und einige Mühe dabei nicht gespart hat" (GM Vorrede 8).

314 "Wer von euch kann zugleich lachen und erhoben sein?
  Wer auf den höchsten Bergen steigt, der lacht über alle Trauer-Spiele und Trauer-Ernste.
  Muthig, unbekümmert, spöttisch, gewaltthätig – so will uns die Weisheit: sie ist ein Weib und liebt immer nur einen Kriegsmann" (Z I Lesen; KSA 4:49).

315 "Komödianten dieses [asketischen] Ideals" (GM III 27).

316 Marsden, Nietzsche and the Art of the Aphorism, 34.

does, as an intersection of femininity, violence, and wisdom that also makes itself manifest in the course of the treatise.[317] But Marsden focuses on the primacy of laughter, and indeed mockery, wondering if Nietzsche mocks even his reader with this call to earnestly "decipher" his text. She might add that Nietzsche appears to do so ironically by actually misquoting Zarathustra's speech,[318] a speech that also declares, "He who writes in blood and proverbs doesn't want to be read, but rather learned by heart" (Z I Reading).[319] This is, however, simply one reading among many enabled by Marsden's account, which, drawing on the image of "rumination" (Wiederkäuen) with which Nietzsche closes the Preface, insists that "[f]or the active reader, the sense of the aphorism changes each time it is revisited."[320] The kind of active reading demanded by the aphorism as understood by Marsden results in an endless perpetuation of interpretation that defies any kind of stabilization or reification of meaning. Nietzsche's model of interpretation, then, demonstrates how one might interpret the aphoristic epigraph prefixed to the treatise, but it provides no final interpretation itself. Unlike the more conservative mode of reading, the cross-textual awareness of Nietzsche's other works in this case does not serve to limit interpretive possibilities, but to blast them open. Knowledge of Nietzsche's other writings doesn't contain the meaning of the aphorism, but dissipates it.[321]

Marsden concludes that Nietzsche's readers are "enjoined to chart a non-teleological path of thought," but the fact is that while the Third Treatise itself may take a few unexpected turns, it actually leads precisely where it says it is going to lead: from the question posed in the title and the opening of Section 1 – "What is the meaning of ascetic ideals?" – to the answer proffered at the end of Section 1 and at the end of treatise – "man would rather will *nothing* than *not* will" (GM III 28).[322] By introducing that final statement with the words "to say again at the end what I said at the beginning," Nietzsche emphasizes that he has concluded exactly where he said he would. If we attempt to chart his progress from the epigraph to the treatise, interpretive possibilities open wide before us; between the conclusion of Section 1 and the conclusion of the treatise as a whole, however, paths appear to narrow, and interpretive options seem much more contained. Marsden's analysis, while not entirely inconsistent with the aphoristic tradition, does not actually concentrate

---

317 See Oliver, Womanizing Nietzsche.

318 Nietzsche leaves out "muthig" (courageous) from the epigraph.

319 "Wer in Blut und Sprüchen schreibt, der will nicht gelesen, sondern auswendig gelernt werden" (Z I Lesen).

320 Marsden, Nietzsche and the Art of the Aphorism, 34. NB: Given Nietzsche's frequent disparaging remarks regarding herd-mentality, this "rumination" (Wiederkäuen) is not without its own strong sense of irony; unlike its English translation, the German term connotes less productive activity than fruitless repetition.

321 I borrow the notion of dissipation from Pichler, Nietzsche, die Orchestikologie und das dissipative Denken.

322 "um es noch zum Schluss zu sagen, was ich Anfangs sagte: lieber will noch der Mensch d a s N i c h t s wollen, als n i c h t wollen..." (GM III 28). Cf. GM III 1.

on how *Nietzsche* reads the epigraph, but rather simply seeks to establish some kind of connection between the epigraph and the greater treatise. This does not so much elucidate Nietzsche's model of interpretation as it establishes the simple possibility that the epigraph should still be considered the aphorism Nietzsche interprets.

Largely ignored in all this are the interpretive maneuvers Nietzsche himself undertakes in expanding the opening aphorism, whether the epigraph or the first section, into the longer treatise. This preoccupation with establishing the possibility of the epigraph's role as the object of Nietzsche's interpretation distracts from any analysis of the actual interpretive model Nietzsche himself provides in the Third Treatise. Those who contend that the first section is the aphorism interpreted do little more to flesh out the art of exegesis Nietzsche claims to present. The arguments of Janaway and Clark seek primarily to identify what aphorism Nietzsche interprets in the Third Treatise; they do not closely examine what this proper identification then tells us about the "model" interpretation itself, other than that there is no longer any need to perform philological marvels or allow undue interpretive freedom in order to get from the aphorism to the treatise that explicates it. Their comments regarding the actual "model" interpretation itself remain general and vague. Wilcox portrays the treatise as a "very careful expansion, 'dilution,' or lengthened version of the aphorism."[323] In similar language, Janaway contends that Nietzsche "is encouraging us to approach any Nietzschean aphorism as a distillation of protracted and diverse thought processes which themselves do not necessarily reach the page."[324]

Neither reading is entirely unproblematic. Advocacy of the epigraph as the aphorism Nietzsche interprets encourages a dissipative mode of interpretation that allows for such a generous understanding of interpretive freedom that it is difficult to determine just how it could function as a *Muster* for Nietzsche's readers. This should not be surprising, because this position relies upon precisely such methodological generosity, given the tenuous connection between the epigraph and the treatise that is supposedly its interpretation. Such a reading promotes an unrestricted in-

---

323 Wilcox, That Exegesis of an Aphorism in Genealogy III, 449.
324 Janaway, Nietzsche's Illustration of the Art of Exegesis, 256. Though they speak in vague generalities on this matter, Wilcox and Janaway together manage to provide more confusion than clarification on this particular point. Janaway claims that these thought processes "must be reconstructed, or constructed *de novo*, or at least paralleled by protracted and patient thought processes in the reader." Though he does not draw attention to the distinction, there would seem to be a big difference between "reconstructing" a thought process (which is what Wilcox suggests Nietzsche would have his reader do) and "constructing" the thought process "*de novo*." While at first blush, they may appear similar, in fact they point in two different directions. To "construct" the thought process *de novo* treats the aphorism as a text which the treatise unfolds (much as the *Einfall* which gives rise to further cogitation). To "reconstruct" this process, on the other hand, figures the aphorism as a condensed form of the treatise (or as an example of *Klärung*). The first situates the aphorism as prior to the treatise, as is fitting, since texts to be interpreted tend to precede their interpretation. The depiction of the aphorism as a "distillation," however, would appear to reflect the reverse and actual sequence of events: the aphorism is a condensed version of that which Nietzsche presents as its interpretation.

terpretive mode because it must, and this in turn reciprocally reinforces the conviction that the epigraph is the aphorism interpreted. At the same time, the argument that Section 1 is the aphorism interpreted itself relies on the assumption that a more conservative mode of reading is itself already somehow more compelling. According to this logic, Section 1 and the Treatise as a whole are structurally and thematically similar, so the mode of reading Nietzsche demonstrates must espouse a structural and thematic similarity between text and interpretation. But this reasoning is likewise circular. Furthermore, reading Section 1 as the aphorism interpreted demands a broadened understanding of interpretation. The fact that Nietzsche allows for the sequence of interpretation to be reversed may neutralize the objection that Section 1 cannot be the aphorism interpreted because it was written only after what is now Sections 2 through 23, but that does not inoculate it from the objection that, in the end, this model of Nietzsche's art of interpretation is itself not an interpretation. Nietzsche may describe *Morgenröte* and *Die fröhliche Wissenschaft* as interpretations literally *avant la lettre*, but he does not present them as a paradigmatic "model" of interpretation. It is far more disinguous to present a text as a model of interpretation when in fact no textual interpretation has actually taken place. Nevertheless, the largely conservative mode of interpretation enabled by the understanding of Section 1 as the object of interpretation aligns itself well with Nietzsche's claim to provide a model of interpretation that could be recognized as such by someone trained in philological exegesis. Even so, it is still not clear what this model of Nietzsche's art of interpretation actually does.

Cross-Textual Interpretation

Neither mode of interpretation entirely eclipses the other. But in fact, examining the mechanics of interpretation Nietzsche actually demonstrates in the Third Treatise does not require that we reach a final decision regarding the aphorism interpreted. Indeed, the key interpretive move, what we might simply call cross-textual interpretation, makes itself apparent regardless of whether one focuses on the epigraph or Section 1, and indeed, it is crucial for both. Though this resembles the mode of "contextual interpretation" advocated by Stegmaier, the latter is more methodical than the mode of interpretation actually exemplified by the Third Treatise.[325] From the outset, Nietzsche positions the treatise within the greater context of his own writings, beginning with the epigraph gleaned from Nietzsche's own *Also sprach Zarathustra*. In fact, the entire book is presented as part of a co-textual network: the reverse of the title page in the printer's manuscript tells us, that *Zur Genealogie der Moral* is "A se-

---

325 Nietzsche's model also differs from the method of "contextual interpretation" in that the aphorism interpreted in GM III does not appear accompanied by other aphorisms, thus Nietzsche does not begin his reading with reference to the immediately surrounding aphoristic co-texts. This does not entail that the two methods are mutually exclusive, but it would be presumptous here to identify the two.

quel to [Nietzsche's] last book, *Beyond Good and Evil*, which it is meant to supplement and clarify" (Dem letztveröffentlichten '*Jenseits von Gut und Böse*' zur Ergänzung und Verdeutlichung beigegeben; see BWN 439; KSA 14:377). The *Genealogie* is thus brought into intimate contact with *Jenseits*. And according to the preface, the book reaches back to ideas developed even earlier, even before *Menschliches, Allzumenschliches.*[326]

Nietzsche does not simply suggest that there is an affinity between the *Genealogie* and his other writings; he openly declares that knowledge of his other writings is crucial for comprehension of the book. The section of the *Genealogie*'s preface which calls for an "art of exegesis" begins:

> If this book is incomprehensible to anyone and jars on his ears, the fault, it seems to me, is not necessarily mine. It is clear enough, assuming, as I do assume, that one has first read my earlier writings and has not spared some trouble in doing so: for they are, indeed, not easy to penetrate. (GM Preface 8)[327]

Nietzsche makes it abundantly clear that even this work, a book comprised primarily of *treatises*, only becomes clear to those familiar with his larger oeuvre. And that larger cross-textual matrix proves integral to the interpretive strategy he presents in the Third Treatise.

As though to emphasize the crucial role of his other works in understanding the *Genealogie*, Nietzsche frequently cites these other works throughout his "model" interpretation. For instance, in Section 1, Nietzsche situates the philosopher and the priest on the same anaphoric list: "in the case of philosophers and scholars [the ascetic ideal means] something like a sense and instinct for the most favorable preconditions of higher spirituality;... in the case of priests the distinctive priestly faith, their best instrument of power, also the 'supreme' license for power." The relationship between the philosopher and the priest, however, remains unarticulated. But in Section 10 of the treatise, Nietzsche establishes a link between the philosopher and the priest that is utterly absent from the opening aphorism itself. He does this through reference to an aphorism from a collection that had been re-issued earlier that year: *Morgenröte*, in particular "Origin of the vita contemplativa" (Herkunft der vita contemplativa; D 42; M 42). Though *Morgenröte* had originally been released six years earlier, its re-issue six months prior to the publication of *Zur Genealogie der Moral* brings the two into close proximity. The outside text furnishes the missing connection by identifying what Nietzsche sees as the origin of the strange power shared by the philosopher and the priest: the life of contemplation that is their common her-

---

326 Admittedly, Nietzsche also mentions Paul Rée's *Der Ursprung der moralischen Empfindungen* (The Origin of the Moral Sensations, 1877) in the preface, but he does so only disparagingly; his comments regarding his own writings, on the other hand, are invariably positive.

327 " – Wenn diese Schrift irgend Jemandem unverständlich ist und schlecht zu Ohren geht, so liegt die Schuld, wie mich dünkt, nicht nothwendig an mir. Sie ist deutlich genug, vorausgesetzt, was ich voraussetze, dass man zuerst meine früheren Schriften gelesen und einige Mühe dabei nicht gespart hat: diese sind in der That nicht leicht zugänglich" (GM Vorrede 8).

itage would have been despised in communities that value action, but it would also have marked them as bearers of an unknown power, thus making them a source of fear. Through this reference to *Morgenröte*, Nietzsche fills a gap *within* the opening aphorism, connecting philosopher and priest, while at the same time opening up the issue of power raised but not elaborated on in Section 1. Since he presents this treatise as a paradigmatic reading, the implication is that the reader should likewise integrate Nietzsche's other writings in order to unfold his aphorisms.

Nietzsche makes overt references to his other publications frequently throughout the Third Treatise, thus aligning the mechanics of his reading method with the demand that the reader also be familiar with his earlier writings. Sometimes the references to his other works are there simply to provide context (as in Section 20, when Nietzsche refers the reader back to the Second Treatise), or to point toward further elaboration on a given topic (as in Section 25, when he refers his reader to the 1886 preface of *Die Geburt der Tragödie* for more on science as a problem). The references also serve to open up otherwise inaccessible avenues of thought. For instance, it is difficult to imagine how one of the treatise's most striking moments – its assertion in Section 27 that Christianity brings about its own destruction through its insistence on the moral value of truth – could be derived from the opening aphorism alone. This is Nietzsche's final blow against the ascetic ideal as the basis of the unconditional will to truth. No amount of exegetical prowess could enable the reader to glean this from the aphorism itself, regardless of whether one sees it as the epigraph or Section 1. Nietzsche, however, introduces this argument by direct reference to another recent text of his, *Die fröhliche Wissenschaft* 357, which he quotes at length in Section 27. Via Book V of *Die fröhliche Wissenschaft*, Nietzsche enables the self-incrimination of the ascetic ideal manifested in Christianity's unquestioning celebration of truth as an absolute value. He implies that the reader, too, might leap the gap from the ascetic ideal's multitude of meanings to the unifying conclusion that humans would "rather will *nothingness* than *not* will," but only through familiarity with his other works.

Traces of Nietzsche's interpretive method are actually incorporated into the structure of Section 1 of the Third Treatise itself, in what is largely seen as a transitional insertion. Wilcox claims that the aphorism Nietzsche explicates does not include all of that section, but rather concludes with the assertion: "it [the human will] will rather will *nothingness* than *not* will." He excludes the closing dialogue that immediately follows and actually concludes the first section: " – Am I understood? ... Have I been understood? ... 'Not at all, my dear sir!' – Then let us start again, from the beginning" (GM III 1; Wilcox, What Aphorism Does Nietzsche Explicate in GM III, 598). Wilcox contends that the dialogue simply separates the aphorism from the rest of the treatise in order to establish a return to the initial question, "What is the meaning of ascetic ideals?" Though this may be true, the dialogue between Nietzsche and himself does more than this; it prepares the reader for the dominant exegetical strategy that Nietzsche will employ throughout the text to follow. Though the dialogue may not have a place in the overarching structural parallel between the aphorism and the bulk of the treatise, it does anticipate the strategy of fre-

quent self-reference, a kind of dialogue with himself, that Nietzsche employs to transform a single aphorism into a sustained treatise.

This mode of reading leads one to approach Nietzsche's writings as one would approach his aphorism collections, namely, as a group of texts that are simultaneously present at all times. Whereas Arthur Danto claims that none of Nietzsche's books "presupposes an acquaintance with any other," leading him to conclude that Nietzsche's works "may be read in pretty much any order, without greatly impeding the comprehension of his ideas,"[328] I would argue that the staggering degree to which the first claim is false actually points to the veracity of the second. Precisely because Nietzsche demands a familiarity with *all* his texts, the order in which one reads them is ultimately immaterial. Paradigmatic for just this kind of cross-textual relationship is the aphoristic collection and the combinatorial freedom it allows. In the aphoristic collection, the relationship between the constituent texts is not so much one of linear development, but rather of spatial simultaneity. The reading practices exemplified in the Third Treatise correspond with those demanded by the aphorism collection, requiring that the reader read between books as one would read between aphorisms. What matters is not so much the order in which information is revealed – narrative and linear argumentation are far more sensitive to this – so long as the co-texts are ready at the reader's disposal. When Nietzsche, in his 1886 preface to *Morgenröte*, admonishes his reader to read him "rück- und vorsichtig" (D Preface 5; D Vorrede 5; KSA 3:17), he describes this cross-textual relationship in spatial terms. Though one could translate this to mean "with consideration and care," the phrase's odd hyphenation invites the reader to consider the words literally, meaning "looking backward and forward." The literalization of the term "vorsichtig" though its pairing with "rücksichtig" (rather than, say, "rücksichtsvoll"), and the highlighting of the visual imagery effected by the dissection of the terms through hyphenation, shift the emphasis from a temporal, that is, sequential understanding of these terms to a spatial image, which implies that the texts occupy that space simultaneously. One may *look* forward and back, but only because the texts are all there to see. This simultaneity is an inherent characteristic of the collection, for within the context of the collection, the individual texts may be presented in a particular numbered sequence, but they have no actual chronology. As a collection they appear simultaneously, regardless of the sequence in which they originated or were collected or are presented.

The cross-textual references Nietzsche weaves throughout the Third Treatise help to establish a network of interconnections across his oeuvre. Even within a single passage, the citation of multiple works can give rise to a knotty complex of cross-textuality. For instance, Section 9, which discusses the philosopher's historic ties to the ascetic ideal, encourages the reader to understand the original contempt for the values of the philosophers in terms of master-and slave-morality. Nietzsche does so not by mentioning the terms by name, nor by referring back to the First Treatise of the

---

328 Danto, Nietzsche as Philosopher, 1.

Genealogie, but by pointing the reader to the first mention of the term in Nietzsche's writing: "(cf. Beyond Good and Evil, page 232)," i.e., BGE 260, JGB 260. He then goes on to quote *Morgenröte* 18, in which he claims that it is "almost impossible for us today to empathize with that vast era of the 'morality of mores' which preceded 'world history'" (D 18)[329]; he describes this era as a time "when suffering was everywhere counted as a virtue, cruelty as a virtue, dissembling as a virtue" (D 18),[330] and so on. Though the contrast of master-morality and slave-morality has its precursor in *Menschliches, Allzumenschliches* 45, it is more fully developed later in *Jenseits* 260; the mention of the latter in the same discussion with *Morgenröte* 18, however, suggests that the idea was at play there as well, thus linking the Third Treatise (and its opening aphorism) not only to *Jenseits* 260 and *Morgenröte* 18, but also to *Menschliches* 45.[331] By bringing these passages into proximity of one another within the discussion of ascetic ideals, Nietzsche suggests that while cross-textual references serve to flesh out the opening aphorism of the Third Treatise, these other works also serve to illuminate one another.

Nietzsche's reading provides a twofold performance of linear narrative-formation derived from a collection of textual nodes both *within* and *between* texts. If we accept that Section 1 is the aphorism Nietzsche explicates, then what Nietzsche does is formulate a coherent narrative from the paratactic structure of the opening aphorism. Out of a disjointed list he conjures a continuous linear development from artist to philosopher to priest, from the will to power and *ressentiment* to the Christian and the scientific will to truth, demonstrating how individual elements can be unified into an integrated chain of thought that follows the contours of the opening passage. And second, he does so by demonstrating how that chain of thought can be forged of material drawn from further texts in the Nietzschean corpus. The individual items that make up the opening aphorism are brought together through narrative cohesion over the following twenty-seven sections of the treatise, providing a model of how the blank spaces left in the aphorism itself can be filled in by the reader through familiarity with Nietzsche's other works. Through reference to other texts in his oeuvre, some aphoristic, others admittedly not, he creates his continuous narrative, i.e., the treatise itself, out of a wider collection of otherwise disjointed claims. In other words, in narrativizing his own aphorism, Nietzsche invites us to narrativize our way through his database of texts. The manner in which Nietzsche brings these various texts together in the reading of this aphorism encourages the reader to see them as a collection of data to be mined for potential argumentative narratives.

But this latter aspect holds for the epigraph as well. Either way, Nietzsche's model reading beckons his reader to seek continuity, both in reading and in thinking,

---

[329] "es [wird] uns fast unmöglich..., mit jenen ungeheuren Zeitstrecken der 'Sittlichkeit der Sitte' zu empfinden, welche der 'Weltgeschichte' vorausliegen..." (M 18).

[330] "wo das Leiden als Tugend, die Grausamkeit als Tugend, die Verstellung als Tugend...in Geltung war!" (M 18).

[331] A similar argument could be made by looking at GM III 25.

by suggesting that his writings can be brought into a coherent narrative. Though he repeatedly expresses a suspicion of systematic philosophy, Nietzsche's aphoristic challenge to the reader as articulated in the *Zur Genealogie der Moral* is to formulate a convincing linear interpretation that develops along the temporal axis out of a non-linear array of spatially organized materials. One could further contend that Nietzsche sustains this exegetical methodology through all three treatises that make up *Zur Genealogie der Moral*, given that he presents the volume as a clarification and supplement to his previous book, *Jenseits von Gut und Böse*, which is itself a non-continuous collection of aphoristic statements. For many, *Zur Genealogie der Moral* presents Nietzsche's most methodical and thereby most philosophically accessible book; in these three treatises, he offers his most coherent discussion of his moral philosophy, which proves inseparable from his theories of knowledge, psychology, and metaphysics. As a clarification and supplement to *Jenseits*, it can be seen to render the aphoristic collection as three distinct philosophical analyses that overcome the blank spaces dividing one statement from the next with narrative cohesion. Thus one might say that not only does the Third Treatise provide a model of exegesis, but all three treatises together do. And together, they encourage the reader to approach Nietzsche's aphorism collections as an unstructured database,[332] requiring that one recognize the lack of necessary linear narrative argumentation while at the same time formulating one from the given materials. Implied by this cross-textual mode of interpretation is the ultimate coherence of Nietzsche's oeuvre. The model of interpretation itself promotes the notion that his writings cohere, that they work together to yield a linear narrative interpretation, whether or not that is actually the case. With this model, Nietzsche encourages his reader to interpret him in such a way that his diverse statements coalesce, but only if the reader takes the time to "decipher" his text and is not satisfied with simply "reading" him.

The Limits of Interpretation

Though many scholars have been drawn to the apparent contradictions in Nietzsche's philosophy,[333] underlying his strategy of frequent and relentlessly positive self-refer-

---

332 Lev Manovich argues that this predilection for the non-hierarchical, non-sequential presentation of data reflects more than just technological developments; he links the appeal of the database over narrative structures directly to the postmodern predicament in the wake of Nietzsche (as well as Lyotard and Tim Berners-Lee), which renders the world itself as "an endless and unstructured collection of images, texts, and other data records" (Manovich, The Language of New Media, 219).

333 Jaspers famously claimed that in Nietzsche "one can almost always also find the opposite of any judgment" (Jaspers, Nietzsche, 17); in his reading, self-contradiction (*Sichwidersprechen*) is the essential characteristic of Nietzsche's thought. This feature determines Jaspers's strategy for approaching Nietzsche's writing, for he considers the "task of interpretation [...] to seek out the contradictions in all forms, never being content until one has *also* found the contradiction" (Jaspers, Nietzsche, 9). The contradictory potential of Nietzsche's writings also informs Heidegger's reading, as

ence is the assumption that his works somehow form a cohesive whole, and the "interpretive" strategy itself promotes precisely this impression of coherence. Nietzsche himself openly asserts this as a priority in the *Genealogie*, portraying himself as one whose writings as a whole exhibit a unity, and this attests to the strength of his philosophy:

> *That* I still cleave to them today [ideas first developed in the *Aphorismen-Sammlung, Menschliches, Allzumenschliches*], [...] that they have become in the meantime more firmly attached to one another, indeed entwined and interlaced with one another, strengthens my joyful assurance that they might have arisen in me from the first not as isolated, capricious, or sporadic things but from a common root, from a *fundamental will* of knowledge. (GM Preface 2)[334]

By invoking a "common root," Nietzsche advocates not only the coherence and unity of his thought, but also its philosophical legitimacy. He goes on to explain what "alone is fitting for a philosopher" in terms that reinforce this priority:

> We have no right to *isolated* acts of any kind: we may not make isolated errors or hit upon isolated truths. Rather do our ideas, our values, our yeas and nays, our ifs and buts, grow out of us with the necessity with which a tree bears fruit – related and each with an affinity to each, and evidence of *one* will, *one* health, *one* soil, *one* sun. (GM Preface 2)[335]

Whereas the earlier aphoristic works celebrated a multifarious heterogeneity, the later Nietzsche insists upon a homogeneous unity to his works. *Zur Genealogie der Moral* supplements *Jenseits von Gut und Böse*, which in turn says the same things as *Also sprach Zarathustra* (see letter to Jacob Burckhardt, 22 Sep 1886, KGB III/3, 254–255, no. 754). Nietzsche went so far as to insist that the printer use the same lay-

---

well as many of the postmodern readings inspired by his analysis. For Wolfgang Müller-Lauter, contradiction is the essence of Nietzsche's thought, as is apparent from the title of his seminal study, *Nietzsche: His Philosophy of Contradictions and the Contradictions of His Philosophy*. But more recent studies from scholars as diverse as Alan Schrift, Brian Leiter and James I. Porter emphasize the continuity and consistency of Nietzsche's thought. And it seems that this search for coherence aligns itself more easily with the image of his own philosophy that Nietzsche promotes in the Third Treatise.

334 "Dass ich aber heute noch an ihnen festhalte, dass sie sich selber inzwischen immer fester an einander gehalten haben, ja in einander gewachsen und verwachsen sind, das stärkt in mir die frohe Zuversichtlichkeit, sie möchten von Anfang an in mir nicht einzeln, nicht beliebig, nicht sporadisch entstanden sein, sondern aus einer gemeinsamen Wurzel heraus, aus einem in der Tiefe gebietenden, immer bestimmter redenden, immer Bestimmteres verlangenden Grundwillen der Erkenntniss" (GM Vorrede 2; KSA 5:248).

335 "So allein nämlich geziemt es sich bei einem Philosophen. Wir haben kein Recht darauf, irgend worin einzeln zu sein: wir dürfen weder einzeln irren, noch einzeln die Wahrheit treffen. Vielmehr mit der Nothwendigkeit, mit der ein Baum seine Früchte trägt, wachsen aus uns unsre Gedanken, unsre Werthe, unsre Ja's und Nein's und Wenn's und Ob's – verwandt und bezüglich allesammt unter einander und Zeugnisse Eines Willens, Einer Gesundheit, Eines Erdreichs, Einer Sonne" (GM Vorrede 2).

out, type, and paper for both the *Genealogie* and *Jenseits*, so that the continuity of the two would be unmistakable (see KGB III/5, 111, no. 877).

The claim to such unity is discernible as a priority in the exegetical "model" Nietzsche provides in the Third Treatise as well. His call for cross-textual awareness reflects this criterion of coherence in interpretation that Nietzsche espouses frequently in his mature writings. By providing a "model" interpretation, Nietzsche acknowledges that even in light of the perspectival nature of exegetical operations, not all interpretations are equal; there is still such a thing as a good interpretation and a bad one. The term "interpretation" may emphasize that our knowledge and experience are not fully "objective" in the sense of being beyond the limitations of perspective – it does not, however, require that we accept all interpretations as equally valid. Again and again, Nietzsche posits unity and coherence as the distinguishing criteria.

The offense of misinterpretation (*falsche Auslegung*; *etwas falsch auslegen*) takes many forms in Nietzsche's critiques, from the peccadillo of "superficial interpretation" (flache Auslegung; BGE 40; JGB 40) to the more serious crimes of scholarly irresponsibility and dishonesty. He chastises physicists, for instance, for their "bad arts of interpretation" (schlechte Interpretations-Künste; BGE 22; JGB 22) and "bad philology" (schlechte[] 'Philologie'), which lead them to such problematic notions as "laws of nature." But Nietzsche finds the most egregious violations of philological exactitude with that manifestation of the ascetic ideal that drew the brunt of his critique throughout his career, Christianity, which earns his ire not so much for being wrong as for being dishonest.

It should be noted that Nietzsche promotes this position long before calling for "an art of exegesis" in the *Genealogie*. In *Morgenröte*, for instance, he attacks the Christians' "art of reading poorly" (Kunst des Schlecht-Lesens; D 84; M 84), dismissing their lapses in philological rigor as an affront to honesty and, somewhat playfully, to decency. Taking aim at what he calls "The Philology of Christianity" (Die Philologie des Christentums), he condemns the reading practices of Christian scholars for being consciously inconsistent:

> Again and again they say "I am right, for it is written –" and then follows an interpretation of such impudent arbitrariness that a philologist who hears is caught between rage and laughter and asks himself: is it possible? Is this honest [ehrlich]? Is it even decent? (D 84)[336]

As an example of this "art of reading poorly," Nietzsche names specifically "that unheard-of philological farce" (jenes unerhörte philologische Possenspiel), the Christians' appropriation of the Old Testament into the Christian Bible. Only through extravagant exegetical maneuvers can the Christian theologian tear the Hebrew Bible from

---

336 "Immer wieder heißt es 'ich habe Recht, denn es steht geschrieben –' und nun folgt eine unverschämte Willkürlichkeit der Auslegung, daß ein Philologe, der es hört, mitten zwischen Ingrimm und Lachen stehen bleibt und sich immer wieder fragt: ist es möglich! Ist dies ehrlich? Ist es auch nur anständig?" (M 84)

the Jews and claim to represent the real chosen people of Israel. Nietzsche condemns such readings not by attacking the methodology, but simply by asking the question, "Has anyone who asserted this ever *believed* it?" (Hat dies jemals jemand ge glaubt, der es behauptete?). He is not interested in the philological (or theological) debate as to whether every piece of wood mentioned in the Old Testament should be understood as a harbinger of the wood of the cross; he does not take issue with such methods directly as a matter of philological error.[337] Rather, he simply holds the indefensibility of such readings to be self-evident, and cannot accept that those who develop and promote them can honestly believe in the validity of such interpretations. Nietzsche rebukes Christian scholarship as philologically unsound due to a lack of integrity that borders on hypocrisy.

Consistency, it would seem, and not truth, is the operative criterion throughout Nietzsche's critique of the ascetic ideal in the Third Treatise. Though the ascetic priest may interpret truth to be of indisputable value, Nietzsche interprets the situation differently. The title of the treatise asks, "What do ascetic ideals mean?" For Nietzsche, they mean that man cannot bear the meaninglessness of suffering, and that the prospect of such suffering threatens him with a suicidal nihilism: "The meaningless of suffering, *not* suffering itself, was the curse that lay over mankind so far – *and the ascetic ideal offered man meaning!* [...] In it, suffering was *interpreted*" (GM III 28).[338] The meaning Nietzsche derives from his analysis of the ascetic ideal is not that the ideal is false, but that it provides evidence of a need for meaning and the presence of an indomitable will that "would rather will *nothingness* than *not will*." This analysis penetrates all the way to the pursuit of truth itself, which is yet another off-shoot of the ascetic ideal, and thus through Nietzsche "the will to truth becomes conscious of itself as a *problem*" (GM III 27).[339] Blind faith in the inestimable value of truth no longer applies, for "the will to truth itself first requires justification" (GM III 24).[340] Nietzsche condemns the ascetic ideal not because it is itself but an interpretation from a particular perspective, and not because it is an expression of the priest's will to power: these are unavoidable in Nietzsche's world. Rather, he attacks the inconsistencies that plague the ascetic ideal's interpretation of the world.

When Nietzsche criticizes the ascetic ideal's denial of life, it is because it actually serves to promote life. Continuing his earlier critiques of Christian philology (e.g., HH I 143; MA I 143), Nietzsche criticizes those who misread affects. The affect he sees as operative behind the ascetic ideal is *ressentiment*, which the priest converts

---

337 Indeed, he might want to avoid it, given his own tendency to read his own works "preposterously."

338 "Die Sinnlosigkeit des Leidens, nicht das Leiden, war der Fluch, der bisher über der Menschheit ausgebreitet lag, – und das asketische Ideal bot ihr einen Sinn! ... In ihm war das Leiden ausgelegt" (GM III 28).

339 "jener Wille zur Wahrheit [wäre] sich selbst als Problem zum Bewusstsein gekommen" (GM III 27).

340 "der Wille zur Wahrheit [bedarf] selbst erst einer Rechtfertigung" (GM III 24).

from suffering into guilt (GM III 15). Doing so may endow the discomfiture of the sufferer with meaning and enhance the power of the priest, but this only alleviates the immediate symptom of suffering; it does not treat its actual cause (GM III 17). The priest's answer to the question of suffering is to diminish the value of life, encouraging withdrawal from worldly concerns. But, Nietzsche points out, the priest's position actually emerges from the impulse to preserve life: it "*springs from the protective instinct of a degenerating life* which tries by all means to sustain itself and to fight for its existence" (GM III 13).[341] Despite the ascetic priests' claim to deny earthly life, they actually espouse the opposite: "life wrestles in it [the ascetic ideal] and through it with death and against death; the ascetic ideal is an artifice for the preservation of life." (GM III 13) Though constantly turning away from the this-worldly, the ascetic priest, "this apparent enemy of life, this denier – precisely he is among the greatest conserving and yes-creating forces of life" (GM III 13). An inherent contradiction emerges between what the ascetic ideal preaches and what this message actually instantiates. In criticizing the ascetic ideal for this, Nietzsche avails himself of, and thereby promotes, the criterion of internal coherence and consistency.

This criterion is also operative in the Third Treatise's critique of the ascetic ideal's portrayal of power. "Every animal," Nietzsche writes, "instinctively strives for an optimum of favorable conditions under which it can expend all its strength and achieve its maximal feeling of power" (GM III 7).[342] This includes the priest of the ascetic ideal, whose denial of power, Nietzsche claims, actually serves to increase his own. To illustrate this point, Nietzsche invokes the slave revolt in morality discussed in the First Treatise: "The will of the sick to represent *some* form of superiority, their instinct for devious paths to tyranny over the healthy – where can it not be discovered, this will to power of the weakest!" (GM III 14)[343] The ascetic ideal serves the ascetic priest's will to power, enabling him to lay low those mightier than he and to establish himself and his interpretation of the world as dominant. In doing so, the ascetic priest himself cannot be seen as representative of his own ideal, but he fits very neatly into Nietzsche's notion of the will to power as the motivating force behind this ideal and the values it advocates.

Finally, the Third Treatise's critique of the will to truth as a manifestation of the ascetic ideal also appeals to the value of consistency, even as it contests the absolute value of truth. According to Nietzsche, one of the ascetic ideal's greatest inconsistencies arises precisely from its demand for and claim to truth:

---

341 "entspringt dem Schutz- und Heil-Instinkte eines degenerirenden Lebens, welches sich mit allen Mitteln zu halten sucht und um sein Dasein kämpft" (GM III 13; KSA 5:366).
342 "Jedes Thier ... strebt instinktiv nach einem Optimum von günstigen Bedingungen, unter denen es seine Kraft ganz herauslassen kann und sein Maximum im Machtgefühl erreicht" (GM III 7; KSA 5:350).
343 "Der Wille der Kranken, irgend eine Form der Überlegenheit darzustellen, ihr Instinkt für Schleichwege, die zu einer Tyrannei über die Gesunden führen, – wo fände er sich nicht, dieser Wille gerade der Schwächsten zur Macht!" (GM III 14).

induction and deduction, taking the specific experience and abstracting it into a general law which the reader is left to formulate, or inversely, taking the general law and imagining its particular applications as supplied by the reader. To peek into the pot, that is, to seek out the biographical origin of the text as its efficient cause, is to short-circuit this process.

Take, for instance, that most popular of Nietzschean aphorisms, "*From Life's School of War. –* What does not kill me makes me stronger" (TI Maxims 8).[353] Here Nietzsche may be considering his own notoriously poor health and the philosophical insights he claims to derive therefrom, and indeed, the aphorism's title suggests that this observation itself is just such an insight (that is to say, he learns from life's school of war that from this "war" there is something to learn). But to read this statement as only a comment on the benefits Nietzsche derives from his own personal suffering may indeed produce a "satisfaction of a vulgar curiosity," but it is in itself both aesthetically and philosophically uninteresting. The title makes it clear, however, that Nietzsche intends the statement to transcend the individual. It is something learned from "Life," in this instance implying both personal experience and a general phenomenon, and indeed, from "Life's School," which suggests a lesson to be passed on and appropriated, not merely a description of the philosopher's own unique existence. Though this general rule may derive from Nietzsche's own personal experiences and observations, its applicability is not limited to these. The statement invites the reader to seek new contexts in which it which it may be effectively applied and against which its validity may be tested.

At the same time, however, the aphoristic statement is also particularly sensitive to issues of authorial source. Harald Fricke's study of the form opens with a telling example, Goethe's maxim that "Once you've missed the first buttonhole, you'll never manage to button up."[354] The statement itself is banal, and indeed, could simply come from a parent teaching a child how to dress. But, as Fricke notes, once we recognize Goethe as the originator of this statement, it takes on an entirely new significance. Such recognition initiates a dialogue with Goethe's other works and beyond. When the source reveals itself, a suspicion begins to take root that there is more to this statement than appears immediately on the surface. A statement like Nietzsche's "God is dead" may be more inflammatory than Goethe's sartorial image, but in itself offers little more than a provocation. Only when situated in the context of Nietzsche's other writings does it adopt actual philosophical character and aesthetic complexity.

Consider once again the aphorism "*From Life's School of War. –* What doesn't kill me makes me stronger." This is perhaps Nietzsche's most famous aphorism, and yet as a description of the world, the statement is certainly flawed. It would be difficult

---

353 "Aus der Kriegsschule des Lebens. – Was mich nicht umbringt, macht mich stärker" (GD Sprüche 8; KSA 6:60).

354 The original, as one can imagine, is somewhat (but not that much) more compelling: "Wer das erste Knopfloch verfehlt, kommt mit dem Zuknöpfen nicht zu Rande," quoted in Fricke, Aphorismus, viii; my translation.

to argue that *all* debilitating injuries lead to an increase in the sufferer's strength; one would have to stretch the definition of strength so broadly that it would become essentially meaningless. Nevertheless, the charm of this declaration is easy to understand: for those confronted with hardship, it provides a degree of comfort, a way to redeem misfortunes that have already been suffered as well as a sense of increasing power at a moment when that power may otherwise seem to be ebbing. Appealing to the will to power, Nietzsche fosters an affirmation of even those things that might otherwise lead one to curse life. In this sense, the above aphorism from *Götzen-Dämmerung* does not so much portray the nature of the world as reflect an attitude towards it, one that aligns well with the notion of *amor fati* Nietzsche had already introduced in *Die fröhliche Wissenschaft*. This attitude enables him to "see what is necessary in things as the beautiful" (GS 276).[355] Later, in *Ecce homo*, he would embellish this notion of loving one's fate:

> My formula for greatness in a human being is *amor fati:* that one wants nothing to be different, not forward, not backward, not in all eternity. Not merely bear what is necessary, still less conceal it [...], but *love* it. (EH Clever 10; BWN 714)[356]

The capacity to reconfigure adversity as an increase of power (regardless of any actual effect it may have on the individual) enables the kind of affirmation Nietzsche associates with *amor fati*. By recognizing that what does not kill actually empowers, one not only recognizes the fortune in misfortune, but affirms the misfortune itself as empowering. Concomitantly, the aphorism responds to that greatest of challenges to unconditional affirmation, the potentially despondent thought of the eternal recurrence of the same. What Nietzsche has learned from life's school of war is thus not some marginal insight; it arises from the very heart of his philosophy.

While this celebrated statement is thoroughly Nietzschean, it can nevertheless also be read as advocating a thoroughly un-Nietzschean value system, one dominated by the ascetic ideal. For those of a more Christian persuasion, the lines offer a redemption of suffering that makes hardship a source of *moral* empowerment. Such a reading would reinforce the ascetic priest's value system, which stands in direct opposition to Nietzsche's *amor fati*. That which seeks to kill me, yet does not, reinforces the sense both that this world is imperfect and that I am somehow superior to it.

Though each reading recognizes an increase in power, they espouse different attitudes toward the world and the threats contained therein. An aphorism in isolation can easily be coopted by disparate camps. The possibility of reading the aphorism in such diametrically opposed ways has probably contributed to its popularity. But only one of these readings qualifies as remotely "Nietzschean" insofar as it reflects posi-

---

355 "das Nothwendige an den Dingen als das Schöne sehen" (FW 276).

356 "Meine Formel für die Grösse am Menschen ist a m o r f a t i : dass man Nichts anders haben will, vorwärts nicht, rückwärts nicht, in alle Ewigkeit nicht. Das Nothwendige nicht bloss ertragen, noch weniger verhehlen [...], sondern es l i e b e n ..." (EH klug 10; KSA 6:297; see also GS 276; FW 276)

tions he actually advocates elsewhere in his writings. The other presents a possible interpretation only when divorced from the larger context of his works. The "ascetic" reading may be defensible in its own right, but it does not represent a position that can easily be ascribed to *Nietzsche*. It is not, one might say, how *Nietzsche* would read it; it's not what *Nietzsche* meant.

The principle of charity demands that in the process of interpretation the reader assume that Nietzsche's statements make the best possible sense, but to criticize the ascetic reading of the above aphorism for not reflecting Nietzsche's other writings goes one step further by insisting that the text make sense *in a particular way*, namely Nietzsche's. That is to say, in interpreting the aphorism, preference is given to the reading that aligns itself most felicitously with those other writings, even when a legitimate alternative reading of the isolated statement suggests itself. This interpretive approach (which typifies all studies that seek to unveil the hidden unity of Nietzsche's writings) presents another face of that conservative mode of reading derivable from Nietzsche's "model interpretation" in the *Genealogie*. Just as the mode of cross-textual self-reference presents a mode of interpretation that demands a thorough familiarity with the entirety of Nietzsche's writings, this common mode of evaluating interpretations relies upon and reinforces the coherence of those works. This demand for coherence provides an intuitive means to control the interpretive heterogeneity permitted by Nietzsche's statements in isolation. Nietzsche's aphorisms may segregate themselves from one another, but the figure of their author provides a regulative context for their interpretation.

In many ways, this figure of Nietzsche enjoys a formal status akin to that of Homer as described in Nietzsche's own inaugural lecture at the University of Basle, "Über die Persönlichkeit Homers" (On the Personality of Homer).[357] Here Nietzsche addresses "the Homeric question," the question of whether the *Iliad* and the *Odyssey* are attributable to a single poet or to many, concluding that "We believe in the one great poet of the *Iliad* and the *Odyssey* – just not in Homer as this poet."[358] The figure of Homer in this reading operates as an "institutionalized function"[359] that reflects generations of "aesthetic judgment" (æsthetisches Urtheil; KGW II/1:263). The unity of this author is important less as a historical reality than as a philological tool and aesthetic phenomenon. Though we may not question the authorship of Nietzsche's works in the same way as he does Homer's, the figure that emerges from Nietzsche's writings is likewise an interpretive construct. The Nietzsche created both in and from his writings must not be confused with the historical writer who exists beyond the confines of his texts and the discourse they generate. This historical writer is less useful to the process of interpretation than what Alexander Nehamas calls the "postulated author," a textual and

---

357 Nietzsche later revised this and published it under the title, "Homer und die klassische Philologie" (Homer and Classical Philology; Basel: Bonfantini, 1869; KGW II/1:248–269).

358 Wir glauben an den einen grossen Dichter von Ilias und Odyssee – d o c h n i c h t a n H o m e r a l s d i e s e n D i c h t e r" (KGW II/1:266).

359 Porter, Nietzsche and the Philology of the Future, 63.

paratextual figure that functions as a provisional guide for interpretative operations rather than as the text's efficient cause.[360] The figure of Nietzsche that emerges from his texts is not identical with the historical Nietzsche, but rather represents a *plausible* Nietzsche whose plausibility is based on correspondence with the texts ascribed to the author whose name appears on the title page.

The conservative mode of reading derivable from Nietzsche's model of interpretation in the Third Treatise of the *Genealogie* relies heavily on precisely such an authorial construction. Nietzsche's database of aphorisms may present an endless hermeneutical challenge, but their number is limited to those ascribed to the writer. Furthermore, Nietzsche identifies only his own other writings as essential for understanding the *Genealogie*; he assumes "that one has first read [his] earlier writings and has not spared some trouble in doing so" (GM Preface 8; GM Vorrede 8), demanding no further cross-textual awareness, either here or in the model reading itself. His cross-textual references always point to his own other writings, and by promoting the coherence of these, he reinforces the impression that they are all the product of "one soil, one sun," and one solitary, identifiable author. The contingency engendered by the possibility of an aphorism's infinite recontextualization and recombination may undermine the reader's sense of stability and control, rendering questionable any reading as a foundation for further interpretive constructions, but absent the arc of argumentation, the figure of the author steps in to unify Nietzsche's aphorisms and limit the chaotic potential of unregulated interpretation. Such an approach appeals to the figure of "Nietzsche" to contend with the aphorism collection's inherently volatile structure in an attempt to reduce a process of interpretation that is ultimately irreducible.

This situation may sound familiar to many readers, for by insisting on the authorial unity of his own work, Nietzsche aligns himself with what Michel Foucault would later dub the "author function." In his seminal essay "What is an Author?" Foucault writes that the author's name "permits one to group together a certain number of texts, define them, differentiate them from and contrast them to others." [361] The author, Foucault writes,

> is not an indefinite source of significations which fill a work; the author does not precede the works; he is a certain functional principle by which, in our culture, one limits, excludes and chooses; in short, by which one impedes the free circulation, the free manipulation, the free composition, decomposition and recomposition of fiction.[362]

The presence of Nietzsche in his writings functions like that of the traditional author of fiction, presenting a strategy for containing the "free circulation" of meaning that allows scholars to speak of the "meaning" of Nietzsche's writings as something de-

---

360 Nehamas, The Postulated Author, 145.
361 Foucault, What is an Author, 107.
362 Foucault, What is an Author, 118–119.

terminable. Foucault describes the author as "the ideological figure by which one marks the manner in which we fear the proliferation of meaning,"[363] and an appeal to this figure of the author reveals a desire to restrict the diversity of possible readings and the potentially limitless play of narratives made possible not only by the structure of Nietzsche's aphorism collections, but indeed, by the irreducibility of interpretation itself.[364] Even Nehamas, a scholar who has written extensively and compellingly on both Nietzsche and the figure of the author,[365] avails himself of the figure of "Nietzsche" when he argues in *Nietzsche: Life as Literature* that the philosopher draws attention to himself in order to avoid the threat of dogmatism. Nehamas has Nietzsche position himself outside of and antecedent to his works in order to avoid sounding dogmatic, but Nehamas's own argument also benefits from this situation. The foregrounding of the author that Nehamas recognizes in Nietzsche's writing actually does double duty in his analysis: explicitly, it responds to problems raised by Nietzsche's perspectivism, but implicitly, it also contributes to Nehamas's objective of discerning the "meaning" of Nietzsche's writing. By asserting Nietzsche's presence in his writings as that of the traditional author, Nehamas adopts a strategy of containment that limits the "free circulation" of meaning, allowing him to speak of the "meaning" of Nietzsche's writings as something determinable. Through his appeal to this figure of the author, Nehamas betrays his desire to restrict the diversity of possible readings and the potentially limitless play of perspectivism. The point here is not to invalidate Nehamas's reading (indeed, the current study is not immune to this criticism), but to illustrate how the figure of Nietzsche operates in accordance with Foucault's "author function" even in the analysis of a scholar whose writings demonstrate that he is clearly cognizant of its operations.

A Wretched Minor Fiction

Nietzsche himself certainly expresses awareness of such operations. As he puts it in *Jenseits von Gut und Böse:* "The 'work,' whether of the artist or of the philosopher, invents the person who has created it, who is supposed to have created it: 'the great,' as they are venerated, are subsequent pieces of wretched minor fiction"

---

363 Foucault, What is an Author, 119.
364 Perhaps this accounts for the perpetual popularity of titles that begin, "Nietzsche and …"; from early studies, like Türck's Friedrich Nietzsche und seine philosophischen Irrwege (1891), through more recent studies, such as Benne, Nietzsche und die historisch-kritische Philologie (2005). This is also typical of the English-language reception, from Ludovici, Nietzsche and Art (1911) to more recent volumes, for example Bishop (ed.), Nietzsche and Antiquity (2004). The number of such titles is substantial.
365 See, for instance, Nehamas, Nietzsche: Life as Literature; Nehamas, The Postulated Author; Nehamas, Writer, Text, Work, Author.

(BGE 269).[366] Through his self-characterization, Nietzsche consciously contributes to the profile that emerges through his works. Yet he also plants a seed of suspicion, for in that same volume he also warns, "To talk about oneself a great deal can also be a means of concealing oneself" (BGE 169).[367] Given the degree to which the mature Nietzsche talks about himself, one is left to wonder what he might be concealing. Indeed, what aspects might the very act of talking about himself itself disguise? What problems does Nietzsche's conspicuous presence in his writings seek to address? Is this perhaps an attempt to maintain authority over a creation that persistently threatens to slip from his grasp?

In the original dedication of *Menschliches, Allzumenschliches*, Nietzsche referred to the work as "monologic," suggesting a unity of voice belied by the multifariousness of the collection itself. Not until after writing *Also sprach Zarathustra* did he make a more concerted effort to form a character within his writing who tied the works together. Beyond the model interpretation in the Third Treatise of the *Genealogie*, the prefaces he added to the aphoristic works insist on the unity of his works as the product of a single, recognizable figure. For instance the preface to *Menschliches*, added in October 1886, begins with a clear claim to this effect:

> I have been told often enough, and always with an expression of great surprise, that all my writings, from *The Birth of Tragedy* to the most recently published *Prelude to a Philosophy of the Future* [i.e., *Beyond Good and Evil*, jw], have something that distinguishes them and unites them together: they all of them, I have been given to understand, contain snares and nets for unwary birds and in effect a persistent invitation to the overturning of habitual evaluations and valued habits. (HH I Preface 1)[368]

Nietzsche thus re-launches *Menschliches, Allzumenschliches* by asserting its coherence with his other writings, lending the claim an air of objectivity by presenting it as a common observation rather than his own reading. The nature of that unity is less pertinent than the fact that Nietzsche considers the notion of unity and coherence important enough to open the re-issue of this early book with this claim. Though his thought may have undergone many developments since *Menschliches* first appeared eight years earlier, these ideas are still the product of a single individual.

---

366 "das 'Werk', das des Künstlers, des Philosophen, erfindet erst Den, welcher es geschaffen hat, geschaffen haben soll; die 'grossen Männer', wie sie verehrt werden, sind kleine schlechte Dichtungen hinterdrein" (JGB 269).

367 "Viel von sich reden kann auch ein Mittel sein, sich zu verbergen" (JGB 169).

368 "Es ist mir oft genug und immer mit grossem Befremden ausgedrückt worden, dass es etwas Gemeinsames und Auszeichnendes an allen meinen Schriften gäbe, von der 'Geburt der Tragödie' an bis zum letzthin veröffentlichten 'Vorspiel einer Philosophie der Zukunft': sie enthielten allesammt, hat man mir gesagt, Schlingen und Netze für unvorsichtige Vögel und beinahe eine beständige unvermerkte Aufforderung zur Umkehrung gewohnter Werthschätzungen und geschätzter Gewohnheiten" (MA I Vorrede 1; KSA 2:13).

For the 1887 release of *Die fröhliche Wissenschaft* in an expanded edition, Nietzsche removed the motto from Emerson, replacing it with the quatrain "Over my door" (Ueber meiner Hausthür). The motto from the original 1882 edition, in quotation marks, reads: "To the poet, to the philosopher, to the saint, all things are friendly and sacred, all events profitable, all days holy, all men divine" (see GS, p. 8).[369] This sentiment anticipates the unconditional affirmation of the eternal recurrence that arises toward the end of the 1882 edition (particularly in "The Greatest Weight," GS 341; FW 341). For the second edition, however, Nietzsche pens his own motto: "I live in my own place, / have never copied nobody even half, / and at any master who lacks the grace / to laugh at himself – I laugh" (GS, p. 31).[370] Nietzsche here replaces a motto that introduces one of the great themes of the work, affirmation, with a motto that thematizes the author's relationship to that work. The plurality of subjects (things, events, days, men) and objects (poet, philosopher, saint) gives way to the unity of the independent, self-generating "I" who is both subject (who laughs) and object (at himself).

The "source" Nietzsche cites, "Over my door," also situates the author as the point of entry, capable of providing access or denying it. This prepares the reader for the discussion of comprehensibility which opens the preface to the new edition of *Die fröhliche Wissenschaft*. The preface begins, "This book may need more than one preface, and in the end there would still remain room for doubt whether anyone who had never lived through similar experiences could be brought closer to the *experience* of this book by means of prefaces." Such a rhetoric of exclusion becomes ever more common in Nietzsche's writings after *Also sprach Zarathustra*. In one of the opening passages of *Die fröhliche Wissenschaft*'s appended Book V, Nietzsche clearly differentiates the addressed reader from those actually capable of comprehending his writing, even if those who comprehend it are not yet sure how to articulate their comprehension:

> *Our question mark.* – But you [ihr] do not understand this? Indeed, people will have trouble understanding us [uns]. We [wir] are looking for words; perhaps we are also looking for ears. Who are we anyway? If we simply called ourselves, using an old expression, godless, or unbelievers, or perhaps immoralists, we do not believe that this would even come close to designating us: we are all three in such an advanced stage that one, that *you* [ihr], my curious friends, could never comprehend how we feel at this point. (GS 346)[371]

---

369 "'Dem Dichter und Weisen sind alle Dinge befreundet und geweiht, alle Erlebnisse nützlich, alle Tage heilig, alle Menschen göttlich.' / *Emerson*" (KSA 3:343; italics original)

370 "Ich wohne in meinem eignen Haus, / Hab Niemandem nie nichts nachgemacht / Und – lachte noch jeden Meister aus, / Der nicht sich selber ausgelacht. / *Ueber meiner Hausthür*" (KSA 3:343).

371 "Unser Fragezeichen. – Aber ihr versteht das nicht? In der That, man wird Mühe haben, uns zu verstehn. Wir suchen nach Worten, wir suchen auch nach Ohren. Wer sind wir doch? Wollten wir uns einfach mit einem älteren Ausdruck Gottlose oder Ungläubige oder auch Immoralisten nennen, wir würden uns damit noch lange nicht bezeichnet glauben: wir sind alles Dreies in einem zu späten Stadium, als dass man begriffe, als dass i h r begreifen könntet, meine Herren Neugierigen, wie es Einem dabei zu Muthe ist" (FW 346).

Although it is unclear in this passage to whom the pronoun "we" [wir] refers (and indeed, the passage is driven by this uncertainty), one thing is clear: the "wir" does not include the readers. To prevent readers from overlooking this distinction and anticipating inclusion in such a presumably elite group, Nietzsche literally emphasizes in the last statement the distinction between "you" (ihr) and "us" (uns) established in the first two sentences. The inserted clarification and emphasis make it unmistakable that, although he refers to his readers congenially, they should not assume that this relationship implies the comprehensibility of his work to them. Lest his reader forget this distinction, Nietzsche peppers his writings with reminders. In *Götzen-Dämmerung*, for instance, he again disparages the reader's association with the term "wir," this time with the parenthetical insertion, "(– I say 'we' out of politeness...)" (ich sage höflicher Weise wir; PN 482; KSA 6:77). Again, Nietzsche makes sure to establish a distance between his "wir" and his readers, maintaining the distinction between those capable of grasping his philosophy and the contemporary reader, even if the comprehending elite themselves are still "looking for words."

This rhetoric of exclusivity contributes both to Nietzsche's self-stylization and to the impression that there is a unity behind his works to which the elect are privy. It shifts the onus to the readers, whose incomprehension reflects a failure on their part, not the author's. In a gesture reminiscent of the emperor's new clothes, Nietzsche thus unifies his philosophy behind a veil of incomprehensibility.

This puts in an odd position those who celebrate the interpretive freedom enabled by Nietzsche's aphoristic texts. In Sarah Kofman's account, for instance, Nietzsche's aphoristic writing presents "an invitation to dance."[372] In this dance the distinction between author and reader becomes confused, for through active participation, the reader becomes in a sense the writer. The aphorism, in Kofman's account, "disseminates meaning and appeals to the pluralism of interpretations and their renewal,"[373] and this possibility is enabled by denying the definitive authority of the author and acknowledging the reader's involvement in the creation of the text. In Kofman's estimation:

> A new reading/writing destroys the traditional categories of the book as a closed totality containing a definitive meaning, the author's; in such a way it deconstructs the idea of the author as master of the meaning of the work and immortalizing himself through it.[374]

This description is consistent with much scholarship devoted to the aphorism insofar as it emphasizes the aphorism's tendency to stimulate the active participation of the reader, though it utterly dismisses the manner in which the later Nietzsche lays claim to his own text. Kofman here denies the applicability of any "author function" and encourages an unrestricted proliferation of interpretations.

---

372 Kofman, Nietzsche and Metaphor, 115.
373 Kofman, Nietzsche and Metaphor, 116.
374 Kofman, Nietzsche and Metaphor, 116.

Yet while Kofman's reading might at first glance seem to promote a democratiza-
tion of reading, she links Nietzsche's use of the aphorism to the play of inclusion and
exclusion, which actually mitigates its liberating potential. Though aphoristic writing
may be an invitation to dance, as with any dance the invitation does not go out to
everyone. As Kofman puts it:

> aphoristic writing [...] aims to discourage the *common* by requiring a reader to be equipped with
> a rigorous philological art. Aphoristic writing wants to make itself understood only by those who
> are linked by having the same refined impressions in common; it wants to banish the *profanum
> vulgus* and attract the free spirits "on to new dance floors."[375]

Here Kofman alludes to one of the prefaces Nietzsche added to an earlier work after
the publication of *Also sprach Zarathustra*. In the preface to the second edition of *Die
Geburt der Tragödie* (1886), in which Nietzsche overtly claims that his is a book for
the "initiates" (Eingeweihte) who share "common and rare aesthetic experiences"
(BT Self-Criticism 3, BWN 19).[376] It seems that the *Pathos der Distanz*, the awareness
of and belief in an "order of rank and differences in value between man and man"
(Rangordnung und Werthverschiedenheit von Mensch und Mensch; BGE 257; JGB
257), is not limited to social or personal development, nor to the development of morality (see GM I 2); that is to say, it is not limited to the content of Nietzsche's works,
but informs the manner in which the reader is to approach those works. The distance
that is recognized between the noble (vornehm) and the *profanum vulgus* also emerges in the relationship between Nietzsche and his reader.[377] By granting interpretive
privilege to a particular audience, this exclusivity operates as a further means to contain the proliferation of meaning necessitated by the perspectival nature of reading.

This puts a different spin on the claims to priority Nehamas discerns in
Nietzsche's writings. In *Nietzsche: Life as Literature*, Nehamas argues that Nietzsche
draws attention to himself throughout his writings because even as he "wants his
readers to accept his views, his judgments and his values [...] he wants them to
know that these are essentially *his* views, *his* judgments, and *his* values."[378] This gesture enables the philosopher to avert the threat of dogmatism by making the perspectival nature of his claims unmistakable. The emphasis Nehamas places on the possessive pronoun echoes a passage from *Jenseits von Gut und Böse*, which Nietzsche
closes with the apparent disclaimer that what he presents are simply *his* truths
(BGE 231; JGB 231). In this passage, he promises to present "something unteachable"
(etwas Unbelehrbares), something that a thinker "cannot relearn but only finish

---

375 Kofman, Nietzsche and Metaphor, 114–115.
376 "gemeinsame und seltene Kunst-Erfahrungen" (GT Versuch 3; KSA 1:14).
377 NB: Strobel also sees the pathos of distance as a leitmotif running through Nietzsche's aphoristic
works and operative in his choice to write aphorisms, but she emphasizes its importance for the
"distance" Nietzsche maintains between the aphoristic utterance and the judgment it expresses; see
Strobel, Das Pathos der Distanz, 163–164.
378 Nehamas, Nietzsche: Life as Literature, 35.

learning – only discover ultimately how this is 'settled' in him" (kann...nicht umlernen, sondern nur auslernen, – nur zu Ende entdecken, was darüber bei ihm "feststeht"). These are the kind of truths that he offers to present; hence he closes the passage with the statement that "these are after all only – *my* truths" (es eben nur – m e i n e Wahrheiten sind). Derrida may read this expression as a denial of unified truth:

> The very fact that 'meine Wahrheiten' is so underlined, that they are multiple, variegated, contradictory even, can only imply that these are not *truths*. Indeed there is no such thing as truth in itself. But only a surfeit of it. Even if it should be for me, about me, truth is plural.[379]

But though Derrida overtly mentions the manner in which the phrase "*my* truths" (m e i n e Wahrheiten) is underlined, he shifts the emphasis in his reading away from the possessive pronoun (*meine*) and to the plurality of truths (Wahrheiten).

Nietzsche himself does not simply say that his reader should not mistake his pronouncements for universal truths; he proclaims that "an unchangeable 'this is I'" (ein unwandelbares "das bin ich") expresses itself in these passages, establishing the very personal nature of its claims. This creates a distance not only between the nature of Nietzsche's claims and those of traditional philosophy (with regard to their truth-status), but between Nietzsche and his reader, for these are not the reader's truths, but Nietzsche's. The emphasis on the author as the source of the text thus does not simply perform the role of a "disclaimer" regarding the multifariousness of truth, but in fact functions as a kind of claim: Nietzsche claims these truths as his own.

In this way, Nietzsche appears to practice precisely the kind of philosophy he associates with the coming philosophers described in *Jenseits* 43. Here the philosopher of the future likewise literally emphasizes an exclusive claim to his position: "'My judgment is *my* judgment': no one else is easily entitled to it – that is what such a philosopher of the future may perhaps say" ("Mein Urtheil ist m e i n Urtheil: dazu hat nicht leicht auch ein Anderer das Recht" – sagt vielleicht [...] ein Philosoph der Zukunft). Nietzsche openly avers earlier in the passage that such philosophers will "not be dogmatists" (keine Dogmatiker sein), and thus this emphasis can be read as a rejection of dogmatism, but Nietzsche here stresses not so much the personal as the possessive nature of the philosopher's judgment. This possessive pronoun again is not a disclaimer, but a claim to possession; the judgment is that of the philosopher, and no one else is easily entitled to it. Rather than simply distinguish the philosopher's judgment from dogmatism, this emphasized possessiveness establishes a distance between the philosopher and an audience that would attempt to claim his claim as their own. Certainly the impression of a disclaimer is reinforced by the adverb "eben nur" (after all only) in the phrase, "eben nur – m e i n e Wahrheiten" (after all only – *my* truths) but then, the idea that Nietzsche uses the posses-

---

379 Derrida, Spurs/Éperons, 103.

sive pronoun to distance himself from his reader does not negate its function as a disclaimer. Certainly he impresses upon his readers that these are not universal truths, but more than that, he would not have them assume to adopt them as truths of their own. Not only would this potentially lead to the kind of dogmatism that the disclaimer seeks to resist, but it would be inconsistent with the perspectivism that lurks behind such a disclaimer. The manner in which Nietzsche foregrounds himself in his writings informs the manner in which the reader approaches his text not simply by reminding the reader that this is *merely* Nietzsche's text, but by reminding the reader that this is *Nietzsche's* text.

Given Nietzsche's rhetoric of exclusion, it would be presumptuous of anyone simply to include oneself in this elite, though such inclusion is perhaps not entirely out of reach. Recall that the section of the *Genealogie*'s preface in which Nietzsche proclaims that the aphorism is not taken seriously enough begins thus:

> If this book is incomprehensible to anyone and jars on his ears, the fault, it seems to me, is not necessarily mine. It is clear enough, assuming, as I do assume, that one has first read my earlier writings and has not spared some trouble in doing so: for they are, indeed, not easy to penetrate. (GM Preface 8).

This demand can be seen to allow for the unavoidability of perspectival interpretation without conceding that all interpretations are equally valid, for Nietzsche here divides his readership into those with the prerequisite knowledge and those without, those who are presumably in a position to comprehend his writings and those who are not. Such differentiation echoes Zarathustra's laments at the incomprehension of his audience,[380] which leads him to turn away from the masses and seek out "companions."[381] The demand that the reader of the *Genealogie* be familiar with his works allows the reader at least the pretense of modeling his own reading on Nietzsche's, as demonstrated in the Third Treatise, while at the same time, this demand performs a strategic rhetorical function, appealing to the reader's own will to power through the promise of inclusion in an elite class. And indeed, the vocabulary Nietzsche uses to describe this differentiation in many ways echoes his descriptions of the masters in *Jenseits* and *Genealogie*. In the fifth book of *Die fröhliche Wissenschaft*, he writes:

> One does not only wish to be understood when one writes [...]. All the nobler spirits and tastes select their audience when they wish to communicate; and choosing that one at the same time erects barriers against "the others." All the more subtle laws of any style have their origin at this point: they at the same time keep away, create a distance, forbid "entrance," understanding, as said above – while they open the ears of those whose ears are related to ours. (GS 381)[382]

---

380 Z Preface 5; Z Vorrede 5.
381 "Gefährten" (Z Preface 9; Z Vorrede 9).
382 "Man will nicht nur verstanden werden [...]. Jeder vornehmere Geist und Geschmack wählt sich, wenn er sich mittheilen will, auch seine Zuhörer; indem er sie wählt, zieht er zugleich gegen 'die Anderen' seine Schranken. Alle feineren Gesetze eines Stils haben da ihren Ursprung: sie halten

Again, the *Pathos der Distanz* that marks the noble's relation to the common man is also discernible in this relation of Nietzsche to his reader. Like the noble described, for example, in the *Genealogie*,[383] Nietzsche positions himself as part of a privileged elite united by common experience from which the reader is excluded, presumably due to a lack of such experience. The *Pathos der Distanz* that recognizes the difference between noble and common emerges in this distinction between those who are capable of comprehending Nietzsche's works and those who are not, and rather than locating his readership in the former group, Nietzsche often relegates it to the latter.

Nietzsche's distinction between the privileged insider and the excluded outsider naturally serves as a rhetorical strategy, and he occasionally appears to throw his reader a bone, hinting at the possibility of inclusion in this inner circle of the comprehending. In the penultimate section of the Third Treatise, for instance, he writes of the meaning of the will to truth as "my problem" (mein Problem; GM III 27) and then immediately modifies it to "our problem" (unser Problem), widening the circle and suggesting that he is perhaps not forever doomed to intellectual isolation. He then clarifies his shift to the plural by addressing (ostensibly) his readers as "my *unknown* friends (for as yet I *know* of no friend)" (GM III 27).[384] This clarification simultaneously counteracts and augments the sense of isolation evident in the passage, reinforcing his self-characterization as a "posthumous" philosopher while at the same time luring his reader with a promise of arcane knowledge.

While throughout his work Nietzsche repeatedly thematizes the author's sense of isolation, this can also be seen to draw the reader into his circle. In the third aphorism of the fifth book of *Die fröhliche Wissenschaft*, he emphasizes his own isolation with the question, "Why is it then that I have never yet encountered anybody, not even in books, who approached morality in this personal way [...]?" (GS 345).[385] And yet the passage closes with an attempt to overcome this isolation through a shift from the first-person singular "ich" to the plural possessive "unser": he declares the questioning of morality as "our task" (unser Werk). The identity of Nietzsche's fellow questioners once again remains unclarified, and one wonders, given the fact that Nietzsche himself has never encountered anyone who has approached morality the way he does, namely *als Person*, what right he has to use the plural. The emphasis on his own isolation in this case seems to suggest that Nietzsche indeed implicates the reader, for no other figures emerge in the passage that could possibly justify this use of the plural; the reader seems the most logical candidate to fill this role, though this could also be just another example of Nietzsche projecting an imaginary audience that does not actually exist.

---

zugleich ferne, sie schaffen Distanz, sie verbieten 'den Eingang', das Verständniss, wie gesagt, – während sie Denen die Ohren aufmachen, die uns mit den Ohren verwandt sind" (FW 381).

383 See, e.g., KSA 5:259f.; BWN 461f.

384 "meine u n b e k a n n t e n Freunde (– denn noch w e i s s ich von keinem Freunde)" (GM III 27).

385 "Wie kommt es nun, dass ich noch Niemandem begegnet bin, auch in Büchern nicht, der zur Moral in dieser Stellung als Person stünde [...]?" (FW 345).

Then again, the unifying figure of "Nietzsche" likewise does not exist as anything more than a figure who, in Nietzsche's later writings, serves to stabilize those writings. Insisting on the unity of this figure enables the reader to limit the corpus of Nietzschean texts and thereby forestall an interpretive free-for-all. It is itself not so much a philosophical posit as a literary trope, less a necessity than a conceit. It does not so much reflect the unity of Nietzsche's writings as promote it.

How different this is from the image Nietzsche notes while working on a preface to *Menschliches, Allzumenschliches* in the fall of 1877. Here he describes the strangeness of being confronted by his own earlier words, as the question poses itself: "Is it me? Is it not me?"[386] He wonders how strange this book must seem to those familiar with his even earlier writings, but upon looking back, he is himself confronted with the alienness of his own text. Such a sense of non-self-identity, however, easily takes root in the aphorism collection, for as much as the aphorism itself often appeals to its authoritative source, the aphorism collection itself can present an assault on that very source. The structure of the aphorism collection, much like Schlegel's fragments, presents a polyphony, an excess of voices, that draws the notion of a unified author into question. The "author function" that is "Nietzsche," much like the conservative reading of Nietzsche's "model" interpretation, exerts a stabilizing counterforce to the pressures of dissipation built into the very structure of the aphorism collection. Yet even without Schlegel's overt attempts to shatter the unity of the individual's authorial voice in the name of *Symphilosophie,* the aphoristic collection is inherently polyphonic.

Coming to terms with Nietzsche's aphorism collection means coming to terms with the figure of "Nietzsche." This figure serves to unite the texts that appear under Nietzsche's name, while at the same time to distinguish them as such. With the aid of this figure, one can contend with the dissipative forces inherent in the aphorism collection. But the figure itself is a construct, and as such is itself subject to the forces against which it operates. It serves a vital function in the process of interpretation, but it is itself a product of interpretation. One may seek to flesh out this figure as completely as possible, and indeed, doing so has been central to scholarship on Nietzsche. This emphasis on the figure of Nietzsche, both by Nietzsche and by scholars of Nietzsche, should come as no surprise, for in emphasizing both coherence and perspective, it offers a stabilizing response to the particular challenges of the aphorism collection. It may be but a wretched minor fiction, but it is nevertheless revealing, and at times even useful.

---

386 "Wenn es schon dem Autor begegnet, dass er, vor sein eigenes Buch hingestellt, demselben mit Befremdung in's Gesicht sieht und ihm die Frage über die Lippen läuft: bin ich's? bin ich's nicht? – um wie viel mehr müssen die Leser seiner früheren Schriften eine solche Empfindung haben, zumal wenn sie den Autor derselben nicht persönlich kennen und er ihnen nur als Geist und Charakter jener Schriften vor der Seele steht...." (NL 25[2], 1877; KSA 8:483).

Part Four. **The Aphoristic Paradigm**

defined by a limit."[399] But this understanding overlooks the concomitant implication of this vocabulary of boundaries, which suggests that the aphorism can also mean "to set beyond a horizon" or "to expand beyond its established context."[400]

This is the same tension that characterizes the aphorism as a genre (discussed in Chapter One). It is a form compromised by the multifariousness of its forms, which transgresses the limits of generic unity, and yet it remains nonetheless a generic tradition. The boundary lines drawn by the notion of genre may be crossed, but they are not erased, and precisely this dynamic of simultaneously acknowledging and disavowing a limit is integral to the notion of excess. Notions of generic identity perform the function of drawing limitations that the aphorism and aphorism collection can be seen to exceed. We can still speak of an aphoristic tradition, but one in which the formal excesses that problematize its generic identity operate as an extension of the genre's association with a critique of systematic discourse.

Whatever form the aphorism takes, its notorious concision actually serves to highlight the form's transgressive potential, making it an apt genre for the "philosopher of excess" who aims "to say in ten sentences what everyone else does *not* say in a book." In his aphoristic works, Nietzsche himself frequently notes that there is more to his writing than meets the eye directly. With reference to the aphorism collection, *Vermischte Meinungen und Sprüche*, he tells his readers outright, "that there is much in it that does not appear on the printed page." Elsewhere in the collection he assumes that his reader is fully cognizant of the fact that his writings are indicative of a much more extensive thought process. He warns his reader against mistaking the product of long contemplation for a flash of inspiration simply due to the precision of its formulation. In the passage, "Against the censurers of brevity," he avails himself of an organic image to distinguish the two:

> Something said briefly can be the fruit of much long thought: but the reader who is a novice in this field, and has as yet reflected on it not at all, sees in everything said briefly something embryonic, not without censuring the author for having served him up such immature and unripened fare. (AOM 127)[401]

Though Nietzsche does not mention the genre of the aphorism by name, the allusion to his own writing, including the aphorism collection in which the statement appears, is unmistakable. And he is by no means alone in his understanding of the aphorism as the product of a lengthy deliberative process that, though not represented in the text itself, is nevertheless present and to be teased out by the reader. Franz Mautner's semi-

---

399 Marsden, Nietzsche and the Art of the Aphorism, 22.
400 See Neumann, Ideenparadiese, 27; Gray, Constructive Destruction, 45.
401 "Gegen die Tadler der Kürze. – Etwas Kurz-Gesagtes kann die Frucht und Ernte von vielem Lang-Gedachten sein: aber der Leser, der auf diesem Felde Neuling ist und hier noch gar nicht nachgedacht hat, sieht in allem Kurz-Gesagten etwas Embryonisches, nicht einen tadelnden Wink an den Autor, dass er dergleichen Unausgewachsenes, Ungereiftes ihm zur Mahlzeit mit auf den Tisch setze" (VM 127).

nal work on the form differentiates between two kinds of aphorism: the "Klärung" (clarification) and the "Einfall" (sudden thought, idea).[402] The image of the aphorism as the conclusion of a chain coincides with the *Klärung*, which situates the aphoristic statement as the closing stage of the cognitive process. The reciprocal notion, the *Einfall*, represents not so much an endpoint as a point of departure, a moment of inspiration that breaks with what came before and initiates new chains of thought.[403] Though Nietzsche does not use the terms Mautner later proposes, he effectively warns against mistaking the mature *Klärung* for the nascent *Einfall*. The novice reader fails to recognize the proper position of the aphorism on the chain of thought. Given the text's insistence that the reader not mistake the ripe thought for the embryonic one, Nietzsche appears to favor the portrayal of the aphorism as *Klärung*, as indicative of an entire chain of thought that is not emergent, but already considered. But the error Nietzsche deplores does not necessarily arise from a superficial reading of the text. Even this novice reader apparently recognizes that the text invokes more than its form contains.

Wittingly or unwittingly, this appeal beyond the confines of the aphoristic text proves a mainstay of aphorism scholarship. Though scholars may not be in agreement as to what constitutes the nature of the aphorism, one characteristic, the aphorism's tendency to transgress the bounds of its own brevity and to "express more than it says,"[404] emerges with striking regularity, and this characterization is frequently articulated in a term of excess. The aphorism is seen to transgress the boundaries or definitions or limits that seek to contain it by activating the further thought and active participation of the reader. The well-wrought aphorism is not contained by its linguistic limitations, but only realizes itself through the extra-textual involvement of the reader.

This leads to scholars frequently invoking images of aphoristic excess. Following the lead of Francis Bacon, the German literature scholar Walter Wehe admonishes scholars not to measure the aphorism according to its number of lines, for the source of the aphorism's effect does not lie in its brevity, but rather in its capacity to stimulate further thought beyond its textual borders.[405] He sees both the appeal and danger of the aphorism as a product of the opposition between the limitedness of the form and the limitlessness of the thought, and this tension between form and content leads to eruption (Entladung). Wehe does not simply speak of the limitlessness of the thought expressed in the aphorism; he sees this limitlessness as challenged by, and transgressing, the limitedness of the form. This tension does not simply reach equi-

---

402 Mautner, Der Aphorismus als Literatur, 285–286.
403 Nietzsche is certainly not immune to the romantic image of the flash of inspiration: he describes the birth of Zarathustra, for instance, thus: "like lightning, a thought flashes up, with necessity, without hesitation regarding its form, – I never had any choice" (wie ein Blitz leuchtet ein Gedanke auf, mit Nothwendigkeit, in der Form ohne Zögern, – ich habe nie eine Wahl gehabt; EH Zarathustra 3; KSA 6:339; BWN 756).
404 Asemissen, Notizen über den Aphorismus, 163; my translation.
405 Wehe, Geist und Form des deutschen Aphorismus, 131.

librium, but in an image reminiscent of Nietzsche, threatens to explode. Such eruptive imagery likewise emerges in Wilhelm Grenzmann's analysis, which portrays aphoristic writing as a tension between formal limitations and the tendency to explode such limitations. Grenzmann uses this image quite directly when he depicts aphoristic writing as a dynamic movement "that explodes fixed borders."[406] In clarifying this image, Grenzmann does not offer any radical new understanding of the aphorism, but rather returns to the conventional image of the aphorism as both a stimulus to further thought and expressing more than it says. Fricke continues in this vein when he describes the aphorism as a kind of "Torso."[407] Here he refers to Rilke's sonnet, "Archaic Torso of Apollo," which resembles the aphorism not so much in its lack of completion, but in its potential to transgress its own recognizable limitations. Like Rilke's torso, the aphorism bursts "all the borders of itself / like a star" (aus allen seinen Rändern / aus wie ein Stern).[408]

These are but a few of the most overt examples of the vocabulary of excess that pervades aphorism scholarship, but in essence they reflect Nietzsche's own attitude toward writing, particularly the writing of that "form of eternity" known as the aphorism. This excessive quality of the aphorism is further reinforced by the two most rigorous analyses of aphorism groups by Nietzsche. Peter Heller devotes over five-hundred pages of small print to the 34 aphorisms that make up the first section of *Menschliches, Allzumenschliches*. And even so, he recognizes that the material is inexhaustible, terminating the discussion of each individual aphorism with lengthy footnotes suggesting further possibilities for discussion. Werner Stegmaier study of Book V of *Die fröhliche Wissenschaft* exceeds even Heller's book in length, and yet Stegmaier is the first to admit that one is never finished reading Nietzsche's text.[409]

The excessive quality of the individual aphorism is further complemented by what can be seen as the excesses of the aphorism collection. As Stegmaier points out elsewhere, with aphorisms, "it is the context and not the system that matters,"[410] but precisely the aphoristic form lends itself to a diversity of contexts. While Mautner discourages the identification of the aphorism with aphorism-like texts removed from their original context, such as drama or narrative, the temptation to do so is understandable, and indeed, the possibility of perpetual recontextualization is manifest in the isolation of the aphorism emphasized by its presentation in the collection. "Aphoristic" remarks, that is, statements with the acerbic concision of a good *maxime*, may originate in all kinds of situations. When the character Max in Arthur Schnitzler's *Anatol* defers an exit with the exclamation, "I can't possibly depart without an aphorism,"[411] one hears a critique of the tendency to litter dramas with aphor-

---

406 Grenzmann, Probleme des Aphorismus, 197; my translation.
407 Fricke, Aphorismus, 8.
408 Rilke, Sämtliche Werke, vol. 1, 557; quoted in Fricke, Aphorismus, 9; my translation.
409 See Stegmaier, Nietzsches Befreiung der Philosophie, vi.
410 Stegmaier, After Montinari, 14.
411 Schnitzler, Die dramatischen Werke, vol. 1, 84; my translation.

istic repartee.[412] In narrative works, aphorisms outside dialogue can present an orienting gesture on the part of the narrator,[413] or possibly a disorienting intrusion into
an otherwise linear account.[414] Mautner may object to using the term "aphorism" for
such statements divorced from their original context, but the notion of "collection"
itself renders questionable the notion of "original context." The very genre of the collection itself suggests that the text has its origins outside the collection, that is, from
whence it was collected. Context plays an important role in the way we make sense
of a given text by limiting the possible interpretations of that text. Within a rational
argument, the meaning of each statement within that argument is limited and focused by the parameters of the argument itself, even if the statement on its own invites diverse interpretations. Context does not necessarily neutralize the interpretive
heterogeneity of a given statement, but it does provide a means to contain interpretive possibilities. In doing so, it prevents these possibilities from approaching infin-
ity, thereby averting the potential dissipation of the statement into nonsense, even as
it undermines the threat of the statement's universalization. Though context does not
necessarily supply determinate meaning, the possibility of perpetual recontextualization inherent in the very notion of the aphorism collection, which defies the notion of
a definitive original or final context, opens the text to continuous reinterpretation.
Stegmaier acknowledges that aphorisms are always relocated or displaced (versetzt),
even when Nietzsche situates them carefully in the context of his aphorism collections.[415] The term "versetzt" carries with it the awareness that these texts always originate elsewhere, that they belong to multiple contexts, one of which is the conscious
context of the aphorism collection. But even these texts invite recontextualization,
and as Stegmaier says, "in a new context, in a new situation under new perspectives
the reader can once again understand them differently."[416] At some point, the reader
who would venture an interpretation must simply draw a limit to contextualization
lest the process continue infinitely.[417] This tension between the demand for a single
context in the process of interpretation and the inescapable plurality of potential
contexts reiterates the dynamic of excess through the drawing of a limit and its in-
evitable transgression through superabundance.

The combinatorial freedom intrinsic to the aphorism collection likewise gives
rise to a dynamic tension that can best be understood in terms of excess. The isolation of the individual texts from one another enables the reader to combine the
aphoristic texts freely, allowing for a diversity of constellations and interpretations

---

412 Gray reads this moment as a critique of the social role of the aphorism (Gray, Constructive
Destruction, 92).
413 Think, for instance, of Annette von Droste-Hülshoff's self-conscious use of aphoristic *Weisheiten*
in her novella, *Die Judenbuche* (The Jew's Beech, 1842).
414 See Pfeiffer, Aphorismus und Romanstruktur, 55.
415 Stegmaier, Nietzsche Befreiung der Philosophie, 11.
416 Stegmaier, Nietzsche Befreiung der Philosophie, 12; translation mine.
417 Stegmaier, Nietzsches Befreiung der Philosophie, 80–81.

to emerge. In contradistinction to the narrative unity one expects from sustained argumentation, such interpretive multiplicity again participates in the dynamic of excess. One might say that the drive to narrative formation constitutes the impulse to contain the formal heterogeneity of the aphoristic collection through linear interpretation, while the structure of the aphorism collection resists such containment by offering a superabundance of narrative possibilities. Again, attempts to determine a single final interpretation are thwarted by the multiplicity that presents itself as a possibility. This possibility does not necessarily undermine the legitimacy of the interpretation, only any potential claim it may stake to finality.

Furthermore, the discontinuousness of the aphoristic collection rendered by the gaps between the individual texts attenuates the borders of the aphorism collection itself. This is apparent in Nietzsche's original plans for *Vermischte Meinungen und Sprüche* to be a continuation of *Menschliches, Allzumenschliches*, complete with continuous pagination and numeration of aphorisms.[418] Likewise, *Die fröhliche Wissenschaft* was originally conceived as a continuation of *Morgenröte*.[419] Though these plans were eventually altered, Nietzsche elsewhere takes advantage of the aphorism collection's seam-riddled structure by effortlessly inserting the last aphorism of *Vermischte Meinungen und Sprüche* at the last minute[420] and, of course, by appending an entire fifth book of forty-one aphorisms to *Die fröhliche Wissenschaft*. At one point during the publication of the latter, printing delays led Nietzsche to demand the return of his manuscript, saying that he would rather use it to enlarge a second edition of *Jenseits von Gut und Böse*, further demonstrating the flexibility of the form.[421] Implied in the very form of the aphoristic collection is the notion that there is always potentially more to collect. Nietzsche's aphoristic collections can thus be said to problematize the integrity of their written, structural limitations by suggesting the continued transgression of their limitations through the possibility of further expansion.

The figure of Nietzsche discussed in the previous chapter could be seen as a means to check rampant expansion by placing a limit on what texts can be legitimately attributed to the Nietzschean corpus, but even this is not entirely unproblematic, as witnessed by discussions regarding the role of his *Nachlass* in the interpretive process. Indeed, while the postulated author may conventionally serve to regulate interpretive possibilities, in the case of the aphorism collection, with its individual and discrete texts, what emerges is not necessarily a single, unified author, but a plurality of voices. The isolation of each individual aphoristic statement prob-

---

418 *Vermischte Meinungen und Sprüche* was to begin with page 379, aphorism 639; see his letter to Schmeitzner, 23 Nov 1878, KGB II/5, 365–366, no. 774; Schaberg, The Nietzsche Canon, 70.
419 See Nietzsche's letter to Gast, 18 Dec 1881, KGB III/1, 149–150, no. 180; in this letter, he refers to current project (GS; FW) as the "Continuation of 'Daybreak' (6th through 10th book)" ("Fortsetzung der 'Morgenröthe' (6. bis 10. Buch)"); see also letter to Gast, 25 Jan 1882, KGB III/1, 158–160, no. 190.
420 See Nietzsche to Schmeitzner, beginning of March, KGB II/5, 390–391, no. 810; cf. Schaberg, The Nietzsche Canon, 70.
421 See letter to Fritzsch, 13 Feb 1887, KGB III/5, 21–22, no. 799.

lematizes a tacit assumption that undergirds more cohesive forms of writing – the assumption that, given the absence of indications to the contrary, the authorial subject of one page can be identified with the authorial subject of the next, even if it is temporally distinct. The collection's written form, when approached as Nietzsche advises, "looking cautiously fore and aft" (rück- und vorsichtig), problematizes such immediate identification. Reading the aphoristic collection thus involves the implementation of a spatially simultaneous understanding of the collection rather than simply a temporally sequential one. This suggests that the subject of each aphoristic statement is not necessarily a single identity expressing itself at distinct consecutive moments, but rather spatially distinct identities expressing themselves simultaneously. This renders the aphorism collection a rich medium for the cultivation of contradiction. Furthermore, this excess of authorial voices renders the authorial voice itself non-self-identical, which, though not by necessity demanding contradiction, opens the door for the introduction of contradiction by providing distinct voices for potentially contradictory views.

The drive to yoke this plurality of voices together under that single name on the title-page ultimately foregrounds the active process required to fabricate a unified author. This tension between the unified authorial figure of "Nietzsche" and the polyphony presented by the aphorism collection can also be understood in terms of excess, for it reflects this twofold gesture of drawing a limit and then challenging that limit through a profusion of possibilities. To understand the authorial voice of the aphorism collection *as excessive* is to posit the figure of the author as self-identical, while at the same time recognizing the fracturedness of this identity. And indeed, this is the situation with which Nietzsche confronts his reader.

This also puts a different spin on Nietzsche's "model" interpretation in *Zur Genealogie der Moral*. That Nietzsche supplies two different texts (the epigraph to the Third Treatise and Section 1) which could each function as the aphorism interpreted provides a further extension of the aphorism understood in terms of excess. Again, where one expects a single, unified identity, one finds a superabundance that undermines interpretive stability literally at its source. This superabundance is then reiterated by the interpretive model's call for cross-textual supplementation. That the aphorism, whether the epigraph or Section 1, demands supplementation from beyond the limits of the isolated texts is itself entirely consistent with the conventional portrayals of aphoristic excess, but Nietzsche intensifies and problematizes this supplementation by rendering the nature of the supplementation itself non-self-identical. The reader may appeal to Nietzsche's other texts in a Nietzsche-centric mode of cross-textual interpretation, but even in this model of interpretation, Nietzsche cannot contain the forces of excess that permeate his writings, leaving his reader with too many options to constitute a unified method. Again, as Stegmaier notes, at some point contexualization just needs to be cut off.

Rather than limiting potential interpretive options, the gesture of containment enabled by the very notion of a model interpretation actually emphasizes the myriad interpretive possibilities not contained by Nietzsche's own reading. As an example of

what Nietzsche's "art of interpretation" might look like, the Third Treatise offers the thrill of "sudden restraint" described in *Jenseits von Gut und Böse* 224; it offers one of

> those moments and marvels when great power voluntarily stopped this side of the immeasurable and boundless, when an excess of subtle delight in sudden restraint and petrification, in standing firm taking one's measure, was enjoyed on still trembling ground. (BGE 224)[422]

The true thrill is not so much in the restraint, but in the transgression that such restraint then allows. For the passage continues: *"Measure* is alien to us; let us admit it; our thrill is the thrill of the infinite, the unmeasured" (BGE 224).[423] Nietzsche draws limits precisely so that he can cross them. But why?

The Ephectic Bent

To understand the critical function of the aphorism and its excesses in Nietzsche's own text, we can take a lead from Nehamas's discussion of Nietzschean hyperbole, a rhetorical form of excess that presents not only a moment of disruption, but also, as Nehamas sees it, a response to potential problems raised by Nietzsche's own perspectivism. Nehamas contends that hyperbole is "what may well be the most consistent and the most conspicuous feature of [Nietzsche's] writing,"[424] even going so far as to say that his writing is "irreducibly hyperbolic"[425] and *"essentially* hyperbolic."[426] He contrasts Nietzschean hyperbole to the self-effacing attitude of Socratic irony, which sets the personality of the speaker in the background, creating the impression of objective disinterest. Such a stance suggests the universalizability of the Socratic claim, thus lending it the air of dogmatic certitude. In the attempt to avoid the dogmatization of his own words, the hyperboles that characterize Nietzsche's self-aggrandizing rhetoric make the author's presence unmistakable, confronting the reader with a personal argument. By saying too much rather than too little, the Nietzschean hyperbole addresses with a similar strategy the same concern that gives rise, in Nehamas' account, to Nietzsche's stylistic pluralism: Nietzsche "wants his readers to accept his views, his judgments and his values as much as

---

422 "jene Augenblicke und Wunder, wo eine grosse Kraft freiwillig vor dem Maasslosen und Unbegrenzten stehen blieb –, wo ein Überfluss von feiner Lust in der plötzlichen Bändigung und Versteinerung, im Feststehen und Sich-Fest-Stellen auf einem noch zitternden Boden genossen wurde" (JGB 224).
423 "Das Maass ist uns fremd, gestehen wir es uns; unser Kitzel ist gerade der Kitzel des Unendlichen, Ungemessenen" (JGB 224).
424 Nehamas, Nietzsche: Life as Literature, 31.
425 Nehamas, Nietzsche: Life as Literature, 22.
426 Nehamas, Nietzsche: Life as Literature, 31.

he wants them to know that these are essentially *his* views, *his* judgments, and *his* values."[427]

Clearly discernible in Nehamas's discussion of hyperbole is the dynamic of excess. Whenever one speaks of hyperbole, one must ask: what statement does this hyperbolic expression exaggerate? What is the statement compared to which this is an over-statement? Nietzsche frequently plays with the prefixes "über-" and "unter-", and in the case of hyperbole (from Greek for "overshooting"), this play continues on the rhetorical level. If we are to understand this gesture as a critique of the philosophical tradition, as Nehamas does, we must not over-simplify the matter by reducing it to a case of a "philosophical content" clad in a "non-philosophical style"; to recognize the critical impact of the hyperbole demands that the traditional philosophical style be present so that we might recognize it as violated. It is not enough that Nietzsche employ exaggerations; they must be recognized as exaggerations, both by Nietzsche and by the reader. If Nietzsche does not recognize them as such, then it would be difficult to say that they operate as a strategy for avoiding dogmatization. If the reader does not recognize them as such, then this strategy simply fails. In recognizing the hyperbole, the reader draws a boundary by determining the statement of which the hyperbole is the over-statement, and the hyperbole transgresses this border.

Yet while foregrounding the role of the author may serve as a disclaimer that addresses the problem of making claims in light of perspectivism, i.e., by drawing attention to Nietzsche as the origin of his claims, it does not address the fact that the reader does not have immediate access to Nietzsche's perspective. To liken Nietzsche's excesses to the phrase "in my opinion" does not effectively address the issue of perspectivism, and indeed, it is potentially misleading with regard to the function of excess in Nietzsche's writing, which foregrounds not Nietzsche as the source of his interpretation, but rather the work as the source of the reader's interpretation. If there is a unity to be discerned in Nietzsche's writing, it resides in the work itself.

The excesses of the aphorism draw the reader back to that work as the source. The aphoristic text may ignite the explosion that is interpretation, but at the same time, the concision of its formulation operates as a gesture of restraint that forces the reader to recognize where the reader begins to transgress the limits of the work. As an object of interpretation, the work may appear multiple, insofar as it constitutes the source for a diversity of interpretations, but to emphasize the particularity of the work does not actually unify its meaning. Rather it highlights the necessary plurality of interpretation, cross-textual, contextual, or otherwise. Indeed, it is the pretense of the work's singularity that enables us to speak of a plurality of interpretation at all. To emphasize the necessarily contingent nature of interpretation in this way fosters a skeptical attitude not so much to Nietzsche's text, but to the reader's own interpretation of that text. It calls for a suspension of ultimate judgment in the process of interpretation that, while perhaps not demanded by Nietzsche's per-

---

427 Nehamas, Nietzsche: Life as Literature, 35.

spectivism, certainly aligns with it felicitously. The body of the work draws the limit transgressed by the process of interpretation. Thus seen, the process of interpretation is inherently excessive. Much as the Dionysian relies upon the Apollinian in order to be comprehensible *as excessive*, the critical function excess is just as much rooted in the positing of limits as in their transgression. The simultaneous assertion and disavowal of boundaries is integral to the dynamic of excess that characterizes Nietzsche's aphoristic writings, and indeed, Nietzsche's writing as a whole. The reader is called upon to recognize the lack of any one interpretation's absolute authority, but this recognition by no means serves to undermine the project of interpretation itself. Nietzsche challenges his readers to engage in the textual excess that is interpretation, while recognizing it as such.

He confronts his reader with a dynamic tension when he presents an aphorism as the object for his "model" for an "art of exegesis" in the Third Treatise. By its very generic identity, his chosen object of interpretation is characterized by this two-part dynamic of excess, both drawing and transgressing boundaries again and again. Through the expectation that a text *express* only as much as it *says* the aphorism blatantly calls upon the reader to exceed the limits of its brevity. Through the expectation that a genre exhibit formal unity, that texts belong to a determinable context, that works have a definite limit, that the writings of a single author present a unified voice, these aspects present dynamic moments of critique. Each of these aspects calls for the reader's intervention, both to recognize the boundary to be exceeded, and then to activate that transgression through the interpretive process. Though the genre of the aphorism itself presents a diversity of excessive qualities that Nietzsche cannot hope to rein in, he nevertheless encourages precisely this ambition through his model reading, and indeed, through the very notion of a "model" reading. With this reading, he promotes the understanding that a larger coherent narrative can be derived from the discrete texts of the Nietzsche's collected writings. In other words, even as he "explodes" the aphoristic text, he sets a limit on interpretive possibilities, which he simultaneously invites his reader to transgress.

The notion of excess requires not the erasure of a limit but its transgression, which demands that the limit itself remain operative, though clearly not absolute.[428] That Nietzsche would turn to a form that engages in this dynamic on so many levels should perhaps come as no surprise when one considers that for him, even "truth" itself proves similarly excessive. In *Menschliches, Allzumenschliches*, Nietzsche claims "the unity of the word guarantees nothing about the unity of the thing" (HH I 14),[429] and in the case of the word "truth," Wahrheit, this unity is destabilized by an excess of possible meanings. In the very title of the early essay "Ueber in Wahrheit und Lüge

---

428 See Michel Foucault, "A Preface to Transgression," where he writes: "The limit and transgression depend on each other for whatever density of being they possess: a limit could not exist if it were absolutely uncrossable and, reciprocally, transgression would be pointless if it merely crossed a limit composed of illusions and shadows" (Foucault, A Preface to Transgression, 73).
429 "die Einheit des Wortes [verbürgt] Nichts für die Einheit der Sache" (MA I 14).

im aussermoralischen Sinne," for instance, Nietzsche draws attention to the fact that he already uses the term "truth" in various "senses." As the title claims, the essay deals with both truth *and* lying in an extramoral sense, indicating that attempts to arrive at a singular understanding of "truth" cannot succeed by means of determining a singular understanding of its antithesis; lying, like truth, can be understood in multiple "senses." Rather than delivering a consistent, unified meaning, the term "truth" indulges in an excess of denotations. That which has been conventionally considered the locus of unity is rendered multiple as a word and as a concept, thus calling into question the conventional association of this word and this concept with coherence and completion.[430]

The reader may attempt to reconcile these various understandings of the word, "Wahrheit," but to do so only throws into relief a semantic phenomenon. The various understandings of the word "Wahrheit" can be distinguished by that to which Nietzsche opposes the word: to lie in a moral sense, to lie in an extramoral sense, to error, to interpretation (WP 616; KSA 12:114), to *shallow* interpretation (BGE 40; JGB 40); but Nietzsche does not provide a distinct term for "Wahrheit" in each of these oppositions. At times he draws attention to the distinction between varying uses of the term by setting it in quotation marks,[431] but this practice is erratic and

---

430 This particular word play is not limited to the essay, "Wahrheit und Lüge." In this text, Nietzsche describes lying (in the moral sense) as using "the valid terms, the words, in order to make the unreal appear real" (die gültigen Bezeichnungen, die Worte, um das Unwirkliche als wirklich erscheinen zu lassen; TL 248; KSA 1:877), but he does not limit the term "lie" to untruths told despite the speaker's awareness of their untruth; he expands it to include erroneous statements made by speakers completely unaware of the falsehood of their claims. Those who call themselves "the good ones" (die Guten), Nietzsche writes in *Also sprach Zarathustra*, also "lie in all innocence" (lügen in aller Unschuld; Z III Return; Z III Heimkehr; KSA 4:234), for "good men never speak the truth" (Gute Menschen reden nie die Wahrheit; Z III Tablets 7; Z III Tafeln 7; KSA 4:251). They are good because they follow convention: they have not said, "that is *my* good and evil" (Das ist m e i n Gutes und Böses; Z III Gravity 2; Z III Schwere 2; KSA 4:243), and precisely because of this failure, they participate in the lie that is convention. In the terms laid out in "Wahrheit und Lüge," they lie in an extramoral sense, but are innocent, for they tell the truth according to the moral economy of truth and lie. Thus when Zarathustra concludes his description of "the good ones" as Pharisees who must crucify those who invent their own virtue with the exclamation "that *is* the truth" (Das i s t die Wahrheit!; Z III Tablets 26; Z III Tafeln 26; KSA 4:266), one cannot help but sense the irony of this statement. One must ask what sense of truth is at play: if the moral sense, then Zarathustra seems to say, "This is what they call truth, these people who claim to possess the truth"; or if in the extramoral sense, he seems to say, "This is the actual truth," but the possibility of the moral interpretation already opens the possibility of irony, and hence one cannot help but recognize the proclamation as problematic. This notion of the innocent lie, because of traditional associations of the term "lie" with conscious falsification, conflates the moral sense of lie with the extramoral sense, which appears more akin to error. But Nietzsche does not make this differentiation: both are lies, and thus any attempt to distinguish between truth as opposed to (moral) lie and truth as opposed to error, however helpful, must deviate from Nietzsche's own usage of the terms *Wahrheit* and *Lüge*.
431 See, e.g., WP 616 (KSA 12:114); GS 373, FW 373; BGE 5, JGB 5.

unreliable.[432] He attenuates the *notion* of truth by endowing the *term* with an excess of meanings, undermining the criterion by which claims are conventionally evaluated, i. e., their truth-value. Faced with an excess of *Wahrheiten*, the reader must determine what the term designates in each individual context and thereby acknowledge the disunity of the term. Where unity is anticipated, the term *Wahrheit* provides a plurality, transgressing the limits of self-identity by assuming multiple identities. "Truth" in Nietzsche's writings proves excessive. And yet he keeps the term in circulation, perpetuating the drive for unity and thereby sustaining a tension between the age-old notion of a single absolute truth and the plurality of perspectival interpretations that form the actual basis of our truths.

It has become commonplace to describe such awareness of the contingent nature of truth and the provisional status of interpretation as "ironic." A pervasive irony is seen to flow through Nietzsche's writing as a result of his attentiveness to the unavoidable contingency of his claims. In such accounts Nietzsche cannot simply say what he means; his writing must also ironically "unsay[] ... what it says."[433] For scholars like Behler and Rorty, an ironic stance marks Nietzsche as the heir to the legacy of early Romanticism and enables him to bypass the potential pitfalls of his own philosophy.[434] By means of irony, Nietzsche can pronounce the veracity of his claims even as he proclaims the illusory nature of truth itself.[435] But unlike, say, Friedrich Schlegel, Nietzsche does not openly cast his own style as ironic.[436] In-

---

432 For example, in BGE 3, JGB 3, Nietzsche objects to the prejudice that, "der Schein weniger werth [ist] als die 'Wahrheit'," firmly setting "Wahrheit" in quotation marks. Yet in BGE 34, JGB 34, he makes essentially the same statement: "Es ist nicht mehr als ein moralisches Vorurtheil, dass Wahrheit mehr wert ist als Schein," this time leaving out the quotation marks, and thereby leaving the reader to question whether another understanding of "Wahrheit" distinct from that in BGE 3, JGB 3 is operative in this passage. If not, then the reader must surmise that while the distinction between *Wahrheit* and *"Wahrheit"* may make a difference within a single passage, this distinction cannot be transferred between passages. One cannot say that Nietzsche consistently distinguishes between "truth" and truth even if he appears to do so within particular passages. In his study of Nietzsche's styles, Derrida writes that, "should the veil [that distinguishes 'truth' from truth] be suspended, or even fall a bit differently, there would no longer be any truth, only 'truth'" (Derrida, Spurs/Éperons, 59). With the multiple meanings of "truth" at play in Nietzsche's writings, the veil does appear to fall differently at different times, but the various meanings of the term discussed here resist any attempt to confine it within a simple binary opposition of "truth" and truth. There can only be "truth," not because it is necessarily secondary to some actual truth, but because the quotation marks foreground the textuality of the word, drawing attention to "truth" as a word that must be contextualized in and as language.

433 Babich, Post-Nietzschean Postmodernism, 253.

434 See Rorty, Contingency, 41; Behler, Irony and the Discourse of Modernity, 112; Behler, Nietzsches Auffassung der Ironie, 11.

435 Such readings echo accounts of Nietzsche's aphoristic writing that see it as an attempt to circumvent the consequences of his linguistic skepticism; see, for example, Krüger, Über den Aphorismus als philosophische Form, 86; Häntzschel-Schlotke, Der Aphorismus als Stilform bei Nietzsche, 20; cf. Meyer, Les moralistes allemands.

436 He reserves the term "irony" more often for Socrates in *contradistinction* to himself; Consider BT Self-Criticism 1, GT Versuch 1; HH I 372, MA I 372; WS 72; TI Socrates 7, GD Sokrates 7. As Norman puts

deed, as a rhetorical stance, irony is hardly in keeping with the unreserved confidence with which Nietzsche presents his philosophy throughout his career.[437] Whereas the irony of the early Romantics arises from the inaccessibility of the absolute, Nietzsche acknowledges no such absolute.[438] There is no compelling reason for his writing to "unsay what it says" when there is no higher order of truth that would require his statements thus to qualify themselves.

To insist upon the "irony" of Nietzsche's writings amounts to an indictment of interpretation; it operates according to the logic that because his writings cannot pretend to the absolute authority of universal truth, they must therefore be ironic. To insist that the only recourse left to Nietzsche in light of his critiques of truth is to adopt an ironic stance is to commit the same error as do those who see Nietzsche's controversial essay "Ueber Wahrheit und Lüge im aussermoralischen Sinne" as a devaluation of human truth.[439] Though Nietzsche undermines the notion of truth as the fundamental criterion distinguishing philosophical and literary language, it would be misleading to say that he thereby brings about a condemnation of truth as such. Rather, he redefines the notion of truth here in a way that acknowledges its lack of universal validity, while at the same time *reinforcing* the value of human truths by rejecting the notion that there is a greater perspective compared to which non-absolute human truths would have to be considered inferior. To say Nietzsche is ironic is to assume that he deliberately avoids claiming the validity of his own interpretations because they fail to achieve a status he does not recognize as valid. But his critique of truth does not demand irony any more than his perspectivism does.

As Nietzsche later puts it in the Third Treatise of the *Genealogie*, to deny the validity of a claim simply because it is an interpretation is itself a manifestation of the ascetic ideal. Here he criticizes "the general renunciation of all interpretation" (jenes Verzichtleisten auf Interpretation überhaupt) in favor of the "will to truth" as part of the ascetic ideal that "expresses [...] as much ascetic virtue as any denial of sensuality" (GM III 24).[440] He does not condemn the ascetic ideal itself for being an interpretation, but rather criticizes the demand for truth that it promotes:

> this unconditional will to truth [...] is *faith in the ascetic ideal itself*, even if as an unconscious imperative – don't be deceived about that – it is the faith in a *metaphysical* value, the absolute

---

it, "the man who wrote *Ecce Homo* had no sympathy for the excessive modesty that Socratic irony was made to serve" (Norman, Nietzsche and Early Romanticism, 518).

437 This leads Nehamas to contrast Socratic irony with Nietzsche's penchant for hyperbole (Nehamas, Nietzsche: Life as Literature, 26).

438 This is Norman's main objection to seeing Nietzsche as the heir to the early romantics.

439 See, e.g., Clark, Nietzsche on Truth and Philosophy, 93.

440 "drückt [...] ebensogut Ascetismus der Tugend aus, wie irgend eine Verneinung der Sinnlichkeit" (GM III 24; KSA 5:400).

value of *truth*, sanctioned and guaranteed by this ideal alone (it stands or falls with this ideal). (GM III 24)[441]

In advocating the absolute value of truth, the ascetic ideal neutralizes potential counter-interpretations, laying claim to a kind of truth that is beyond interpretation. It claims knowledge of a different order, compared to which anything characterized as interpretation must be considered *merely* interpretation. Thus, according to Nietzsche, this widespread understanding of truth as objective and thereby unquestionable operates as an expression of the ascetic's will to power. Precisely for that reason, "the value of truth must for once be experimentally *called into question*" (GM III 24).[442] The absolute privileging of truth is also simply (rather than *merely*) another interpretation, and as such, is subject to the scrutiny of other interpreters and to the requirements of rigorous interpretation.

Late in his career Nietzsche gave the resulting stance a name drawn from his original discipline of philology. He describes an alternative attitude that, like irony, recognizes the contingency of interpretation, but does so without subjugating interpretation to a higher order of knowledge. Though scholars (and the current study) frequently point out that Nietzsche's understanding of interpretation stretches beyond textual interpretation, it should not be forgotten that it still includes textual interpretation. And in discussing such interpretation, Nietzsche identifies a stance that proves appropriate for one who has determined the irrelevance of absolute truth. In *Der Antichrist*, Nietzsche condemns the theologian for a presumptuousness akin to that of the ascetic priest, who not only posits the absolute value of truth, but claims to possess it. The theologian's offense, however, is rendered not in terms of morality, but of philology. The criteria of Nietzsche's criticism reveal an alternative stance toward the irreducibility of interpretation that, unlike irony, does not rely upon a notion of the absolute that has no place in Nietzsche's thought:

> Another sign of the theologian is his incapacity for philology. What is here meant by philology is, in a very broad sense, the art of reading well – of reading facts without falsifying them by interpretation, without losing caution, patience, delicacy, in the desire to understand. Philology as *ephexis* in interpretation: whether it is a matter of books, the news in a paper, destinies, or weather conditions – not to speak of the "salvation of the soul" ... The manner in which a theologian, in Berlin as in Rome, interprets a "verse of Scripture" or an event – for example, a victory of the armies of the fatherland, in the higher light of the Psalms of David – is always so audacious that a philologist can only tear his hair. (A 52; PN 635)[443]

---

441 "jener unbedingte Wille zur Wahrheit, das ist der Glaube an das asketische Ideal selbst, wenn auch ein unbewusster Imperativ, man täusche sich hierüber nicht, – das ist der Glaube an einen metaphysischen Werth, einen Werth an sich der Wahrheit, wie er allein in jenem Ideal verbürgt und verbrieft ist (er steht und fällt mit jenem Ideal)" (GM III 24; KSA 5:400).

442 "der Werth der Wahrheit ist versuchsweise einmal in Frage zu stellen..." (GM III 24; KSA 5:401).

443 "Ein andres Abzeichen des Theologen ist sein Unvermögen zur Philologie. Unter Philologie soll hier, in einem sehr allgemeinen Sinne, die Kunst, gut zu lesen, verstanden werden, –

To be clear, Nietzsche's admonition here against "falsifying [facts] by interpretation" is not a devaluation of interpretation. For Nietzsche, interpretation is not a peaceful exercise – it necessarily involves "forcing, adjusting, abbreviating, omitting, padding, inventing, falsifying"; these activities belong to the "*essence* of interpreting" (GM III 24).[444] But again, interpretation itself is not a problem. What the theologian lacks is the appropriate *evaluation* of his interpretive endeavors. He does not adopt the interpretive stance that Nietzsche advocates here – he does not practice "*ephexis* in interpretation.*"

But what does Nietzsche mean by "*ephexis* in interpretation"? Porter describes the ephectic attitude as "an infinite patience in interpretation"[445] and the "paradigmatic gesture" of Nietzsche's philology of the future, "a philology that forever lies in wait, suspended in time."[446] The term *ephexis* does not appear in most dictionaries, English, German or Greek, though the adjectival form *ephektikos*, holding back, is not uncommon.[447] Nietzsche describes the "ephectic bent" as one of the virtues of philosophers in the Third Treatise of the *Genealogie*, the adjective "ephectic" referring to a stance that holds back, reserves judgment, waits, and doubts (GM III 9). As Nietzsche well knew, Diogenes Laertius and Sextus Empiricus referred to the Pyrrhonic Skeptics as "ephectics" who opposed dogmatism of any kind, in particular the *dogmata* of the Stoics.[448] The root substantive is not ἔφεξις, but ἐποχή; both, however, are derived from the verb *epichein*, meaning "to hold back" or "to check."[449] These two terms, *ephexis* and *epochē*, each connote a suspension of judgment, and though not all sources equate the two, [450] Nietzsche certainly drew the connection.

A note from the summer of 1885 provides insight into Nietzsche's understanding of the term and the stance he associates with "reading well." In an entry titled "*The*

Tatsachen ablesen können, o h n e sie durch Interpretation zu fälschen, o h n e im Verlangen nach Verständnis die Vorsicht, die Geduld, die Feinheit zu verlieren. Philologie als E p h e x i s in der Interpretation: handle es sich nun um Bücher, um Zeitungs-Neuigkeiten, um Schicksale oder Wetter-Thatsachen, – nicht zu reden vom 'Heil der Seele' ... Die Art, wie ein Theolog, gleichgültig ob in Berlin oder in Rom, ein 'Schriftwort' auslegt oder ein Erlebniss, einen Sieg des vaterländischen Heers zum Beispiel unter der höheren Beleuchtung der Psalmen Davids, ist immer dergestalt k ü h n, dass ein Philolog dabei an allen Wänden emporläuft" (AC 52; KSA 6:233).

444 "Vergewaltigen, Zurechtschieben, Abkürzen, Weglassen, Ausstopfen, Ausdichten, Umfälschen und was sonst zum W e s e n alles Interpretirens gehört" (GM III 24).

445 Porter, Nietzsche and the Philology of the Future, 58.

446 Porter, Nietzsche and the Philology of the Future, 80.

447 See Sommer, Friedrich Nietzsches Der Antichrist, 510 ff.

448 See Sommer, Friedrich Nietzsches Der Antichrist, 510, fn. 61.

449 See Berry, Perspectivism as Ephexis in Interpretation, 32; also Benne, Nietzsche und die historisch-kritische Philologie, 197 ff.

450 In Victor Brochard's *Les sceptiques grecs* (Paris, 1887), a study Nietzsche esteemed, the term ἔφεξις does not appear as a synonym for ἐποχή; see Sommer 510 – 511.

Bibliography

Abbey, Nietzsche's Middle Period
    Ruth Abbey, *Nietzsche's Middle Period*. Oxford: Oxford University Press, 2000.
Adorno, Der Essay als Form
    Theodor W. Adorno, "Der Essay als Form," in: *Schriften II: Noten zur Literatur*, ed. Rolf
    Tiedemann. Frankfurt/M.: Suhrkamp, 1974, 9–33.
Andreas-Salomé, Friedrich Nietzsche in seinen Werken
    Lou Andreas-Salomé, *Friedrich Nietzsche in seinen Werken*. Frankfurt/M., Leipzig: Insel, 1994.
Andreas-Salomé, Looking Back
    Lou Andreas-Salomé, *Looking Back: Memoires*. New York: Paragon House, 1991.
Asemissen, Notizen über den Aphorismus
    Hermann Ulrich Asemissen, "Notizen über den Aphorismus," in: Neumann (ed.), Der
    Aphorismus, 159–176.
Babich, Post-Nietzschean Postmodernism
    Babette Babich, "Post-Nietzschean Postmodernism," in: Clayton Koelb (ed.), *Nietzsche as
    Postmodernist: Essays Pro and Contra*. Albany, NY: SUNY Press, 1990.
Bacon, Works
    Francis Bacon, *Works*, ed. James Spedding, R. L. Ellis, and D. D. Heath. 14 vols. London,
    1857–74.
Behler, Confrontations
    Ernst Behler, *Confrontations: Derrida, Heidegger, Nietzsche*, trans. Steven Taubeneck.
    Stanford: Stanford University Press, 1991.
Behler, Irony and the Discourse of Modernity
    Ernst Behler, *Irony and the Discourse of Modernity*. Seattle: University of Washington Press,
    1990.
Behler, Nietzsches Auffassung der Ironie
    Ernst Behler, "Nietzsches Auffassung der Ironie," in: *Nietzsche-Studien* 4 (1975), 1–35.
Benne, Nietzsche und die historisch-kritische Philologie
    Christian Benne, *Nietzsche und die historisch-kritische Philologie*. Monographien und Texte
    zur Nietzsche-Forschung 49. Berlin/New York: De Gruyter, 2005.
Berry, Perspectivism as Ephexis in Interpretation
    Jessica Berry, "Perspectivism as *Ephexis* in Interpretation," in: *Philosophical Topics* 33:2
    (2005), 19–44.
Besser, Die Problematik der aphoristischen Form
    Kurt Besser, *Die Problematik der aphoristischen Form bei Lichtenberg, Fr. Schlegel, Novalis
    und Nietzsche*. Berlin: Junker und Dünnhaupt, 1935.
Bishop, Nietzsche and Antiquity
    Paul Bishop (ed.), *Nietzsche and Antiquity*. Rochester: Camden House, 2004.
Borsche, System and Aphorismus
    Tilman Borsche, "System und Aphorismus," in: Mihailo Djurić and Josef Simon (eds.),
    Nietzsche und Hegel. Würzburg: Königshausen & Neumann, 1992, 48–64.
Brobjer, Nietzsche's Philosophical Context
    Thomas H. Brobjer, *Nietzsche's Philosophical Context: An Intellectual Biography*. Urbana:
    University of Illinois Press, 2008.
Brochard, Les sceptiques grecs
    Victor Brochard, *Les sceptiques grecs*. Paris: Imprimerie nationale, 1887.
Burgard, Figures of Excess
    Peter J. Burgard, "Figures of Excess," in: Peter J. Burgard (ed.), *Nietzsche and the Feminine*.
    Charlottesville: University Press of Virginia, 1994, 1–32.

Del Caro, Nietzsche contra Nietzsche
Adrian Del Caro, *Nietzsche contra Nietzsche: Creativity and the Anti-Romantic.* Baton Rouge: Louisiana State University Press, 1989.

Chaouli, The Laboratory of Poetry
Michel Chaouli, *The Laboratory of Poetry: Chemistry and Poetics in the Work of Friedrich Schlegel.* Baltimore: Johns Hopkins University Press, 2002.

Claesges, Der maskierte Gedanke
Ulrich Claesges, *Der maskierte Gedanke: Nietzsches Aphorismenreihe "Von den ersten und letzten Dingen."* Würzburg: Königshausen & Neumann, 1999.

Clark, From the Nietzsche Archive
Maudemarie Clark, "From the Nietzsche Archive: Concerning the Aphorism Explicated in *Genealogy* III," in: *Journal of the History of Philosophy* 35:4 (1997), 611–614.

Clark, Nietzsche on Truth and Philosophy
Maudemarie Clark, *Nietzsche on Truth and Philosophy.* Cambridge: Cambridge University Press, 1990.

Cohen, Science, Culture, and Free Spirits
Jonathan Cohen, *Science, Culture, and Free Spirits: A Study of Nietzsche's Human, All-Too-Human.* Amherst, NY: Humanity, 2010.

Cox, Nietzsche: Naturalism and Interpretation
Christoph Cox, *Nietzsche: Naturalism and Interpretation.* Berkeley: University of California Press, 1999.

Danto, Nietzsche as Philosopher
Arthur C. Danto, *Nietzsche as Philosopher.* New York: Columbia University Press, 1980.

Danto, Philosophy as/and/of Literature
Arthur C. Danto, "Philosophy as/and/of Literature," in: *Proceedings and Addresses of the American Philosophical Association* 58:1 (1984), 5–20.

Derrida, Spurs/Éperons
Jacques Derrida, *Spurs: Nietzsche's Styles; Éperons: Les Styles de Nietzsche,* trans. Barbara Harlow. Chicago/London: University of Chicago Press, 1979.

Donnellan, Friedrich Nietzsche and Paul Rée
Brendan Donnellan, "Friedrich Nietzsche and Paul Rée: Cooperation and Conflict," in: *Journal of the History of Ideas* 43 (1982), 595–612.

Donnellan, Nietzsche and the French Moralists
Brendan Donnellan, *Nietzsche and the French Moralists.* Bonn: Bouvier, 1982.

Ebner-Eschenbach, Aphorismen
Marie von Ebner-Eschenbach, *Aphorismen.* Stuttgart: Reclam, 1988.

Faber, The Metamorphosis of the French Aphorism
Marion Faber, "The Metamorphosis of the French Aphorism: La Rochefoucauld and Nietzsche," in: *Comparative Literature Studies* 23:2 (1986), 205–217.

Fedler, Der Aphorismus: Begriffsspiel zwischen Philosophie und Poesie
Stephen Fedler, *Der Aphorismus. Begriffsspiel zwischen Philosophie und Poesie.* Stuttgart: Metzler, 1992.

Fieguth, Nachwort
Gerhard Fieguth, "Nachwort," in: *Deutsche Aphorismen.* Stuttgart: Reclam, 1978, 352–392.

Förster-Nietzsche, The Lonely Nietzsche
Elizabeth Förster-Nietzsche, *The Lonely Nietzsche,* trans. Paul V. Cohn. New York: Sturgis and Walton, 1915.

Foster, Heirs to Dionysus
John Burt Foster, *Heirs to Dionysus: A Nietzschean Current in Literary Modernism.* Princeton, NJ: Princeton University Press, 1981.

Foucault, What is an Author
　　Michel Foucault, "What is an Author?" in: Paul Rabinow (ed.), *The Foucault Reader*. New York: Pantheon, 1984, 101–120.
Foucault, A Preface to Transgression
　　Michel Foucault, "A Preface to Transgression," trans. Donald F. Bouchard and Sherry Simon, in: Paul Rabinow (ed.), *The Essential Works of Foucault 1954–1988*. 3 vols. New York: New Press, 1997–99. Vol. 2, 69–87.
Franco, Nietzsche's Enlightenment
　　Paul Franco, *Nietzsche's Enlightenment: The Free-Spirit Trilogy of the Middle Period*. Chicago/London: University of Chicago Press, 2011.
Frank, Unendliche Annäherung
　　Manfred Frank, *"Unendliche Annäherung": Die Anfänge der philosophischen Frühromantik*. Frankfurt/M.: Suhrkamp, 1997.
Frank, Über Stil und Bedeutung
　　Manfred Frank, "Über Stil und Bedeutung. Wittgenstein und die Frühromantik," in: *Stil in der Philosophie*, Stuttgart: Reclam, 1992. 86–115.
Fricke, Aphorismus
　　Harald Fricke, *Aphorismus*. Sammlung Metzler 208. Stuttgart: Metzler, 1984.
Frow, Reproducibles, Rubrics, and Everything You Need
　　John Frow, "'Reproducibles, Rubrics, and Everything You Need': Genre Theory Today," in: *PMLA* 122:5 (2007), 1626–1634.
Gemes, Nietzsche's Critique of Truth
　　Ken Gemes, "Nietzsche's Critique of Truth," in: *Philosophy and Phenomenological Research* 52 (1992), 47–65.
Gilman/Parent, Conversations with Nietzsche
　　Sander L. Gilman and David J. Parent, *Conversations with Nietzsche: A Life in the Words of his Contemporaries*. Oxford: Oxford University Press, 1897.
Granger, Argumentation and Heraclitus' Book
　　Herbert Granger, "Argumentation and Heraclitus' Book," in: *Oxford Studies in Ancient Philosophy* 26 (2004), 1–17.
Gray, Constructive Destruction
　　Richard T. Gray, *Constructive Destruction: Kafka's Aphorisms, Literary Tradition, and Literary Transformation*. Tübingen: Niemeyer, 1987.
Greiner, Friedrich Nietzsche
　　Bernhard Greiner, *Friedrich Nietzsche: Versuch und Versuchung in seinen Aphorismen*. Zur Erkenntnis der Dichtung, vol. 11. Munich: Fink, 1972.
Grenzmann, Probleme des Aphorismus
　　Wilhelm Grenzmann, "Probleme des Aphorismus," in: Neumann (ed.), Der Aphorismus, 177–208.
Häntzschel-Schlotke, Der Aphorismus als Stilform bei Nietzsche
　　Hiltrud Häntzschel-Schlotke, *Der Aphorismus als Stilform bei Nietzsche*. Diss. Heidelberg, 1967.
Heidegger, Nietzsche
　　Martin Heidegger, *Nietzsche*. 2 vols. Pfullingen: Neske, 1961.
Heit, Abel, and Brusotti, Nietzsches Wissenschaftsphilosophie
　　Helmut Heit, Günter Abel, and Marco Brusotti, *Nietzsches Wissenschaftsphilosophie: Hintergründe, Wirkungen und Aktualität*. Berlin/Boston: De Gruyter, 2012.
Heller, Von den ersten und letzten Dingen
　　Peter Heller, *"Von den ersten und letzten Dingen": Studien und Kommentar zu einer*

Aphorismenreihe von Friedrich Nietzsche. Monographien und Texte zur Nietzsche-Forschung 1. Berlin/New York: De Gruyter, 1972.

Heller, Nietzsches Scheitern am Werk

Edmund Heller, *Nietzsches Scheitern am Werk*. Freiburg: Alber, 1989.

Helsloot, Vrolijke Wetenschap

Niels Helsloot, *Vrolijke Wetenschap. Nietzsche als Vreind*. Baarn: Agora, 1999.

Higgins, Comic Relief

Kathleen Marie Higgins, *Comic Relief: Nietzsche's "Gay Science."* Oxford: Oxford University Press, 2000.

Hofmannsthal, Ein Brief

Hugo von Hofmannsthal, "Ein Brief," in: *Gesammelte Werke in Einzelausgaben. Prosa II*. Frankfurt/M.: S. Fischer, 1951, 7–22.

Hofmannsthal, A Letter

Hugo von *Hofmannsthal*, "A Letter," in: *Selected Prose*, trans. Mary Hottinger and Tania & James Stern. New York: Pantheon, 1952, 129–141.

Janaway, Beyond Selflessness

Christopher Janaway, *Beyond Selflessness: Reading Nietzsche's "Genealogy."* Oxford: Oxford University Press, 2007.

Janaway, Nietzsche's Illustration of the Art of Exegesis

Christopher Janaway, "Nietzsche's Illustration of the Art of Exegesis," in: *European Journal of Philosophy* 5:3 (1997), 251–268.

Janz, Friedrich Nietzsche

Curt Paul Janz, *Friedrich Nietzsche: Biographie*. 3 vols. Munich/Vienna: Hanser 1978–79.

Jaspers, Nietzsche

Karl Jaspers, *Nietzsche: Einführung in das Verständnis seines Philosophierens*. Berlin: De Gruyter, 1947.

Johnston, The Vienna School of Aphorists

William M. Johnston, "The Vienna School of Aphorists 1880–1930: Reflections on a Neglected Genre," in: Gerald Chapple and Hans H. Schulte (eds.), *The Turn of the Century: German Literature and Art 1890–1915*, The McMaster Colloquium on German Literature II. Bonn: Bouvier, 1981.

Kaufmann, Nietzsche

Walter Kaufmann, *Nietzsche: Philosopher, Psychologist, Antichrist*. 4th ed. Princeton: Princeton University Press, 1974.

Kelterborn, Erinnerungen

Louis Kelterborn, "Erinnerungen" (1901), in Sander Gilman (ed.), *Begegnungen mit Nietzsche*. Bonn: Bouvier, 1985, 103–123.

Kirk/Raven, The Presocratic Philosophers

G. S. Kirk and J. E. Raven, *The Presocratic Philosophers*. Cambridge: Cambridge University Press, 1962.

Klein, Wesen und Bau des deutschen Aphorismus

Johannes Klein, "Wesen und Bau des deutschen Aphorismus, dargestellt am Aphorismus Nietzsches," in: *Germanisch-Romanische Montatsschrift* 22 (1934), 358–369.

Kofman, Nietzsche and Metaphor

Sarah Kofman, *Nietzsche and Metaphor*, trans. Duncan Large. Stanford: Stanford University Press, 1993.

Krüger, Über den Aphorismus als philosophische Form

Heinz Krüger, *Über den Aphorismus als philosophische Form*. Munich: edition text + kritik, 1988 (from his dissertation of the same title, Frankfurt/M., 1956).

Kuhn, Friedrich Nietzsches Philosophie des europäischen Nihilismus
  Elisabeth Kuhn, *Friedrich Nietzsches Philosophie des europäischen Nihilismus*. Berlin/New
  York: De Gruyter, 1992.
Lacoue-Labarthe, Apocryphal Nietzsche
  Philippe Lacoue-Labarthe, "Apocryphal Nietzsche," in: *The Subject of Philosophy*, trans.
  Timothy D. Bent. Minneapolis: University of Minnesota Press, 1993.
Lacoue-Labarthe/Nancy, The Literary Absolute
  Philippe Lacoue-Labarthe and Jean-Luc Nancy, *The Literary Absolute*, trans. Philip Barnard
  and Cheryle Lester. Albany, NY: State University of New York Press, 1988.
Lamping, Der Aphorismus
  Dieter Lamping, "Der Aphorismus," in: Otto Knörrich (ed.), *Formen der Literatur*. Stuttgart:
  Kröner, 1981, 21–27.
La Rochefoucauld, Réflexions ou Sentences et Maximes morales
  François de La Rochefoucauld, "Réflexions ou Sentences et Maximes morales / Moral
  Reflections or Sententiae and Maxims (fifth edition, 1678)," in: *Collected Maxims and Other
  Reflections*, trans. E. H. and A. M. Blackmore and Francine Giguère. Oxford: Oxford University
  Press, 2007, 1–138.
La Rochefoucauld, The Maxims
  François Duc de la Rochefoucauld, *The Maxims*, trans. F. G. Stevens. The World's Classics
  482. London: Oxford University Press, 1940.
Leiter, Nietzsche on Morality
  Brian Leiter, *Nietzsche on Morality*. London: Routledge, 2002.
Lichtenberg, Vermischte Schriften
  Georg Christoph Lichtenberg, *Vermischte Schriften. Neue Original-Ausgabe*. 8 vols. Göttingen:
  Dieterich, 1867.
Lichtenberg, Georg Christoph Lichtenbergs Aphorismen
  Georg Christoph Lichtenberg, *Georg Christoph Lichtenbergs Aphorismen*, ed. Albert
  Leitzmann. 5 vols. Berlin: B. Behr, 1902–08.
Lichtenberg, Sudel-
  Georg Christoph Lichtenberg, *Schriften und Briefe*, ed. Wolfgang Promies. 3 vols. Munich:
  Hanser, 1980.
Liddel/Scott, A Greek-English Lexicon
  Henry George Liddel and Robert Scott, *A Greek-English Lexicon*, revised by Henry Stuart
  Jones. Oxford: Clarendon, 1940.
Lucka, Der Aphorismus
  Emil Lucka, "Der Aphorismus," in: *Das literarische Echo* 21 (1918/19), col. 17–20.
Ludovici, Nietzsche and Art
  Anthony Mario Ludovici, *Nietzsche and Art*. London: Constable, 1911.
Magnus, Nietzsche's Mitigated Skepticism
  Bernd Magnus, "Nietzsche's Mitigated Skepticism," in: *Nietzsche Studien* 9 (1980), 260–267.
Manovich, The Language of New Media
  Lev Manovich, *The Language of New Media*. Cambridge: MIT University Press, 2001.
Marsden, Nietzsche and the Art of the Aphorism
  Jill Marsden, "Nietzsche and the Art of the Aphorism," in: Keith Ansell-Pearson (ed.), *A
  Companion to Nietzsche*. Oxford: Blackwell, 2006, 22–37.
Mauthner, Beiträge zu einer Kritik der Sprache
  Fritz Mauthner, *Beiträge zu einer Kritik der Sprache*. 3 vols. Frankfurt/M.: Ullstein, 1982
  (reprint of 1923 edition).

Mautner, Der Aphorismus als literarische Gattung
Franz H. Mautner, "Der Aphorismus als literarische Gattung," in: Neumann (ed.), Der Aphorismus, 19–74.

Mautner, Der Aphorismus als Literatur
Franz H. Mautner, "Der Aphorismus als Literatur," in: Franz H. Mautner, *Wort und Wesen*. Frankfurt: Insel, 1974, 279–299.

Mautner, Der Aphorismus
Franz H. Mautner, "Der Aphorismus," in: Klaus Weissenberger (ed.), *Prosakunst ohne Erzählen: Die Gattungen der nicht-fiktionalen Kunstprosa*, Tübingen: Niemeyer, 1985, 7–26.

Mieder, Sprichwörtliche Aphorismen
Wolfgang Mieder, *Sprichwörtliche Aphorismen: von Georg Christoph Lichtenberg bis Elazar Benyoëtz*. Vienna: Edition Praesens, 1999.

Meijers, Gustav Gerber und Friedrich Nietzsche
Anthonie Meijers, "Gustav Gerber und Friedrich Nietzsche: Zum historischen Hintergrund der sprachphilosophischen Auffassungen des frühen Nietzsche," in: *Nietzsche-Studien* 17 (1988), 369–390.

Menninghaus, Unendliche Verdopplung
Winfried Menninghaus, *Unendliche Verdopplung: Die frühromantische Grundlegung der Kunsttheorie im Begriff absoluter Selbstreflexion*. Frankfurt: Suhrkamp, 1987.

Meyer, Les moralistes allemands
Urs Meyer, "Les moralistes allemands? La naissance de l'aphorisme dans la litterature allemande et la réception des moralistes français au XVIIIe siècle," in: Marie-Jeanne Ortemann (ed.), *Fragment(s), fragmentation, aphorisme poétique*. Nantes: Centre de recherche sur les identités nationales et l'interculturalité, 1998.

Miller, Aphorism as Instrument of Political Action in Nietzsche
J. Hillis Miller, "Aphorism as Instrument of Political Action in Nietzsche," in: *parallax* 10:3 (2004), 70–82.

Montinari, Nietzsche lesen
Mazzino Montinari, *Nietzsche lesen*. Berlin/New York: De Gruyter, 1980.

Müller-Lauter, Nietzsche. Seine Philosophie der Gegensätze und die Gegensätze seiner Philosophie
Wolfgang Müller-Lauter, *Nietzsche. Seine Philosophie der Gegensätze und die Gegensätze seiner Philosophie*. Berlin/New York: De Gruyter, 1971.

Müller-Lauter, Nietzsche: His Philosophy of Contradictions and the Contradictions of His Philosophy
Wolfgang Müller-Lauter, *Nietzsche: His Philosophy of Contradictions and the Contradictions of His Philosophy*, trans. David J. Parent. Chicago: University of Illinois Press, 1999.

Musil, Tagebücher, Aphorismen, Essays und Reden
Robert Musil, *Tagebücher, Aphorismen, Essays und Reden*. Hamburg: Rowohlt, 1955.

Nehamas, The Postulated Author
Alexander Nehamas, "The Postulated Author: Critical Monism as a Regulative Ideal," in: *Critical Inquiry* 8 (1981), 131–149.

Nehamas, Nietzsche: Life as Literature
Alexander Nehamas, *Nietzsche: Life as Literature*. Cambridge, MA/London: Harvard University Press, 1999.

Nehamas, Writer, Text, Work, Author
Alexander Nehamas, "Writer, Text, Work, Author," in: William Irwin (ed.), *The Death and Resurrection of the Author?* New York: The Greenwood Press, 2002, 95–116.

Neumann, Einleitung
Gerhard Neumann, "Einleitung," in: Neumann (ed.), Der Aphorismus, 1–18.

Neumann (ed.), Der Aphorismus
    Gerhard Neumann (ed.), *Der Aphorismus: Zur Geschichte, zu den Formen und Möglichkeiten einer literarischen Gattung.* Darmstadt: Wissenschaftliche Buchgesellschaft, 1976.
Neumann, Ideenparadiese
    Gerhard Neumann, *Ideenparadiese: Untersuchungen zur Aphoristik von Lichtenberg, Novalis, Friedrich Schlegel und Goethe.* Munich: Fink, 1976.
Nietzsche Research Group (Nijmegen), Nietzsche-Wörterbuch
    Nietzsche Research Group (Nijmegen) led by Paul van Tongeren, Gerd Schank and Herman Siemens (eds.), *Nietzsche-Wörterbuch.* Vol. 1: Abbreviatur—einfach. Berlin/New York: De Gruyter, 2004.
Norman, Nietzsche and Early Romanticism
    Judith Norman, "Nietzsche and Early Romanticism," in: *Journal of the History of Ideas* 63:3 (2002), 501–519.
Oliver, A Dagger through the Heart
    Kelly Oliver, "A Dagger through the Heart: The Ethics of Reading Nietzsche's *On the Genealogy of Morals,*" in: *International Studies in Philosophy* 25 (1993), 13–28.
Oliver, Womanizing Nietzsche
    Kelly Oliver, *Womanizing Nietzsche: Philosophy's Relation to the "Feminine."* London: Routledge, 1995.
Pfeiffer, Aphorismus und Romanstruktur
    Peter C. Pfeiffer, *Aphorismus und Romanstruktur: Zu Robert Musils "Der Mann ohne Eigenschaften."* Bonn: Bouvier, 1990.
Pichler, Nietzsche, die Orchestikologie und das dissipative Denken
    Axel Pichler, *Nietzsche, die Orchestikologie und das dissipative Denken.* Vienna: Passagen, 2010.
Pippin, Nietzsche, Psychology, and First Philosophy
    Robert B. Pippin, *Nietzsche, Psychology, and First Philosophy.* Chicago: University of Chicago Press, 2010.
Porter, Nietzsche and the Philology of the Future
    James I. Porter, *Nietzsche and the Philology of the Future.* Stanford: Stanford University Press, 2002.
Rée, Basic Writings
    Paul Rée, *Basic Writings,* ed. and trans. Robin Small. Urbana/Chicago: University of Illinois Press, 2003.
Rée, Psychologische Beobachtungen
    Paul Rée, "Psychologische Beobachtungen," in: Rée, *Gesammelte Werke,* 59–125.
Rée, Gesammelte Werke
    Paul Rée, *Gesammelte Werke 1875–1885,* ed. Hubert Treiber. Supplementa Nietzscheana 7. Berlin/New York: De Gruyter, 2004.
Richardson, Nietzsche's System
    John Richardson, *Nietzsche's System.* Oxford: Oxford University Press, 1996.
Richardson, Nietzsche's New Darwinism
    John Richardson, *Nietzsche's New Darwinism.* Oxford: Oxford University Press, 2004.
Riehl, Friedrich Nietzsche: Der Künstler und der Denker
    Alois Riehl, *Friedrich Nietzsche. Der Künstler und der Denker. Ein Essay.* Stuttgart: Frommann, 1897.
Ries/Kiesow, Von Menschliches, Allzumenschliches bis zur Fröhlichen Wissenschaft
    Wiebrecht Ries and Karl-Friedrich Kiesow, "Von *Menschliches, Allzumenschliches* bis zur *Fröhlichen Wissenschaft* (1878–1882)," in: Henning Ottmann (ed.), *Nietzsche-Handbuch: Leben – Werk – Wirkung.* Stuttgart/Weimar: Metzler, 2000, 91–119.

Rilke, Sämtliche Werke
  Rainer Maria Rilke, *Sämtliche Werke*, ed. E. Zinn. 6 vols. Frankfurt: Insel, 1955.
Rorty, Contingency, Irony, and Solidarity
  Richard Rorty, *Contingency, Irony, and Solidarity*. Cambridge: Cambridge University Press, 1989.
Ryan, The Vanishing Subject
  Judith Ryan, *The Vanishing Subject: Early Psychology and Literary Modernism*. Chicago: University of Chicago Press, 1991.
Schaberg, The Nietzsche Canon
  William H. Schaberg, *The Nietzsche Canon*. Chicago: University of Chicago Press, 1995.
Schacht, Nietzsche
  Richard Schacht, *Nietzsche*. London: Routledge and Kegan Paul, 1983.
Schalk, Aphorismus
  Fritz Schalk, "Aphorismus," in: Joachim Ritter (ed.), *Historisches Wörterbuch der Philosophie*. 13 vols. Basel/Stuttgart: Schwabe, 1970. Vol. 1, 438.
Schildknecht, *Philosophische Masken*
  Christiane Schildknecht, *Philosophische Masken: Literarische Formen der Philosophie bei Platon, Descartes, Wolff und Lichtenberg*. Stuttgart: Metzler, 1990.
Schlegel, KA
  Friedrich, Schlegel, *Kritische Friedrich-Schlegel-Ausgabe*. Ed. Ernst Behler with Hans Eichner and Jean-Jacques Anstett. 35 vols. Munich/Paderborn/Vienna: Ferdinand Schoningh, 1958–.
Schmidt/Gessmann, Philosophisches Wörterbuch
  Heinrich Schmidt and Martin Gessmann (eds.), *Philosophisches Wörterbuch*. Stuttgart: Kröner, 2009.
Schnitzler, Die dramatischen Werke
  Arthur Schnitzler, *Die dramatischen Werke*. 2 vols. Frankfurt: Fischer, 1962.
Schöne, Aufkärung aus dem Geist der Experimentalphysik
  Albrecht Schöne, *Aufkärung aus dem Geist der Experimentalphysik. Lichtenbergsche Konjunktive*. Munich: Beck, 1982.
Schopenhauer, Über Philosophie und ihre Methode
  Arthur Schopenhauer, "Über Philosophie und ihre Methode," in: *Parerga und Paralipomena*, ed. Julius Frauenstädt. 2 vols. Leipzig: Brockhaus, 1878. Vol. 2, 3–21.
Schrift, Nietzsche and the Question of Interpretation
  Alan D. Schrift, *Nietzsche and the Question of Interpretation*. New York: Routledge, 1990.
Shapiro, Nietzschean Aphorism as Art and Act
  Gary Shapiro, "Nietzschean Aphorism as Art and Act," in: *Man and World* 17 (1984), 399–429.
Small, Nietzsche and Rée
  Robin Small, *Nietzsche and Rée: A Star Friendship*. Oxford: Oxford University Press, 2005.
Smith, Einleitung zu einer Sammlung englischer Aphorismen
  Logan Pearsall Smith, "Einleitung zu einer Sammlung englischer Aphorismen," in: Neumann (ed.), *Der Aphorismus*, 144–158.
Sommer, Friedrich Nietzsches Der Antichrist
  Andreas Urs Sommer, *Friedrich Nietzsches "Der Antichrist". Ein philosophisch-historischer Kommentar*. Basel: Schwabe, 2000.
Spicker, Aphorismen über Aphorismen, Fragen über Fragen
  Friedemann Spicker, "Aphorismen über Aphorismen, Fragen über Fragen – Zur Gattungsreflexion der Aphoristiker," in: *Zeitschrift für deutsche Philologie* 113:2 (1994), 161–198.

Spicker, Der Aphorismus
  Friedemann Spicker, *Der Aphorismus. Begriff und Gattung von der Mitte des 18. Jahrhunderts bis 1912*. Berlin/New York: De Gruyter, 1997.
Spicker, Kurze Geschichte des deutschen Aphorismus
  Friedemann Spicker, *Kurze Geschichte des deutschen Aphorismus*. Tübingen: Francke, 2007.
Stegmaier, After Montinari
  Werner Stegmaier, "After Montinari: On Nietzsche Philology," in: *The Journal of Nietzsche Studies* 38 (2009), 5–19.
Stegmaier, Der Tod Gottes und das Leben der Wissenschaft
  Werner Stegmaier, "Der Tod Gottes und das Leben der Wissenschaft. Nietzsches Aphorismus vom tollen Menschen im Kontext seiner *Fröhlichen Wissenschaft*," in: Carlo Gentili and Cathrin Nielsen (eds.), *Der Tod Gottes und die Wissenschaft. Zur Wissenschaftskritik Nietzsches*. Berlin/New York: De Gruyter, 2010, 1–16.
Stegmaier, Nietzsches Befreiung der Philosophie
  Werner Stegmaier, *Nietzsches Befreiung der Philosophie. Kontextuelle Interpretation des V. Buchs der "Fröhlichen Wissenschaft."* Berlin/Boston: De Gruyter, 2012.
Stephenson, On the Widespread Use of an Inappropriate and Restrictive Model of the Literary Aphorism
  R.H. Stephenson, "On the Widespread Use of an Inappropriate and Restrictive Model of the Literary Aphorism," in: *Modern Language Review* 75 (1980), 1–17.
Stingelin, Unsere ganze Philosophie ist Berichtigung des Sprachgebrauchs
  Martin Stingelin, *"Unsere ganze Philosophie ist Berichtigung des Sprachgebrauchs". Friedrich Nietzsches Lichtenberg-Rezeption im Spannungsfeld zwischen Sprachkritik (Rhetorik) und historischer Kritik (Genealogie)*. Munich: Fink, 1996.
Strobel, Das Pathos der Distanz
  Eva Strobel, *Das "Pathos der Distanz". Nietzsches Entscheidung für den Aphorismenstil.* Würzburg: Königshausen & Neumann, 1998.
Teichmann, Georg Christoph Lichtenberg
  Jürgen Teichmann, "Georg Christoph Lichtenberg: Experimental Physics from the Spirit of Aphorism," in: Gerd Biegel, Günther Oestmann and Karin Reich (eds.), *Neue Welten – Wilhelm Olbers und die Naturwissenschaften um 1800* (exhibition catalog). Wolfenbüttel: Heckner Print-Service, 2001, 192–201.
Thönges, Das Genie des Herzens
  Bernd Thönges. *Das Genie des Herzens. Über das Verhältnis von aphoristischem Stil und dionysischer Philosophie in Nietzsches Werken.* Stuttgart: M & P, 1993.
van Tongeren, Reinterpreting Modern Culture
  Paul van Tongeren, *Reinterpreting Modern Culture*. West Lafayette, IN: Purdue University Press, 2000.
Treiber, Erläuterungen
  Hubert Treiber, "Erläuterungen," in: Rée, Gesammelte Werke, 385–409.
Türck, Friedrich Nietzsche und seine philosophischen Irrwege
  Hermann Türck, *Friedrich Nietzsche und seine philosophischen Irrwege*. Dresden: Glöss, 1891.
Vaihinger, Nietzsche als Philosoph
  Hans Vaihinger, *Nietzsche als Philosoph*. Berlin: Reuther & Richard, 1902.
Vickers, Francis Bacon and Renaissance Prose
  Brian Vickers, *Francis Bacon and Renaissance Prose*. Cambridge: Cambridge University Press, 1968.
Warnock, Nietzsche's Conception of Truth
  Mary Warnock, "Nietzsche's Conception of Truth," in: Malcolm Pasley (ed.), *Nietzsche's Imagery and Thought: A Collection of Essays*. Berkeley: University of California Press, 1978.

Wehe, Geist und Form des deutschen Aphorismus
  Walter Wehe, "Geist und Form des deutschen Aphorismus" (1939), in: Neumann (ed.), Der Aphorismus, 130–143.
Westerdale, Zarathustra's Preposterous History
  Joel Westerdale, "Zarathustra's Preposterous History," in: *Nietzsche Studien* 35 (2006): 47–69.
Westerdale, Zur Ausdifferenzierung von Sentenz und Aphorismus
  Joel Westerdale, "Zur Ausdifferenzierung von Sentenz und Aphorismus in 'Jenseits von gut und böse' (1882) und *Jenseits von Gut und Böse* (1886)," in: Marcus A. Born and Axel Pichler (eds.), *Texturen des Denkens: Nietzsches Inszenierung der Philosophie in "Jenseits von Gut und Böse."* Nietzsche heute 5. Berlin/Boston: De Gruyter, 2013.
Widmann, Feuilleton: Nietzsche's gefährliches Buch
  Joseph Victor Widmann, "Feuilleton: Nietzsche's gefährliches Buch," In: *Der Bund* (Bern), 16–17 September 1886.
Wilcox, Truth and Value in Nietzsche
  John T. Wilcox, *Truth and Value in Nietzsche: A Study of His Metaethics and Epistemology.* Ann Arbor: University of Michigan Press, 1974.
Wilcox, What Aphorism Does Nietzsche Explicate in GM III
  John T. Wilcox, "What Aphorism Does Nietzsche Explicate in *Genealogy of Morals*, Essay III?" in: *Journal of the History of Philosophy* 35:4 (1997), 593–610.
Wilcox, That Exegesis of an Aphorism in Genealogy III
  John T. Wilcox, "That Exegesis of an Aphorism in *Genealogy* III: Reflections on the Scholarship," in: *Nietzsche-Studien* 27 (1998): 448–462.

Index

Made in the USA
Las Vegas, NV
21 December 2023

83372712R00116